Developing Arms Transparency: The Future of the UN Register

Bradford Arms Register Studies

The Bradford Arms Register Studies (BARS) series is the result of an ongoing research project based at the Department of Peace Studies, University of Bradford and supported by the Ford Foundation. Studies published so far include:

1. Malcolm Chalmers and Owen Greene, *Implementing and Developing the United Nations Register of Conventional Arms*, May 1993

2. Malcolm Chalmers and Owen Greene, *The United Nations Register of Conventional Arms: An Initial Examination of the First Report*, October 1993

3. Malcolm Chalmers and Owen Greene, *Background Information: An Analysis of Information Provided to the UN on Military Holdings and Procurement through National Production in the First Year of the Register of Conventional Arms*, March 1994 (reprinted April 1995)

4. Malcolm Chalmers, Owen Greene, Edward J. Laurance, and Herbert Wulf (eds.) *Developing the UN Register of Conventional Arms*, May 1994

5. Malcolm Chalmers and Owen Greene, *Taking Stock: the UN Register After Two Years*, June 1995

6. Malcolm Chalmers, *Confidence-Building in South-East Asia*, 1996

BARS Working Papers:

No. 1: Malcolm Chalmers and Owen Greene, *The UN Register of Conventional Arms: Examining the Third Report*, November 1995

No. 2: Malcolm Chalmers and Owen Greene, *The UN Register in its 4th Year: Part A, analysing the 4th year replies; Part B, priorities for the 1997 Review*, November 1996

No. 3: Malcolm Chalmers and Owen Greene, *In the Background: reporting national procurement and military holdings to the UN Register 1993-97*, March 1997

Bradford Arms Register Studies
Department of Peace Studies
University of Bradford,
West Yorkshire BD7 1DP
United Kingdom
Telephone: +44 1274 38 5235
Facsimile: +44 1274 38 5240

Developing Arms Transparency: The Future of the United Nations Register

Edited by

Malcolm Chalmers, Mitsuro Donowaki, Owen Greene

Bradford Arms Register Studies No. 7

1997

University of Bradford

and

Centre for the Promotion of Disarmament and Non-Proliferation, Japan Institute For International Affairs

ISBN 1-85143-165-9

Typeset by Jeannie Grußendorf

Cover design by Jenny Braithwaite and Simon Covey

Printed in Great Britain on acid-free paper

by Redwood Books, Trowbridge, Wiltshire

Contents

List of tables, figures and appendices

Chapter 14

CHAPTER 1

Introduction

Malcolm Chalmers, Mitsuro Donowaki, Owen Greene

The development of the UN Register

The United Nations Register of Conventional Arms remains the only global cooperative agreement relating to conventional arms. This in itself is a testament to the difficulty of tackling the security problems associated with the accumulation and transfer of conventional arms at an international level.

Launched at the end of the cold war, and in the immediate aftermath of the 1991 Gulf War, the UN Register is now in its fifth year of operation. In spite of some initial scepticism about its prospects and value, it has become well-established as an important international transparency and confidence-building measure. Over 130 states have participated, with a core group of about 75 states (including almost all major arms suppliers and most major importers) participating regularly. They have provided information on their annual imports and exports of seven categories of major conventional arms, so that the Register has almost certainly covered well over 90% of the annual international trade in such weapons. About 30 states now also regularly provide information on their military holdings and domestic arms procurement.

The Register has not only revealed substantial new information on international arms transfers but has also provided an important basis for developing regional or global security dialogues and confidence-building measures. It has stimulated improvements in national systems for monitoring and controlling arms transfers, and has also helped to promote domestic openness and accountability within participating states.

Nevertheless, this new transparency regime is still far from achieving its full potential in contributing to international security. Moreover, it has some continuing weaknesses and the regime remains vulnerable to loss of political momentum and interest. Further measures are needed to promote effective implementation and to strengthen and expand the Register.

The United Nations decided to carry out a major review in 1997 of the operation and further development of the Register. This is the second such review: the first in 1994 helped to maintain the Register but failed to achieve agreement on ways to substantially strengthen or develop it. The 1997 review therefore provides a key opportunity to improve and expand the new transparency regime. Central to this review is the 1997 UN Group of Governmental Experts, consisting of representatives of 25 states, selected to include key states and to ensure good geographical representation. The 1997 Group of Experts is due to meet three times for formal discussions and negotiations (in March, June and August), to prepare recommendations for consideration by the UN First Committee and General Assembly in the autumn of 1997. Consensus recommendations from the Group of Experts are very likely to be adopted globally.

The Book

This book aims to contribute to the 1997 review of the UN Register. It aims to clarify and examine the key issues, and to promote the prospects for successfully strengthening and developing existing transparency arrangements. The chapters have been developed from papers first presented at an international workshop on this topic held in Tokyo in May 1997, in which nearly all members of the UN Group of Experts participated. This workshop provided a unique opportunity for the members of the Group of Experts to examine and explore key issues informally, together with a number of non-governmental specialists. We hope that the book will prove useful and interesting for all government experts, officials, analysts and members of the public who are interested or involved in debates about the further development of the arms transparency measures.

Part A of the book aims to provide key contextual and background material, and to identify the main issues and priorities for the operation and development of the UN Register in 1997. Chapter 2, by Malcolm Chalmers and Owen Greene, examines the development and operation of the UN Register up to Spring 1997, through its first four years of operation. This chapter briefly outlines the historical development of the Register, and then it examines: participation in the Register, the character and significance of the submitted information, and emerging strengths and weaknesses. In chapter 3 Raphael Grossi provides a personal view of the issues and priorities for the 1997 UN review process, from his perspective as Chair of the 1997 UN Group of Experts and also Argentina's representative in both the 1994 and 1997 UN review processes. In the following chapter, Chalmers and Greene outline their own assessment of the significance of the Register and of the tasks and priorities for the 1997 Group of Experts, from their perspective as two non-governmental experts who have closely observed the development and operation of the Register since it began.

One of the most important challenges is to identify and agree ways to expand the scope of the UN Register to cover not only international arms transfers but also states' military holdings and arms procurement from national production. This question has been central since the Register was first proposed, and is the focus of Part B of the book.

In chapter 5, Mitsuro Donowaki, Japan's representative on the Group of Experts and closely involved with the development of the Register throughout its existence, describes and assesses the history of how the issue of expanding the Register has been addressed up to now. In chapter 6, Ravinder Pal Singh examines national arms procurement processes, and identifies some key themes and lessons for the development of international transparency and domestic accountability in this important but relatively secretive area. Next, Terry Taylor describes in chapter 7 the approaches and challenges involved in compiling information on states' military holdings for the International Institute of Strategic Studies' *Military Balance* - a widely used and authoritative non-governmental source for such data. Finally, in this section, Malcolm Chalmers and Owen Greene examine the priorities and means for expanding the scope of the UN Register. In chapter 8, they argue that it is important for the 1997 Group of Experts to identify and agree ways to substantially expand the scope of the Register in 1997, and identify a number of options which could be adopted to achieve this goal.

There are many other important areas in which the Register could be usefully improved, which need to be addressed in the 1997 review. Part C of the book focusses on examining ways in which the transfers Register could be strengthened in itself, on the significance of this new transparency regime for promoting security and accountability, and on ways to promote the effective use of the Register.

In chapter 9, Giovanni Snidle, US representative on the 1997 Group of Experts, proposes some ways in which the existing Register of arms transfers could be usefully strengthened. In the following chapter, Malcolm Chalmers and Owen Greene discuss the same question: identifying and assessing a range of proposals for strengthening the Register and discussing relative priorities for the 1997 review. In Chapters 11 and 12, Jasjit Singh and Herbert Wulf respectively provide an Indian and a European view of the significance of the UN Register for international security and accountability, and of the priorities for promoting its effectiveness and use.

The UN Register is a global transparency arrangement. Yet it is clear that developments in transparency and confidence-building processes at the regional level are of critical importance for improving security. It is a major aim for the Register to promote conflict prevention, cooperation, restraint and accountability at the national and regional level, and to stimulate the development of regional confidence-building measures (such as complementary regional registers). Conversely, states' willingness to participate in the Register, and to develop it further, is shaped by local and regional circumstances.

Part D of the book thus examines regional developments in arms transparency and security cooperation. It focusses particularly on recent developments in three key regions: East Asia, Latin America and the area of the former USSR. In chapter 13, Amitav Acharya examines developments in East Asia, particularly the significance and dynamics of the ASEAN Regional Forum. In chapter 14, Ricardo Mario Rodriguez examines recent trends in Latin America, including the significance and role of arms transparency and constraint in the region and important recent agreements within the Organisation of American States. Finally, in chapter 15 Alexander Nikitin reviews trends in arms transfer controls, transparency, and cooperation in the countries of the former Soviet Union, and particularly amongst CIS countries. All chapters in this part of the book discuss trends and issues relating to participation in the UN Register by countries in the relevant region, and identify key linkages between domestic accountability and international transparency.

The UN Register covers seven categories of major conventional weapons systems. There are concerns also to promote transparency in other areas of armaments, and questions have been raised about whether the existing Register should itself be expanded to cover some of these. Two of the categories of armaments that have been most prominently discussed in this context are 'light' weapons (or small arms) and nuclear weapons. For example, concerns that international measures need to be taken to address the proliferation of light weapons are reported for several regions discussed in Part D of the book.

The last part of the book (Part E) therefore addresses the questions of developing international transparency arrangements for light weapons and nuclear weapons. In chapter 16, Mitsuro Donowaki (who is Chair of the UN Panel on Small Arms) provides a personal view on issues and priorities for addressing small arms problems, and reviews some recent developments and proposals for international action. Natalie Goldring provides another perspective on these issues in chapter 17, reviewing some recent international debates, identifying and assessing several options for establishing international transparency arrangements for light weapons, and discussing associated control measures. Finally, in chapter 18, Harald Müller and Katja Frank examine the possibilities for establishing nuclear weapon registers, designed to promote confidence and facilitate broader progress towards nuclear disarmament, and discuss the complex questions relating to the involvement of nuclear 'threshold' states and the appropriate international forum in which to develop such nuclear weapon registers.

Overall, the book examines all the key issues on the agenda for the 1997 review of the implementation and further development of the UN Register, and a number of major associated issues relating to the development and use of arms transparency and confidence-building measures at a regional level and also relating to light weapons and nuclear arms. The chapters approach these issues from a number of perspectives. We have not aimed to ensure a single consistent line of argument throughout the book, but rather to ensure that the chapters reflect the range of key themes and positions on arms transparency and the Register. We hope that everybody involved or interested in the policy debates will find it stimulating and informative.

One central message that emerges for us from the book is that the Register is still far from reaching its full potential in its contribution to promoting transparency, accountability and security. There is a substantial and promising agenda for the future development and use of the Register and other associated arms transparency arrangements. Moreover, weaknesses in the existing Register need to be tackled. These points were recognised by the 1994 UN Group of Experts, but it proved impossible at that time to achieve consensus on ways and means to pursue them. Three years on, the Register has now been established, with good levels of participation, for about five years. We believe that the time is right in 1997 to take steps to strengthen and expand the Register, and to promote its wider use. The challenge for the 1997 UN Group of Experts is to take the opportunities to achieve this.

A range of people and institutions contributed substantially to this book, and to the workshop from which it emerged. As noted at the beginning of this introduction, the workshop aimed to provide an opportunity for the members of the 1997 UN Group of Experts to meet with non-governmental specialists, and to examine and discuss papers on key topics relevant to the review. It was jointly organised by: the Department of Peace Studies, University of Bradford (UK); the Ministry of Foreign Affairs (Japan); and the Centre for the Promotion of Disarmament and Non-Proliferation (CPDNP), Japan Institute for International Affairs (Japan). Owen Greene and Malcolm Chalmers of Bradford University took primary responsibility for arranging the workshop programme and non-governmental participation. Ambassador Mitsuro Donowaki and his colleagues in the Arms Control and Disarmament Division of the Ministry of Foreign Affairs, Japan (particularly Hitoshi Ozawa, Takeshi Matsunaga, and Tamotsu Kidono) invited the members of the UN Group of Experts, arranged accommodation and excellent facilities for the workshop, and organised a short meeting for the UN Group of Experts immediately after the workshop. CPDNP co-sponsored the workshop and this book, and the consistent support of Ambassador Tomoya Kawamura (Director of CPDNP) and his staff contributed significantly to all phases of the project.

Above all, the success of the workshop depended on the quality of the contributions of the participants (listed in Appendix 1). We thank the members of the UN Group of Experts for devoting the substantial time and attention required to participate in the workshop - only a very few could not attend due to other commitments - and particularly Mr Raphael Grossi, Chair of the 1997 UN Group of Experts, for his invaluable support and advice, for chairing two sessions and contributing to several others. Similarly, we thank the non-governmental experts and paper-givers for their excellent papers and presentations, and for their cooperation and effectiveness in responding to our editorial requests in presenting and rapidly revising their papers for this book.

It was an important aim for us that this book would be completed, published, and distributed in time to feed in to the deliberations of the UN Group of Experts well before their final meeting began in July 1997, as well as to provide a timely resource for the wider interested policy community and public. This meant that the entire process had to be completed within about 6 weeks. This could not have been achieved without the cooperation of many people. In addition to the cooperation, speed and grace of the contributors noted above, we would like to give special thanks to Jeannie Grußendorf, for all of her help in editing and formatting the book at Bradford. In addition, we thank Jenny Braithwaite and Chris Bowers for their role in preparing the book covers, and Doris Coombs, Simon Covey and all the other staff at Redwood Books for their efficiency and cooperation in the speedy printing of the book.

For the editors, the workshop and book are part of an on-going engagement with the development and operation of the UN Register and associated confidence-building measures, started before the Register was established in 1992. Ambassador Mitsuro Donowaki has been closely involved with the process as Japan's representative. Malcolm Chalmers and Owen Greene have contributed as academics and non-governmental experts, not least through their books and reports in the Bradford Arms Register Studies (BARS) series of which this book is a part. Their work in this area has greatly benefited from interactions with many colleagues, in academia, non-governmental organisations, governments, and the UN and other international organisations. The cooperation of the UN Centre for Disarmament Affairs, particularly Provoslav Davinic, Hannelore Hoppe, Tamara Malinova, Anita Ng and their colleagues, has been consistent and invaluable, and we heartily thank them for this.

The Ford Foundation and Ploughshares Fund have generously provided funding to support Malcolm Chalmers and Owen Greene in their work in this area for several years. Specifically, they also provided essential financial support for the Tokyo workshop (including non-governmental participation) and for this book, which is gratefully acknowledged. The editors would also like to thank the Ministry of Foreign Affairs of Japan and the CPDNP for co-sponsoring the workshop, and also for providing substantial resources to not only help with the workshop organisation and provide excellent accommodation and facilities for the workshop, but also to contribute to the travel costs of governmental representatives from developing countries. Japan's consistent support for, and interest in, the UN Register has been an important factor in its development.

Malcolm Chalmers, Mitsuro Donowaki, and Owen Greene

June 1997

Part A: Reviewing the Register

CHAPTER 2

The Register in its first four years

Malcolm Chalmers and Owen Greene

Introduction

The United Nations Register of Conventional Arms was established in 1992, with the first submissions of data due to be submitted to the UN by 30 April 1993. Thus, at the time of writing (June 1997), the Register had operated for four years, and was entering its fifth year of operation. Debates on whether and how to strengthen and develop it should, clearly, be based on a knowledge and understanding of how the Register has operated so far. This chapter aims to provide this, by outlining and examining experience with the Register in its first four years.

The chapter examines participation in the Register, and discusses some global and regional trends. It then analyses its operation, examining the numerical and qualitative information submitted on arms transfers and the issue of discrepancies between data provided by exporting and importing states. Finally, a number of conclusions are provided. Firstly, however, a short historical outline of the establishment of the Register and the UN Review processes are provided in the next two sections.

Establishing the UN Register

During the Cold War, there was widespread scepticism as to the political feasibility of a UN Register of Conventional Arms, given the opposition of many developing and Soviet bloc countries. The prospects for the register concept changed dramatically after the end of the Cold War, and particularly in the aftermath of the Gulf War in early 1991, which created intense pressure on governments to 'do something' about the arms trade. In this context, support for the concept strengthened greatly, particularly amongst OECD states, the USSR and East European countries, and numerous developing countries (particularly from Latin America). In the summer and autumn of 1991, the European Community and Japan took the lead in the UN in preparing and promoting support for a UN General Assembly resolution to establish an UN register of arms transfers.[1]

In the course of the debates that followed, several developing countries expressed concern that an exclusive focus on arms transfers would discriminate in favour of those states that were largely self-sufficient in arms production. In response to these concerns, the revised resolution submitted to the First Committee on 15 November 1991 accepted in principle that a UN Register should include military holdings and procurement through national production as well as arms transfers, and called for the establishment of a Panel of Technical Experts to review this and other questions. The name of the Register was changed from Register of Conventional Arms Transfers to Register of Conventional Arms. The resolution as amended then passed the First Committee by a vote of 106 to 1 (Cuba), with eight abstentions (China, North Korea, Iraq, Myanmar, Oman, Pakistan, Singapore and Sudan). The General Assembly passed the resolution on 9 December by 150 votes to nil, with two abstentions (Cuba and Iraq).

The Panel of Technical Experts met four times through 1992, presenting a consensus report to the First Committee in October 1992, which was subsequently endorsed by consensus (without a vote) by the General Assembly in December 1992. The Report included a standardised form for the submission by each country of entries on its arms imports and exports, together with detailed guidelines on what data should be provided and in what form. Each year, countries were (and are) asked to provide data on their imports and exports of seven categories major conventional arms during the previous calendar year. Each participating state should report the number of arms in each category that it has transferred between each (named) supplier or recipient country during that year, together with further qualitative information (on weapons types and roles, for example) as they see fit.

The inclusion in the Register of similar data on military holdings and procurement from national production was deferred for future consideration. Though the principle of including such data had been accepted, there was no consensus on ways and means of doing so. In practice, several key states were not yet prepared to report such information, and even some strong supporters of the Register felt that there was a risk of overloading the new and fragile transparency arrangement. They successfully argued that it was better to launch a relatively limited Register and secure wide participation. Once this was achieved, the question of expanding it to include military holdings and procurement from national production would be reviewed. In the meantime, governments were simply invited to supplement their annual reports on arms transfers with 'available background information' on their military holdings and procurement from national production, as they saw fit.

UN Reviews of the Register

Thus the Register was initially established in 1992 primarily as a register of international transfers of seven categories of major conventional arms. However, the question of developing the Register, and particularly of expanding its scope, has continued to be raised since then. Indeed, support for including military holdings and procurement from national production widened substantially once the Register had been launched, as previously-sceptical western governments endorsed the proposal.

In 1994, the UN established its first review of the operation and further development of the UN Register. A UN Group of Experts representing 23 states was established, which met through the spring and summer of 1994 to negotiate and agree ways in which the Register could be strengthened or expanded. Since the Group of Experts included the key states and had good geographical representation, any consensus recommendations were very likely to be accepted by the UN General Assembly and come into effect. It considered many issues (as identified in chapter 1, 3 and 4 of this book), with proposals to include military holdings and procurement from national production providing a central focus for negotiations. Unfortunately, although the Group endorsed the Register and usefully clarified certain issues, no consensus could be reached on any substantial measure to revise, strengthen or expand the transparency regime.[2]

Several states argued that it was too early in the life of the Register for such measures to be appropriate. The 1994 review took place at a time when most participants had scarcely completed their data submissions for the second year. It therefore took place before the accumulation of much experience with operating the Register, and before many states had had time to become comfortable with the new transparency arrangements.

The UN decided to carry out a second major review of the Register in 1997. A new UN Group of Experts was convened for this purpose, consisting of representatives of 25 states. It held its first meeting on 3 - 7 March 1997, with two subsequent meetings on 16 - 27 June and 4 - 15 August (in addition to the informal workshop in Tokyo in May 1997 from which this book emerged). As in 1994, it is essentially a negotiating group: any consensus recommendations are very likely to be adopted by the UN General Assembly.

Four Years of Reporting: an overview

Every year, states in the UN system are requested to submit data for the Register to the UN Secretariat at the Centre for Disarmament Affairs by 30 April, on their major arms transfers during the previous calendar year. Their submissions are subsequently compiled and published in an annual report of the UN Secretary-General on the United Nations Register of Conventional Arms. In practice, most states have missed the 30 April deadline, and the Secretary-General's report has been delayed until late summer, so that it can include late submissions. Every year, a few states have missed even this extended deadline, and submitted their replies after the Secretary-General's report has been published. These replies are published as Addenda to the annual report (similarly, Corrigenda are published if states find errors in their initial submissions).

Thus, the fourth annual Report of the UN Secretary General on the United Nations Register of Conventional Arms was released on 3 October 1996, providing information on countries' imports and exports of major conventional arms during 1995.[3] In previous years, the UN had delayed publication until the end of October, in order to provide some additional time for further submissions. The relatively early publication in 1996 meant that a number of important regular participants had not made submissions in time to be included in that year's annual report. Nevertheless, 85 countries were included in the 1996 Report, compared to 84 in the previous year. By 22 October, late submissions had been made by Australia, Azerbaijan, Belarus, Russia, Tanzania and Thailand. In addition, it was decided that the Cook Islands should be recorded in the total number of replies, despite the fact that it is not a UN member. This brought the total number of countries providing information for the Register in its fourth year to 92.[4] Further replies were received from Sri Lanka in December 1996 and Pakistan in January 1997.

The annual report of the UN Secretary General is widely used as the key source on annual participation in the Register, and for the information reported. However, the above discussion shows how this practice can be misleading. Late submissions, particularly by key states, mean that any analysis of Register participation and data focused solely on the annual reports would be incomplete. We have therefore used a cut-off date of mid-November to analyse the replies. Experience indicates that this provides a substantially more complete and consistent picture.

Table 1 summarises participation in the UN Register during its first four years. Participation rates have gradually increased from year to year.

Moreover, every year nearly all of the top arms exporting countries and most major importers have participated. This means that the Register has consistently covered over 90% of the international trade in major conventional arms.

Table 1: Total number of Register replies received

	1993	1994	1995	1996
Included in annual report	80	81	84	85
Received by November 14	82	84	87	92
Received by March 31, next year	83	88	92	94

As Table 1 shows, even the mid-November cut-off date can omit some late entries. In the third year, for example, five additional countries made submissions between mid November and the end of March in the following year: Belize, Burkina Faso, Chad, Iran and Nepal.[5] In the fourth year, Pakistan and Sri Lanka similarly reported after our November reference date, as noted above. The situation is made even more complex by the fact that new or lapsed participants in the Register are encouraged to submit data on previous years as well as for the current one. Thus, when Sri Lanka reported in December 1996, it provided information for 1993 and 1994 as well as for 1995. In practice, reporting to the Register has thus developed into a continuous process, though the official deadline and publication of the annual Secretary-General's report continues to provide an important stimulus and guideline for the great majority of participating states.

Participation

About 50% of states have participated in the Register each year. Moreover, the number of participants has gradually but discernibly increased each year. Altogether 92 states had submitted reports on their activities in 1995 by 14 November 1996. As Table 1 shows, this compares with 87 states replying by the same stage in 1995 (covering transfers during 1994), 84 in 1994 (relating to 1993) and 82 in 1993 (relating to 1992).

However, this upward trend conceals substantial and continuing 'turnover' in participation. For example, twelve countries reported in 1996 for the first time: Andorra, Monaco, Cook Islands, St Kitts and Nevis, Azerbaijan, Kyrgystan, Latvia, Turkmenistan, Central African Republic, Ethiopia, Gabon and, in December 1996, Sri Lanka. A further 11 countries reported in 1996 which had not participated in the Register in its third year (by November 1995), but which had reported in a previous year. But these new or 'returnee' participants were largely offset by 17 countries which did participate in the third year, but have not done so in this year. The relatively high rate of turnover that characterised the first three years of the Register thus shows no sign of ending.

The high turnover in participation means that a total of 134 states participated in the Register at least once in its first four years (rising to 138 by June 1997 as Guatemala, Brunei, Macedonia and Honduras submitted reports for the first time for the fifth year). This represents almost three quarters of all UN member states. Appendix 1 lists all of the countries that have participated in the Register, according to year.

A number of significant non-participants, such as North Korea, Nigeria and several Middle Eastern states, probably cannot be expected to participate unless there are substantial changes in the orientation of national policy. However, there are as many as twenty or more UN members (such as Costa Rica) that are widely seen as 'norm-abiding', 'responsible', states, and have not yet participated in the Register, even though they have regularly endorsed it at the UN General Assembly and have no obvious political problems with submitting reports. It seems reasonable to expect that most such states will decide to participate in the Register within the next three years, though efforts need to continue to persuade them to do so. Otherwise, efforts to increase participation in the Register must increasingly focus on persuading (or enabling) 'lapsed' participants to submit reports every year.

Most of the states which are not yet regular participants in the Register are not heavily engaged in the international trade in major conventional arms. However, the submission of a 'nil report' itself conveys significant information, as well as providing an important indication of active political support for, and participation in, the Register. Moreover, many 'smaller' states are actually significantly involved in the arms trade. As discussed below, many of the smaller states in sub-Saharan Africa and Latin America - where turnover in participation in the Register is greatest - have imported significant conventional arms recently. Over a period of years, such imports accumulate and their overall significance may increase. Thus, it remains important to increase participation in the Register by these countries.

Regional Participation

Participation of the countries of **Europe** in the Register is high. The Holy See and San Marino have yet to submit reports. However, by the end of the fourth year, the major gap in participation was the lack of replies from four of the five countries that have emerged from the former Yugoslavia: Bosnia, Croatia, Macedonia and Yugoslavia (Serbia & Montenegro). In previous years, Croatia and Yugoslavia participated by submitting (implausible) 'nil returns', but they apparently decided against this course of action in 1996. In a welcome recent development, Macedonia reported for the first time in 1997, providing data for the fifth year.[6] Hopefully, the other three remaining former Yugoslavian states will also prove willing to submit reports now that UN sanctions against them are being relaxed and the peace process is in place.

One of the most positive developments over the four years has been the increased participation in the Register by the countries of the **former Soviet Union**. In 1996, 13 of the 15 states in this region participated, compared to only five in the first two years and nine in year three. This appears to reflect increased awareness of the Register and improved administrative capacity, and perhaps also increased attention to arms export controls.[7] Alongside their improved participation in the Register, these countries are typically becoming more active in UN and international affairs. In 1996, only Uzbekistan and Georgia had not submitted reports by mid-November. Georgia participated in each of the first three years of the Register's operation, and it is not clear why this changed in 1996. However, Georgia submitted a reply in June 1997 relating to 1996. Uzbekistan, however, has yet to participate. According to SIPRI, its exports were valued at $406 million in 1994 and $464 million in 1995, largely due to exports of military transport aircraft to China.[8]

Russia has consistently found it difficult to submit its annual reports on time, though it is by no means unique in this respect. Alongside the continued turbulence in the Russian government and bureaucratic complexities, there appears to be continuing resistance amongst some influential groups in Russia to providing reports on arms exports. Nevertheless, every year these problems have been overcome, and Russia has submitted a substantial report to the UN. For example, the fourth year's report included several transfers in 1995 to countries that do not participate in the Register (armoured personnel carriers to Algeria, Kuwait

and the United Arab Emirates), some of which had not previously been
noted in other publicly available sources (such as SIPRI).

Table 2: Participation in the UN Register by region

Region	1992 replies by November 1993	1993 replies by November 1994	1994 replies by November 1995	1995 replies by November 1996	Countries in region
Europe	30	31	31	32	38
Asia & Oceania	18	20	21	21 (1)	34
America	14	14	19	15	35
Former Soviet Union	5	5	9	13	15
Sub-Saharan Africa	8	11	5	9	48
Middle East	7	3	2	2	18
Total	82	84	87	92	188

(1) Note however, that in December 1996 Sri Lanka provided submissions for 1993, 1994
and 1995, and in January 1997 Pakistan provided a report for 1995. Thus, by spring 1997,
the participation rate in Asia and Oceania for 1995 had reached 23.

Participation in the **Middle East** remains low. Israel and Jordan regularly
submit timely reports, but they are alone in this in the region. A few other
states participate irregularly, but in the context this too is welcome. Iran
provided a late submission in 1994 (covering its imports in both 1992 and
1993), and in January 1996 it provided data on its imports in 1994. In each
case, the imports Iran reported precisely matched the information that had
already been reported to the Register by its suppliers. In the third year of
operation, Libya also participated (submitting a 'nil report'). After some
initial uncertainty, however, most other countries in the region appear to
have deliberately decided not to participate in the Register, and seem to be
unlikely to reverse their position without a significant change in the
domestic or regional political situation.

Since nearly all arms exporting countries do participate, the Register still includes substantial amounts of information on imports into this region. In fact, about 90% of the total arms transfers to non-participating states in 1995 that were reported to the Register by exporters were to the Middle East. Most of the non-participating Middle East countries were reported to be recipients of arms exports, and in some cases their imports were very substantial. Only four countries are not reported by exporters to have imported major arms during 1995: Iraq, Libya, Syria, and Morocco. The first three of these were reportedly in the same position in the previous year (1994), but the USA reported exporting 120 tanks to Morocco that year.

Egypt - which, thanks largely to US military aid, is an important arms importer - continues to suspend its participation in the Register. It took part in the first year, but subsequently refused to participate further because of its dissatisfaction with the outcome of the 1994 UN Group of Experts. Egypt had wanted the Register to be expanded to include nuclear arms transparency as a reflection of its concerns about Israeli capabilities. It had also expressed concern at the failure to include military holdings, procurement through national production, and military high technology. When no progress was made on any of these issues in the 1994 Group of Experts, the Egyptian expert on the Group reserved his position on the report: the only member to do so.[9]

Participation rates in **Asia and Oceania** are mixed, but remain fairly stable. In East Asia most countries now regularly participate in the Register.[10] One of the most significant and positive developments since 1992 has been the increasing participation by ASEAN states. In the first year, only half of these participated. However, as of 1997, all ASEAN states submit reports.[11] However, the three candidate ASEAN members - Cambodia, Laos and Myanmar - remain non-participants.[12] In North East Asia, China, Japan, South Korea, Russia and Mongolia have submitted full reports from the beginning. North Korea remains the only UN member in the sub-region which does not participate in the Register.

Taiwan is not asked to provide data for the Register because it is not a UN member. Since Taiwan was the third largest importer of conventional arms into East Asia in 1991-1995 (after China and Japan),[13] this significantly limits the coverage in the Register of arms transfers into the region. In the first three years of the Register's operation, this gap was compounded by the practice of major arms exporters not to report their exports to Taiwan to the Register. In the fourth year, however, the USA made an important contribution to transparency by reporting to the Register the export to

Taiwan of 21 battle tanks, 1 ACV, 10 attack helicopters and 254 missiles and missile launchers. Presumably in order to emphasise Taiwan's different status, the information was included as a footnote to the US's export table, rather than in the table itself. In order for this arrangement to provide full coverage of Taiwan's imports, it will be necessary for other suppliers to adopt a similar arrangement. This is of particular relevance for France, which is in the process of delivering six Lafayette missile frigates and 60 Mirage 2000-5 aircraft to Taiwan, but has not so far declared any exports to the island.[14]

In Oceania, participation continues to be mixed. Australia and New Zealand are consistent participants. Fiji, Papua New Guinea, and Samoa have also become consistent participants. However, the Marshall Islands allowed its participation for the first three years to lapse in 1996, whereas Vanuatu resumed participation after a year's absence in 1995. The Cook Islands submitted a report for the first time in 1996, and the UN included it in the total number of replies reported in the annual report. However, since the Cook Islands is not a member of the UN, its report was not included in the UN's standardised table of replies for that year.

In South Asia, India, Pakistan, Nepal, Bhutan and the Maldives consistently submit reports. In 1996, there was concern for a period when Pakistan did not provide a submission. However, it submitted a late reply on 13 January 1997. The delay apparently occurred while national authorities checked a discrepancy between their records of imports and the submission by the UK for that year: a useful example of how the Register can help states to check and improve their national control systems.[15] Afghanistan reported once in 1993 (to say that it could not provide reliable data to the data in the context of civil war). Encouragingly, Sri Lanka replied for the first time in December 1996, reporting the import of 3 KFIR aircraft from Israel in 1995 (and also providing reports for previous years). However, Bangladesh has remained a non-participant throughout.

In the **Americas**, the overall participation rate has been modest, at between 14 and 19 countries out of a possible 35.[16] In 1996, 15 countries from the Americas had submitted reports for the fourth year by mid-November 1996. However, the major states in the hemisphere (including Canada, USA, Mexico, Brazil, and Argentina), have consistently fully participated. Amongst the medium regional powers, however, participation remains mixed. Chile, Peru and Cuba have been consistent participants. But Uruguay and Venezuela have not submitted reports, Bolivia and Colombia allowed their participation to lapse after the first year, and Ecuador's and Paraguay's participation lapsed in 1996.

Turnover in participation amongst small states in this hemisphere has remained high. For example, in 1996 fewer of these countries renewed their participation than those that allowed their participation to lapse, bringing the overall participation rate in the hemisphere down to below the 1995 figure. This turnover probably reflects a lack of bureaucratic capacity and government awareness of the Register in these small states more than any particular dissatisfaction with it.

Finally, in **Sub-Saharan Africa**, participation has remained disappointingly low. Participation rates have varied between five and eleven, out of a possible total of 48 states in the region. In 1996, nine countries submitted reports. Burkina Faso, Mauritius, South Africa and Tanzania have become consistent participants. Otherwise, there is a regular turnover of participants, with Madagascar and Namibia resuming reporting and the Central African Republic, Ethiopia and Gabon making a submission for the first time in 1996.

Apart from problems of lack of administrative capacity and government awareness, it is sometimes argued that sub-Saharan African states also choose not to participate because the Register deals only with major weapons, which are not relevant to these states' security. As discussed in Part E of this book, there is a strong case for developing UN transparency measures covering light weapons (though not necessarily as part of the UN Register itself). In reality, however, this argument for non-participation may in some cases be more of a justification than a real reason. There were considerable transfers of major conventional weapons to the region during the last four years, as exporters' reports to the Register demonstrate. However, it appears that those African countries who are involved in imports of major weapons are less, not more, likely to report to the Register. Each of the 35 separate replies on imports made by sub-Saharan African countries since the Register began have been 'nil returns'. Yet, over the same four year period, exporting states have reported transfers of weapons in the Register categories to 15 of the countries of sub-Saharan Africa. There are also well-documented reports of significant shipments of conventional arms during this period to Angola, Botswana, Zimbabwe, and Nigeria, none of which have been reported to the UN by recipient states. With the significant exception of South Africa, therefore, it appears that only those African countries that are not involved in transfers of major conventional weapons have been willing to participate in the Register. This has not generally been the case in most other regions of the world.

One of the explanations for different rates of regional participation in the Register may lie with the relative strength of regional confidence-building processes. In East Asia, improving participation in the Register has been a focus of ASEAN Regional Forum recommendations, and this is thought to have played a role in persuading Indonesia, Thailand and Vietnam to participate.[17] All the countries of the former Soviet Union are members of the OSCE, and many are also associated with Nato's Partnership for Peace programme, both of which emphasise military transparency. The security dialogues in South America, especially in the Southern cone, appear to be playing a role in encouraging participation amongst key states.[18] In sub-Saharan Africa, by contrast, there is a relative lack of autonomous regional or sub-regional confidence-building arrangements. Finally, in the Middle East, problems with Arab-Israeli peace-building, together with attempts by Arab states to create linkages between the development of confidence-building measures in the conventional and nuclear weapons spheres, has so far contributed to a low level of participation.

Examining the Transfers Data

The major exporters and importers

In all four years of operation of the Register so far, nearly all of the main conventional arms exporters submitted a report for the Register. For example, of the top 20 arms exporters during 1991-95 listed by SIPRI (ranked by trend-indicator value of their exports of major weapons), all but two (North Korea and Uzbekistan) reported in 1996.[19] The data provided by the major exporters to the Register confirm the continuing dominance of the world arms market by NATO and European countries. The United States' position as the largest arms exporter has been consolidated, and it now accounts for well over half of reported global exports. By 1995, Russia had overtaken Germany for second place as the 'cascading' of surplus weapons from Germany winds down. Central and Eastern European producers are also significant exporters, as are the UK, France and Canada. In comparison, overall exports of major weapons by 'emerging' suppliers such as South Africa, Israel, and South Korea are relatively small in number and value. In total, only 22 countries reported any exports at all during 1995, for example (see Table 3).

Table 3: Complete listing of exporters of conventional arms 1995 (based on exporters' submissions to the Register)

Country	Tanks	ACVs	Artillery	Combat aircraft	Attack helos	Warships	MML	TOTAL (excluding MML)
NATO								
USA	437	1090	152	128	35	-	3287	1842
Germany	-	335	15	-	20	6	-	376
Canada		294					-	294
UK	12	137	55	12	1	1	-	228
Belgium		118		1			-	119
France	25			3	6		11	34
Italy			18				-	18
Netherlands						1	-	1
OTHER EUROPE								
Russia		451	210	46		1		708
Czech Republic		62	70	21			-	153
Romania		81	1				-	82
Ukraine	64	8		4			159	76
Poland	72						-	72
Slovakia	6	57	6				-	69
Finland		31					-	31
Switzerland		10					-	10
Kazakhstan				6			-	6

OTHER								
China	51	20				1	18	72
South Korea		47		3			-	50
South Africa		43					-	43
Argentina			18				-	18
Israel				3			20	3
Total 1995	667	2784	545	227	62	10	3495	
Total 1994	1255	3856	976	232	12	36	2098	

It is important to emphasise that raw numbers of weapons exported, even if entirely accurate, are not a good guide to the relative value of exports from different countries. Some countries' exports are composed mainly of relatively low-value exports of tanks, ACV's and artillery, some of which may in any case be second-hand. Similarly, the category of 'missiles and missile launchers' is particularly difficult to interpret on the basis of numbers alone, and they are thus excluded from the indicative numerical totals in Table 3 of countries' arms exports.

Similarly, most major arms importers also participated in the Register in each of its four years of operation. For example, 18 of the 25 top importers during 1991-95 (according to SIPRI) provided reports in 1996.[20] Amongst the top importers, Egypt, Saudi Arabia, Kuwait, and the United Arab Emirates do not participate. Because it has not been asked for information, neither does Taiwan. Other important importers that do not participate include Algeria, Angola, Lebanon, Uganda, Uruguay and Venezuela.

Since almost all arms exporters participate in the Register, it includes much information on exports to non-participating states, including all of the major importers listed above. To illustrate this, Appendix 2 details this information for 1995.

Nil Returns

Each year, about 50% of the participants have provided 'nil reports'. For example, 44 of the 92 states that had submitted a report for the fourth year by mid-November 1996 reported nil returns for both imports and exports.

This reflects the fact that the trade in major conventional arms is concentrated amongst a relatively small number of suppliers and recipients.

Exports to regions of tension

The Register provides substantial information on exports to regions of tension, which are a particular concern for international security. For example, as Table 4 shows, the Register has detailed large scale transfers of arms to Greece and Turkey, between whom the level of tension remains dangerously high. This transfer process has largely been associated with the 'cascading' of surplus weapons from richer NATO members. The level of reported imports slowed significantly in 1995. Given the ambitious procurement plans of both countries, however, it remains to be seen whether this is only a temporary pause.

Similarly, the Register confirms that major conventional arms continue to be transferred in large quantities to the Middle East. Since few of the main recipients in this region participate in the Register, most of the data on this in the register has been provided by suppliers. However, the data from exporters appears sufficiently comprehensive to provide a fairly complete picture for most importers in the region.

Table 4: Imports by Greece and Turkey 1992-1995
(according to importers' replies)

Country	Tanks	ACVs	Artillery	Combat aircraft	Attack helos	Warships	Missiles and Missile Launchers
Greece 1992	447	151	249	16		11	21
Greece 1993	450	-	12	44		4	33
Greece 1994	43	933	222	33		3	
Greece 1995	-	100	9	24	20	5	16
Turkey 1992	427	119	69	26	6		24
Turkey 1993	539	433	3	15	25	5	10
Turkey 1994	62	151	131	19	1	4	
Turkey 1995	-	70	-			1	

The Register also reveals information on arms exports to countries with internal conflicts or where there is a risk that the weapons may be used against internal rebels. For example, in 1996 the Algerian government was reported to have received 150 ACV's from Russia and 49 ACVs from Slovakia. In addition to 3 patrol boats from Germany, Indonesia was reported to have received 27 ACVs from the UK (which were not included in the Indonesian submission for that year). Arms exports to Turkey also cause some controversy, because of concern about Turkish military actions against Kurdish groups.

New information in the Register

When the Register was first established, it was sometimes suggested that it would reveal little new information on transfers of major armaments. Authoritative unofficial sources of information on the arms trade already existed, such as Jane's, IISS and the SIPRI arms trade data-base. It was often argued that these already provided reasonably comprehensive and reliable information, and in any case states would not reveal information on their transfers that was not already in the public domain. The first years of the Register quickly demonstrated that these sceptics were wrong. The Register revealed significant new information on transfers occurring during 1992-3, particularly in relation to land-based systems (tanks, armoured combat vehicles, heavy artillery) and helicopters.[21]

Since then, the Register has continued to provide information that was not previously available in public sources. For transfers in 1994 (covered by the Register in its third year of operation), we have identified some 59 transfers reported to the UN Register which were not listed by SIPRI in its published data-base.[22] Similarly for 1995, we have found 57 separate transactions that had not been included in the 1996 SIPRI Yearbook but were featured in the Register replies in 1996.[23] In some of these, the Register itself may be inaccurate. Although it provides official information, governments may sometimes erroneously report transfers that have yet to take place. Moreover, some of these newly revealed transfers were quite small. In other cases, however, they were substantial. For example, in 1996 Russia reported exports of 201 artillery systems to India and 150 ACV's to Algeria. Neither transfer is included in SIPRI's 1996 Yearbook.

This is not to imply any criticism of the annual SIPRI Register, which plays a vital role in promoting transparency in the arms trade. It often provides more details on transfers, has wider scope, and includes significant transfers not included in UN Register replies. Some of the omissions from the SIPRI Register are a result of appropriate caution about including unconfirmed reports. Our comparison does indicate, however, that the UN Register is producing added value: revealing information that was not previously in the public domain as well as officially confirming existing information.

Qualitative information in the Register

The extent to which the Register contributes to transparency of arms transfers depends significantly on whether it includes qualitative information on the types and models of the weapons involved and their intended role. According to agreed UN guidelines, countries are invited to provide qualitative data on each transfer in the 'comments' columns of the Register's standardised reporting forms. However, this is optional: participating countries are only obliged to provide numerical information for each category of weapons transferred to a particular country.

Many participating states reporting transfers have routinely included some qualitative information in their submissions. The major Latin American countries have, for example, provided types data from the beginning. Moreover, since the 1994 review, a number of states have overcome their initial caution on providing data on the types and models of weapons transferred. Only six of the 13 states which did not provide types data in 1993 (the Register's first year) were still declining to do so by early 1997.[24] France provided types data on its exports for the first time in 1996. The UK similarly included types data (for all categories except missiles and missile launchers) in their 1997 submission for the fifth year of the Register. This means that all members of the EU are now providing information on weapon types for at least six of the Register's arms categories. Similarly, ASEAN states in particular appear to be moving towards a norm of providing types data on their imports. Indonesia, Malaysia and the Philippines have always done so. The first 'non-zero' return from Vietnam, submitted in 1996, included types data on its import of combat aircraft from Russia. In a change to previous practice, Singapore and Thailand also began to provide types data in 1996.[25]

This trend is welcome and important. The further development of reporting on qualitative information on transfers is an important issue on the agenda of the 1997 Group of Experts' review of the Register. China, India, Japan, Russia, and the US now stand out as countries which still do not supply qualitative information. Of these, Japan at least has indicated that it would supply such data if the USA also did so. A change of policy in this respect by the USA and any of the other three countries noted above would go a long way towards securing a new global norm on providing data on weapons types in the Register.

Discrepancies in the submitted data

In the first four years of operation of the Register, there were many discrepancies between transfers reported by the importer and exporter. Discrepancies between exports reported by the US and the imports reported by its recipient countries were particularly frequent. Since the US is by far the largest arms exporter, this practice had a serious impact on the Register as a whole. For example, our analysis of the third year of the Register included a general comparison of the extent to which the replies of different exporting states matched those of their trading partners.[26] The results of this analysis found that only a small proportion of the replies of the US in 1995 matched those of its Register-participating trading partners, while a very high proportion of those of Germany did match. The records of the UK and France were closer to that of Germany in this respect than those of the US. Other exporters - almost all European - appeared to find it about as difficult as the US to match the replies of their importers.

A similar examination of the replies from the major exporters in 1996 indicated that the problem of discrepancies remains serious. In Table 5, we start with the exports reported by the exporting states themselves, and tabulate how many of these reported exports are: (a) confirmed by the import returns of the appropriate countries ('matches'); (b) not confirmed by the importing state despite its participation in the Register ('non-matches'); (c) not confirmed because the importing state in question did not participate in the Register ('not taking part'). The 'match rate' then shows what proportion of the transfers reported by exporting states matched up with the submissions from importers participating in the Register. On this basis, for example, one of France's reported exports was matched by the report from the relevant importing state, three failed to match with reports from importers, three were to states not taking part in the Register.

However, the analysis in Table 5 fails to take account of those exports which are not reported by the exporter, but are reported by an importing state. Table 6 does take this into account. It starts by arranging all imports (as reported by importing states) according to the reported supplier country. It then assesses how many of these imports were reported by the appropriate exporting state. In the three cases of imports from non-participants, no matches are possible. In all other cases, the 'match rate' denotes the proportion of imports reported by importing states which are matched by identical replies by the exporting state.

Table 5: Matching of the returns of exporting states for 1995

Exporting countries	Matches	Non-matches	Match rate %	Not taking part in Register	Total transfers
Germany	8	0	100%	-	8
Russian Federation	6	2	75%	4	12
Other West European	4	3	57%	-	7
UK	3	4	43%	10	17
Central and Eastern European	6	10	37%	13	29
France	1	3	25%	3	7
US	6	33	15%	16	55
Other Register participants	1	5	17%	11	17
Total	35	60	37%	57	152

Table 6: Matching of the returns of importing states for 1995

Countries from which imports reported	Matches	Non-matches	Match rate %	Not taking part in Register	Total transfers
France	1	-	100%		1
Germany	9	1	90%		10
Russian Federation	6	6	50%		12
UK	3	3	50%		6
Other West European	4	4	50%		8
Central and Eastern					

European	5	9	36%		14
US	5	21	24%		26
Other Register participants	1	4	20%		5
Exporters not in Register				3	3
Total	34	48	41%	3	85

This analysis indicates that the overall rate of discrepancies between reports from exporters and importers has actually worsened somewhat between the third and the fourth years. The proportion of exporters' replies that match with those of importers declined from 53% in 1995 to 37% in 1996; and a similar decline can be seen if one looks at importers' reports. Once again, moreover, the US had the worst matching rate of all the major exporters in 1996, with only 15% of the transfers it reports to other Register participants being matched by the replies from the importing state. Only 24% of the reports of imports from the US match those made by the US itself.

One of the reasons for the high level of discrepancies is undoubtedly the failure of the 1994 UN Group of Experts to reach agreement on a common definition of what constitutes an arms transfer. Many countries even fail to make clear which definition they have chosen to use. For example, the failure of the US to report the export of a Knox-class warship to Thailand in 1994 (which was reported by Thailand) may be the result of the US's practice of using 'transfer of title' as the criterion for transfer. The US has interpreted this criterion to exclude the lease of military equipment to foreign armed forces. This helps to explain why four countries reported imports of warships from the US in 1995, but the US did not report the export of any warships during the same year. Taking a longer period, obligatory reports to Congress show US exports of 5 destroyers, 34 frigates and 13 tank-landing ships over the four years since the Register began in 1992. But only four exports of warships were reported to the Register by the US during this same period.[27]

Background Information

In addition to information on their transfers, states are also invited to provide additional 'background information' on their military holdings and procurement from national production (and also on relevant national arms transfers regulations and guidelines). Experience with reporting 'background information' on military holdings and procurement from national production is discussed more fully in chapter 8, as a basis for analysing the opportunities and prospects for expanding the Register to include such information more fully. However, for completeness, we briefly summarise below how states have responded to the invitation to provide such 'background information' during the last four years.

In the first year of operation, some 33 states chose to provide at least some background information to the Register. This number increased significantly to 36 in the second year. Thereafter, however, this number stabilised, at 33 in the third year and 31 for the fourth year.

Each year, more states provided information on their military holdings than on procurement from national production, partly because several countries that report on their holdings are not arms producers. The number of countries providing at least some data on their military holdings was 24 in the first year, 31 in the second, and 29 and 28 in the following two years. Compared with this, the number of countries providing data on their procurement from national production was 16, 17, 20 and 20 respectively.

Thus the overall situation appears to be stable in this context. A significant number of states now routinely provide data on their military holdings and procurement from national production. However, they provide a variety of types of information, and in a range of format, making comparisons difficult. In the absence of a further initiative to promote globally the practice of providing such data, there is little evidence that this number will increase substantially.

Conclusions

After four years of operation, participation in the Register continues to increase gradually. By the time of writing (June 1997) 94 states had reported for its fourth year, and 138 states had participated at least once since 1993. Of these, about 70 states now consistently provide reports, and can be classed as 'core' participants. These include almost all major arms exporters, most major importers, and a reasonable number of countries from most geographical regions. A further 60 states only report occasionally, and 52 states have still never submitted replies. Since the Register began, participation rates have been consistently high amongst OECD and European states. Participation has increased steadily in East Asia and the former Soviet Union, and is now at a high level. Participation in South Asia and Latin America is still quite good, though marked by high 'turnover' or the absence of some regional powers. However, it remains low in both sub-Saharan Africa and the Middle East.

Overall, the Register has become established as an important source of official information covering more than 90% of the international trade in major conventional arms, and revealing significant new information on arms transfers. Moreover, an increasing number of states voluntarily include qualitative as well as quantitative information on their arms transfers. The Register thus continues to develop and provides an important basis for developing international security dialogues and confidence-building measures in most regions of the world. Some of the problems in its operation, such as discrepancies between importers' and exporters' submissions, remain. Furthermore, although a substantial number of countries now routinely provide background information on their military holdings or procurement from national production, this number does not appear to be increasing. In this and other key respects, the Register appears to require further development of its guidelines, scope and institutions if it is to achieve its full potential in contributing to international security.

Appendix: 1995 Exports to non-participants (in the fourth year) reported to the Register

Destination	Exporter	Number	Weapon
MIDDLE EAST			
Algeria	Russia	150	ACV
Algeria	Slovakia	48	BVP-2 ACV
Algeria	Slovakia	1	OT-66
Bahrain	US	6	attack helicopters
Egypt	US	274	battle tanks
Egypt	US	299	ACV
Egypt	US	7	artillery
Egypt	US	31	combat aircraft
Egypt	Czech Rep	1	advanced jet trainer L-59
Iran	Poland	70	T-72 tank
Iran	China	18	MML
Kuwait	US	16	battle tanks
Kuwait	UK	66	ACV
Kuwait	US	46	ACV
Kuwait	Russia	91	ACV
Kuwait	Russia	9	artillery
Lebanon	US	319	ACV
Oman	UK	12	battle tanks
Oman	UK	3	ACV
Oman	UK	4	combat aircraft
Oman	France	1	ITL 70 missile/missile launcher, via UK

Qatar	France	2	ITL70 missile/missile launcher, via UK
Saudi Arabia	US	89	battle tanks
Saudi Arabia	US	306	ACV
Saudi Arabia	Canada	212	Light armoured vehicle
Saudi Arabia	US	4	combat aircraft
Tunisia	Czech Rep	6	advanced jet trainer L-59
United Arab Emirates	France	25	tanks Leclerc
United Arab Emirates	Russia	122	ACV
United Arab Emirates	UK	4	combat aircraft
United Arab Emirates	US	12	attack helicopters
Yemen	Ukraine	4	Su-22 aircraft
ASIA & OCEANIA			
Bangladesh	Czech Rep	8	advanced jet trainer L-39ZA
Taiwan	US	21	battle tanks
Taiwan	US	1	ACV
Taiwan	US	10	attack helicopters
Taiwan	US	254	missiles & launchers
Destination	Exporter	Number	Weapon
SUB-SAHARAN AFRICA			
Angola	South Africa	3	Casspir mine protected ACV

Botswana	UK	10	ACV
Botswana	UK	3	artillery
Cote D'Ivoire	South Africa	3	ACV: RG12 Riot Control Vehicle
Cote D'Ivoire	South Africa	10	11 man Mamba APC
Gabon	UK	1	ACV
Sierra Leone	Poland	2	T-72 tank
Uganda	Ukraine	60	T-55 tank
Uganda	South Africa	10	11 man Mamba APC
Uganda	Ukraine	2	ACV: BTC-4 tractor
AMERICA			
Colombia	US	2	attack helicopters
Ecuador	Slovakia	6	122 mm BM vs. 70
Haiti	UK	2	ACV
Uruguay	Czech Rep	60	APC type OT-64
Venezuela	Argentina	18	105 mm gun
THE UN			
UNPROFOR	Slovakia	6	T-66 tank, adapted as deminer for sappers
UN	South Africa	15	11 man Mamba APC
UN	South Africa	2	7 man Mamba APC

---

1   A detailed account of the historical development of the UN
       Register is provided in: Malcolm Chalmers and Owen Greene,

Implementing and Developing the UN Register of Conventional Arms, Bradford Arms Register Studies (BARS) 1, Peace Research Report No 32, Bradford University, May 1993; E. Laurance, S. Wezeman and H. Wulf, *Arms Watch: SIPRI Report on the first year of the United Nations Register of Conventional Arms*, SIPRI Research Report No 6, Oxford University Press, 1993; H. Wagenmakers, 'Transparency in Armaments: the United Nations Register of Conventional Arms as a proud member of a family of efforts', in M. Chalmers, O. Greene, E. Laurance, and H. Wulf (eds), *Developing the UN Register of Conventional Arms*, Bradford Arms Register Studies No 4, Westview Press, London, 1994; and Malcolm Chalmers and Owen Greene, *Taking Stock: the UN Register after two years*, Bradford Arms Register Studies No 5, Westview Press, London, 1995.

2   For a detailed discussion of the discussions and outcomes of the 1994 UN Group of Experts, see: Malcolm Chalmers and Owen Greene, *Taking Stock: the UN Register After Two Years*, BARS 5, op. cit. 1995 (especially chapter 6); or E. Laurance and H. Wulf, 'The 1994 Review of the United Nations Register of Conventional Arms', *SIPRI Yearbook 1995*, Oxford University Press, Oxford, 1995.

3   *UN Register of Conventional Arms: Report of the UN Secretary-General*, General Assembly Document A/51/300, United Nations, New York, 20 August 1996.

4   *UN Register of Conventional Arms: Report of the UN Secretary-General*, General Assembly Document A/51/300/Add.1, 16 October 1996 (Australia, Azerbaijan, Belarus, Russia, Tanzania); A/51/300/Add.2, 24 October 1996 (Thailand). No further replies had been received by 20 November. The UN report, together with late submissions (Addenda) and revisions (Corrigenda) has, for the first time, become available on the Internet, on http://www.un.org/Depts/dpa/cda/register/register.htm.

5   *UN Register of Conventional Arms: Report of the UN Secretary-General*, General Assembly Document A/50/547/Add.2, 20 December 1995 (Belize and Burkina Faso); A/50/547/Add.3, 12 January 1996 (Chad and Iran); A/50/547/Add.4, February 1996 (Nepal).

6   Communication from UN Centre for Disarmament Affairs, June
        1997.

7   For further discussion of participation in the Register amongst
        states in the area of the former Soviet Union, see chapter 15 in this
        book.

8   *SIPRI Yearbook 1996, op cit*, p. 465

9   Edward J. Laurance and Herbert Wulf, 'The 1994 review of the
        United Nations Register of Conventional Arms', in Stockholm
        International Peace Research Institute, *SIPRI Yearbook 1995*,
        Oxford University Press, 1995, pp. 566-567.

10   For further discussion of recent developments in transparency in
        East Asia, see Amitav Acharya's chapter in this book (chapter 13).

11   Brunei, until recently the only ASEAN member not to have
        submitted a report, provided information to the Register in 1997,
        for its fifth year of operation.

12   SIPRI reports significant deliveries of combat aircraft and battle
        tanks from China to Myanmar in 1995. *SIPRI Yearbook 1996, op
        cit*, p. 511. China's report on its exports in 1995 does not include
        any transfers to Myanmar.

13   *Ibid,* p. 466.

14   For those with an interest in the arcane complications for reporting
        to the Register, another set of potentially complex sovereignty
        issues may arise in relation to Hong Kong. These arise from the
        seizure in 1996 by Hong Kong authorities of a shipment of arms en
        route from North Korea to Syria, reported to include 155 mm
        cannon (*Straits Times*, 22 September 1996). Should the UK (as the
        authority responsible for Hong Kong) declare this as an import in
        its 1997 submission? What should be reported by China in relation
        to Hong Kong in subsequent years, bearing in mind that the UK
        will be handing over sovereignty in 1997 (only a few weeks after
        the Register deadline of 30 April)?

15   Apparently, Pakistan Ministry of Defence officials noted a
        discrepancy between their draft submission and the UK's report to
        the Register of exports of three armoured personnel carriers to

Pakistan in 1995. The Ministry and armed forces could find no record of these imports. After extensive internal investigations, it was found that these vehicles had been imported by Sind paramilitary forces to support the policing of Karachi. Pakistan then revised its submission to the register accordingly, as well as tightening its national monitoring procedures for the future. See Malcolm Chalmers and Owen Greene, *Developments in Official Transparency on Conventional Arms in East and South Asia, particularly relating to Procurement, Holdings and Procurement,* Research Report, Centre for Promotion of Disarmament and Non-Proliferation (CPDNP), Japan Institute for International Affairs, Tokyo, May 1997.

16   For further discussion of participation in the UN Register and the development of associated regional transparency and confidence-building measures, see Ricardo Mario Rodriguez' chapter in this book (chapter 14).

17   See Malcolm Chalmers, *Confidence-Building in South-East Asia,* Westview Press, 1996, p. 172, and also Amitav Acharya, chapter 13 of this book. For analyses of confidence-building and transparency in South-East Asia, also see Bates Gill, J.N. Mak and Siemon Wezeman, *ASEAN Arms Acquisitions: Developing Transparency,* Malaysian Institute of Maritime Affairs / SIPRI, 1995; Ralph Cossa (ed), *Towards a Regional Arms Register in the Asia Pacific,* Pacific Forum / CSIS Occasional Papers, 1995; Ralph Cossa (ed), *Promoting Regional Transparency: Defense Policy Papers and the United Nations Register of Conventional Arms,* Pacific Forum / CSIS Occasional Papers, 1996; Malcolm Chalmers, 'Openness and Security Policy in South-East Asia' *Survival,* 38, 3, 1996; Bates Gill and J. N. Mak (ed), *Arms Trade, Transparency and Security in South-East Asia,* SIPRI Research Report, Oxford University Press, forthcoming 1997

18   See Ricardo Mario Rodriguez, chapter 14 of this book.

19   *SIPRI Yearbook 1996, op cit,* p. 465

20   *Ibid,* pp. 466-467

21   For further details, see Malcolm Chalmers and Owen Greene, *Taking Stock: The UN Register After Two Years,* Westview Press,

1995, Chapter 4. For a detailed comparison of the UN Register in its first year with the SIPRI Register, see Edward J. Laurance, Siemon T. Wezeman and Herbert Wulf, *Arms Watch: SIPRI Report on the first year of the United Nations Register of Conventional Arms*, SIPRI Research Report Number 6, Oxford University Press, 1993.

22   Malcolm Chalmers and Owen Greene, *The United Nations Register of Conventional Arms: Examining the Third Report, op cit*, pp. 25-26. Based on comparisons with John Sislin and Siemon Wezeman, *1994 Arms Transfers: A Register of Deliveries from Public Sources*, Monterey Institute of International Studies, March 1995. It is important to note that the fact that a transfer reported in the UN Register is not included in the SIPRI's published data-base does not necessarily mean that no unofficial information on that transfer already existed in the public domain. SIPRI, for example, normally only includes an unofficial report of a transfer in its published data base if that report is reasonably consistent with at least one other such report.

23   Malcolm Chalmers and Owen Greene, *The United Nations Register in its Fourth Year*, Bradford Arms Register Studies (BARS) Working Paper 2, Bradford University, UK, November 1996. The methods used for this comparison were the same as for 1994 (discussed in the previous footnote).

24   China, India, Japan, Pakistan, Russia, and USA.

25   Thailand only provided descriptions for six of its eight reported 1995 imports.

26   Malcolm Chalmers and Owen Greene, *The United Nations Register of Conventional Arms: Examining the Third Report, op cit*, pp. 14-17.

27   Paul Pineo and Lora Lumpe, *Recycled Weapons: American Exports of Surplus Arms 1990-1995*, Federation of American Scientists, 1996. Our thanks to Lora Lumpe for her help on this issue.

CHAPTER 3

Issues and Priorities for the Group of Experts

Rafael Mariano Grossi

In this chapter, I aim to present a succinct introductory review of the issues before the 1997 Group of Experts. It is not an easy task in view of the complexities and the interrelated nature of the different components of the Register.

Firstly, however, it has been an honour for me to take part in the Tokyo workshop on Transparency in Armaments, organised jointly by the Ministry of Foreign Affairs of Japan, the University of Bradford, and the Centre for Promotion of Disarmament and Non-Proliferation of the Japan Institute for International Affairs. As Chairman of the 1997 Group of Governmental Experts and a member of the UN Governmental Expert Groups in 1992 and 1994, I would like to emphasise how valuable such informal workshops have been.

Back in 1992, once the General Assembly established the framework for the creation of the Register, the Japanese authorities had the idea of bring together the governmental experts with representatives of other sectors and concerned countries. The informal setting provided the experts with an opportunity to exchange views freely, understand better each others' positions and also provide those not represented at the negotiating table with an opportunity to present their views and influence the review process in a concrete manner. In 1994, the experience was repeated, with informal workshops organised in Japan by the Japanese government and also at Monterey by a non-governmental team including the University of Bradford.

Now for a third time, Japan has played an active and positive role by hosting the Tokyo workshop, which has facilitated and informed our work in 1997. Let me express special gratitude to Ambassador Mitsuro Donowaki, with whom I have had the privilege to work for a number of years. It is also a privilege to take part with Drs Owen Greene and Malcolm Chalmers from Bradford University, whose early interest in the Register has allowed the international disarmament community and all those concerned with international security to benefit from their acute assessments relating to all aspects of the Register, particularly through their well-known Bradford Arms Register Studies.

Issues for the Group of Experts

At the outset, it is important to bare clearly in mind that the Group of Experts does not operate in a vacuum. We have clear terms of reference to carry out our work embodied in a mandate stemming from paragraph three of the General Assembly Resolution 51/45 H, which says that we have to assist the Secretary General to prepare his report on the continuing operation of the Register and its further development.

This already indicates the two main areas of our work. Namely, the actual way in which the Register has performed, and the way ahead.

As far as the **operation of the Register** is concerned, our points of departure are the results of the four years of reporting to the Register.

In this sense, I feel justified in saying that by now, we have an instrument which can no longer be considered a novelty or an experiment, the results of which are yet to be seen.

Five consecutive years have helped to establish the Register as the unique intergovernmental source of official information covering more than 90% of the international trade in major conventional weapons. In itself, this stands as a clear example of the institutional importance of the Register, a unique characteristic that puts the Register above any other similar existing instruments, even those with a more comprehensive scope.

The Register provides a seal of credibility to information previously available from private sources only, and this in itself is invaluable for governments in their own national reading of the international situation.

The Group of Experts has already started to analyse in a systematic way, the operation of the Register. This comprises a **quantitative** assessment of submissions of data on arms transfers as well as a **qualitative** analysis.

On the **quantitative** side, we will of course look at figures and what they reveal to us in terms of percentages, bearing in mind the important aspects of relevancy of the Register in different regions and its impact on a given regional circumstance.

The **quality** assessment evokes difficult and rather technical problems linked to the definition of transfers, the existence of mismatches and discrepancies in returns, and the description of export and import data. To put it clearly, here we are talking about degrees of transparency applied to data being submitted.

In its present form, the Register gives participating states the possibility to submit information on imports and exports at different degrees of detail. An important issue for the group to consider will be the possibility of introducing certain changes that could add an element of clarity to the information that is currently provided. Since 1992, states have approached this matter in different ways: some have chosen a simple return with no further details attached, while others have made use of the opportunity to provide more information. It will be necessary to draw the pertinent conclusions from this experience.

This part of our work will give us an opportunity to address the technical difficulties that participating states may have found in implementing the Register. We know that national bureaucracies, the people actually filing out reports, have interesting suggestions to make -- based on their experience -- in order to render the Register a truly 'user-friendly' device.

Our efforts will of course be directed in this spirit. But we are conscious of the fact that an excess of detail or an undue emphasis on technicalities risks diverting our energies from other equally important tasks before us. The approach here will ideally aim at striking the right balance, which I personally identify with practical changes, and avoiding what the French so rightly describe as an 'excès de zèle".

The further development of the Register will bring us to the heart of our review. Here again, we will have to address the different dimensions connected with its development, namely the **categories of weapons** covered by the Register and their adjustments, the **expansion of the scope** of the Register, and possible **new categories and types**.

As far as the **categories already covered** by the Register are concerned, there are many sides to this topic that need consideration. In fact, technical adjustments could be useful as a way to redress discrepancies but also, more substantively, as a measure designed to broaden the present categories by lowering thresholds, extending ranges, readjusting tonnages, and so on. So there is a distinction to be made between adjustments to existing categories and those considered completely new.

In the past, similar efforts proved particularly difficult. In view of this, the ideal would be to concentrate on those adjustments capable of commanding consensus. The problem is not an easy one, as technical adjustments can be seen as a way to improve the efficient and effective operating way of the Register, but at the same time, there can be substantive reasons behind preferences for additions. These two sides of the same coin have to be carefully weighed in view of these two potentially conflicting goals.

Already in 1992, when the first Group of Experts worked on the modalities to set the Register in motion, and again in 1994, concrete proposals for adjustments were considered. However, none could be agreed. The matter is still under review and once again it will be our job to find an adequate solution that will take care of useful adjustments while avoiding those that could affect the integrity of the existing categories without which the value of the Register as an analytical tool could be weakened.

The **expansion of the scope** of the Register is of course one of the greatest challenges for the Group of Experts. It is important to recall that the principle of early expansion of the Register has been reaffirmed by the General Assembly. There is therefore an agreement on the final goal which solves half of the problem.

This brings us to the crucial consideration of **military holdings and procurement** from national production. As it stands, countries are invited to submit data on holdings, but reporting on production and holdings is not institutionalized in the Register as it is for imports or exports.

The question of whether and how to address this situation deserves careful consideration. Since 1991 when the Register was originally debated, there have been lengthy discussions on it, based on evaluations and sometimes re-evaluations by countries on how to tackle this question. At present a significant number of countries are already providing information on both holdings and national procurement. But the situation is far from ideal in the absence of a stronger indication of how to address this problem, not to mention the fact that even those willing and able to provide such information do not have the necessary guidance on how to do it.

I look forward to the exchange of views that I am sure will take place on this issue. Debates about the different options and possibilities for expanding the scope of the Register were, as is well-known, at the heart of the discussions of the 1994 Group of Experts.

New categories and types are also an integral part of our discussions. They reflect a desire to develop transparency measures to address the two extremes of the existing weaponry represented by small arms on the one hand and weapons of mass destruction on the other.

I would be remiss if I omitted other important subject matters before us, as represented, for example, by the **regional approach** and what we call the implementation of the Register on the regional level. We are considering ways in which the Register could be supported through existing regional arrangements and agencies. At the same time the enhancement of its implementation at the regional level is being discussed. There are interesting examples we could look at, such as the efforts made by the ASEAN Regional Forum or the Council for Security and Cooperation in the Asia Pacific.

In Africa, for example, there are growing indications of a trend towards measures to foster transparency and interstate cooperation on security matters. The Central African subregion is one of the areas where such initiatives are being explored. Another example is provided by the initiatives carried out in this regard in West Africa. Recent meetings in Bamako (Mali) have helped to promote movement towards agreement in that area on measures with regard to light weapons and the UN Register.

In the Americas, the Committee on Hemispheric Security of the OAS has also taken up the relevancy of the Register, in an effort to promote participation and increase the understanding of this instrument.

There are other similar examples. So it is necessary to look into these developments, and see how these parallel efforts could combine in a synergetic way to make sure that the 'family of efforts' on transparency will not be a diaspora but a rather coherent set of mutually reinforcing actions.

Lastly, I am satisfied to see that already at this early stage of our work, the experts seem to be developing a convergence of views on questions related to the **access to data and information**. The idea is to give more visibility to the Register by exploring alternatives like the use of the world-wide web, contacts between member states, academies, and NGO's as a concrete way to make the information more easily accessible for states and individuals. The role of the Centre for Disarmament Affairs will require a thorough examination, as much of what can be done at this level will undoubtedly require the active involvement of the UN Secretariat. At a time of streamlining and budgetary austerity, this acquires special implications.

In conclusion, I have aimed to outline some of the outstanding issues facing the Group of Experts. We are conscious of the importance of our work, as a failure in achieving the objectives set out for us by the General Assembly could endanger one of the most promising exercises on transparency in an area - conventional weapons - where consensus has historically been infrequent.

It is my conviction that progress has to be made this time to preserve an instrument that gives member states an opportunity to provide tangible proof of their attachment to the principles and objectives of the UN Charter.

Preserving the succeeding generations from the scourges of war is still a universally shared principle. I am convinced that this lofty goal will be easier to reach if we have a robust Register on Conventional Arms operating. In spite of the difficulties of our task, I feel reassured by the outstanding personalities we have as national experts as well as the excellent spirit in which we have been operating since our first session in March 1997. The Tokyo workshop consolidated this commitment even further and gave us the opportunity to listen to those presenting new ideas and options to explore. When we return to the negotiating table in New York we will do so enriched and enlightened by our discussions in Tokyo.

CHAPTER 4

Issues and Priorities for the 1997 Review

Malcolm Chalmers and Owen Greene

Achievements so far

The United Nations Register of Conventional Arms has established itself as an important global transparency regime. It is worth reviewing its significance and recalling what it has achieved.

The Register is the first global co-operative regime addressing the problem of potentially destabilising accumulations of conventional arms. Indeed, it is still the only substantial global instrument of this kind. It is a politically-binding transparency arrangement, not the legally-binding control measure which some would prefer. However, it is important to recognise how difficult it is to achieve any international agreements in this area. There is no negotiable global measure to limit major conventional arms transfers or holdings in prospect. Moreover, transparency arrangements are themselves important: they can contribute significantly to confidence-building, conflict prevention and restraint. The UN Register itself has great potential to contribute to international security.

In this context, the UN Register has broken new ground in international affairs in at least four major ways.

The first, and central, achievement of the UN Register so far is that it has in practice established, on a global scale, a norm of transparency in relation to conventional arms - particularly in relation to international transfers of major weapons systems. Although participation in the Register is still far from universal, it is relatively high and most arms exporters and importers do regularly participate. This reflects and strengthens the principle that states' rights to procure arms for their own defence must be accompanied by a responsibility to exercise that right with restraint and with due regard to the concerns of others. Given the traditional reluctance of states to allow openness in this area, this is a significant step forward.

Second, the Register involves the provision of information on conventional arms transfers, as well as on military holdings and procurement through national production, on an official basis. Unofficial estimates of data have already been available as a result of the excellent work of organisations such as SIPRI and IISS. But the Register has revealed a significant body of information that has not before been publicly available. It has also stimulated governments to monitor their own arms transfers more systematically and rigorously. Even more significantly, the Register has provided *official* information. This gives a 'seal of credibility' to the data it contains, allowing the information to be used more effectively as a basis for development of security-dialogues between states, on a bilateral or multilateral level. It thus contributes an important building block for confidence-building processes.

Third, Register information is publicly available, even when - as is the case with 'available background information' - it is not published by the UN. This is of considerable significance, not least because of the growing realisation of the relationship between domestic accountability in security policy and international security. A similar trend is seen in the support by regional organisations for greater public openness in security policy in other areas. For example, the ARF has urged the publication of annual defence statements by member states. NATO's Partnership for Peace has, as an important part of its work, the development of transparency and domestic accountability in defence and security policy.

Fourth, in comparison with many global arms control and disarmament regimes - such as those relating to weapons of mass destruction - the Register has at least some relevance to a much larger number of states: nearly all states possess major conventional arms in the seven Register categories, and most are involved to some extent in the international arms trade. The UN Register is sometimes criticised by states in Latin America and sub-Saharan Africa because it does not cover systems, such as small arms and light weapons, that are of more pressing concern to them. There is some merit in this criticism. Yet, for example, the Register did include reports of transfers of major conventional weapons to 15 countries in sub-Saharan Africa during its first four years. Moreover, the Register can be used as a starting point for taking further account of such concerns (for example by revising or adding categories or including military holdings).

The operation and further development of the Register

As discussed in chapter 2, the operation of the Register remains far from perfect, and there are continuing weaknesses which need to be addressed by the 1997 UN Group of Experts. Nevertheless, the Register of transfers is now established as an operational and useful arrangement, covering over

90% of the trade in major conventional arms and revealing substantial information that was not previously publicly-available.

Despite its status as a voluntary international instrument, and the continuing sensitivity of many states about arms transparency, the Register rapidly achieved and maintained very respectable levels of participation. In any one year, the Register has only gained the participation of about half of the UN's full membership. But this in itself is substantial compared to many other international reporting arrangements, and compares well with reporting levels in many other international agreements addressing less politically-sensitive areas. Moreover, participation has been steadily rising: from 82 in the first year, to 92 in the fourth year. Regular participants now include all major arms exporters, together with a majority of major importers. Participation has been consistently high in Europe, has risen to high levels in East and South Asia and the former Soviet Union, and includes most of the major military powers of Latin America. By contrast, participation remains low in the Middle East and sub-Saharan Africa. Overall, 138 countries have participated at least once.

The Register is still far from reaching its full potential. It is important that the 1997 Group of Experts succeeds in correcting some of its present weaknesses and in agreeing ways to develop it further. The agenda for the 1997 review is much the same as it was for the 1994 review. It includes: ways and means of improving participation; revising existing weapons categories; adding possible new weapons categories; strengthening and improving existing reporting guidelines, to reduce discrepancies and promote submission of qualitative data on weapons types and roles; promoting more effective use of the Register; and whether and how to expand the scope of the Register to cover military holdings and procurement from national production. These issues are identified and discussed further by Rafael Grossi in chapter 3.

The key challenge for the 1997 Group of Experts is to avoid the failure of the previous review exercise and succeed in agreeing ways of developing and strengthening the Register. The fact that the Register has now been operating reasonably successfully for over four years should improve the prospects for agreement compared to 1994, when the Register was still very young. More experience has been gained. Countries have had time to become more familiar and comfortable with arms transparency arrangements. The Register is more 'ripe' for development. Nevertheless, obstacles to achieving agreement on substantial measures still exist. Unless there is real political commitment to developing the Register, and unless care is taken to avoid the pitfalls of the 1994 exercise, the 1997 Group of Experts could still fail.

At this point, the prospects for achieving at least some progress appear quite good. According to reports, a constructive atmosphere seems to have been established at the first meeting of the Group of Experts, and several of the countries involved have developed and revised their approach over the last three years.

Nevertheless, it is important to recognise that the key challenge for the Group of Experts remains finding ways and means to expand the scope of the Register to include military holdings and procurement from national production. For many, progress on this issue is the key indicator of the success or failure of the 1997 review. Issues and options for achieving progress in this area are discussed in detail in Part B of this book. The key point here is that achieving agreement on minor if useful revisions to Register categories or reporting guidelines is no substitute for taking a significant step forward in expanding the scope of the Register.

Participation and scope

It is sometimes argued that the scope of the Register cannot be expanded until a much higher number of countries are taking part. But this argument needs to be assessed in the context of the fact that 138 UN members have so far (as of June 1997) taken part in the Register at least once: thus indicating their acceptance of the arrangement in principle. Of those remaining, a significant number are probably staying out because they are unclear of its relevance to their own situation (for example the Holy See and Costa Rica) or due to bureaucratic inertia or for legal reasons (for example, Venezuela). A second significant group of states - such as Iraq, Myanmar and North Korea - are unlikely to take part before there is a major change in their domestic or regional circumstances.

If participation is to increase, efforts must be focused on this first group of countries, seeking to persuade countries that are generally recognised as being responsible members of the international community to participate on a regular basis.

There is a link between participation and scope. But it does not relate so much to these potential new members - whose reluctance to participate so far is not clearly linked to the particular scope of the Register - as to those key participants in the existing Register that may be reluctant to reveal more information than they are currently making available.

Thus, in considering possible expansion of scope, it is important to do so in a way that preserves the present participation levels, and particularly of the major exporters and importers that currently take part. This should be done even if it means going at a slower pace than one at which some countries would be more comfortable. However, the composition of the Group of Experts reflects this constraint and concern. Any recommendation agreed by the states represented in this Group is likely to command wide support from existing Register participants, and is highly unlikely to provoke damaging reductions in existing participation levels. On the other hand, if the Group of Experts fails to agree to develop and expand the Register, there is a risk that the political momentum that has established and sustained the Register so far could be lost. Thus, the Group of Experts should concentrate on finding agreement amongst themselves on ways to carry the expansion of the Register forward.

Qualitative development

In reviewing the progress of the Register so far, it is important to review the quality as well as the number of submissions. From its inception, the Register has served as a catalyst for transparency rather than a rigid blueprint. It provides a basic framework of obligations, but complements this with opportunities for individual states to do more. Both in reporting on transfers, and on national procurement and military holdings, the record has been one of steady and continuing improvement in the quality of information provided. As governments have become more comfortable with Register reporting, they have learnt from others' experience and overcome some of their initial concerns about the security implications of disclosure.

This steady improvement in the quality of information provided appears to be reaching its limits in some areas, necessitating a development of the framework itself, as discussed above. But it also highlights the continuing responsibility all governments have to continue to review whether they can each do more within the Register framework. The Register is, after all, a voluntary arrangement not a legally-binding regime. It therefore depends on the willing co-operation of its members. In reviewing what can be done to develop the Register through multilateral agreement, therefore, states should not forget the considerable potential for progress that also exists at the national and regional levels.

Part B: Expanding the Scope of the Register: Military Holdings and Procurement

CHAPTER 5

The Expansion of the Scope of the Register: Background and Future Prospects

Mitsuro Donowaki

The question of the expansion of the scope of the UN Register was a hotly debated issue from the time of the introduction of Resolution 46/36L in the General Assembly in 1991 which established the Register. As a matter of fact, Japan and the member states of the European Community (who originally prepared two separate drafts as early as June of that year, but eventually merged them into one draft resolution by September), intended to establish a "Register of International Conventional Arms Transfers". This was the title used in the draft resolution introduced by Japan and the EC nations in the First Committee on the 31st of October as document A/.C/46/L.18. It was not until a few days before the voting in the middle of November that a revised text of the draft resolution stated to use the title of a "Register of Conventional Arms".

As is well known, the experience of the Gulf War earlier in 1991 prompted a number of world leaders, among them the then Prime Minister Toshiki Kaifu of Japan, to advocate the establishment of a UN Register of international arms transfers. This was largely because of the realization that Iraq imported nearly US $50 billion of conventional arms between 1983 and 1990, which represented about a half of Iraq's total imports, an astonishingly high figure, and the realization that the absence of any restraint on the part of major arms exporters played no little part in facilitating such an excessive and destabilizing accumulation of armaments by Iraq.

Therefore, it was only natural that the original sponsors of the idea of a UN register were not quite prepared to include in the register data on procurement from national production and data on military holdings in addition to data on arms transfers. When a series of heated and prolonged negotiations started in New York from the middle of October between the representatives of the original sponsors and the representatives of Non-Aligned nations, it was the Non-Aligned nations who made a strong case for the inclusion of data on procurement through national production and on military holdings. Otherwise, countries which could produce most of their arms without relying much on imports would have little to report to the Register, while other nations which relied heavily on imports might be endangering their security interests by "going transparent" about such imports. If the Register was to promote confidence among nations, then there should be no discrimination between large importers nations of arms and countries that could produce their own weapons.

This was a forceful and convincing argument, to which the original sponsors could not easily turn deaf ears. However, looking back, it appears that this was the lowest common denominator the Non-Aligned nations could agree upon in order to counter the position of the original sponsors of the resolution. Indeed, there were diverse views held among them. Some of them were more concerned about the transparency in weapons of mass destruction. Others were questioning the transfer of high technology with military application. Still others were more concerned about the illicit trade in small arms. On these points, I will not have to go into details here because they will be discussed elsewhere in this volume.

What was truly remarkable was the agreement arrived at after nearly one month's laborious negotiations between the representatives of the original sponsors and the Non-Aligned nations. Both sides exhibited the spirit of compromise and flexibility to the maximum extent. In the end, it was agreed that the "Register of Conventional Arms" would consist of two parts, namely with a section on "data on international arms transfers", and another section on "information on military holdings, procurement through national production and relevant policies". As to the former "data", Member States were "called upon" to provide relevant data, while Member States were only "invited" to provide the latter "information" as a part of the "available background information", and as an interim measure "pending the expansion of the Register". (See operative paragraphs 7, 8 and 10 of Resolution 46/36 L.)

The term "invited" as compared to "called upon" was generally understood to be used in describing norms that were less obligatory and more voluntary. Furthermore, according to paragraph 5 of the Annex to the Resolution, the annual consolidated report of the Secretary-General on the Register was to include "data registered, together with an index of the other interrelated information". This meant that the Register would consist of a detailed "data" section on arms transfers and an "information" section with an index only. This was because it was thought that "information" to be supplied by Member States could consist of such voluminous documents as defense white papers.

As to the procedure for the expansion of the Register by inclusion of "data" on military holdings and procurement through national production, it was stated in the resolution that a panel of governmental experts, to be established in 1992, should report on the modalities for such an expansion. Eventually, the 1992 Panel's Report did enumerate some of the points that ought to be considered in carrying out such an expansion, but did not recommend the expansion itself because it was understood at that time that the question would be addressed a few years later. What the Panel did do, however, was to agree upon standardized forms to be used in submitting "data" on transfers, and to state that "information" on procurement and holdings may be submitted "in any form" Member States may wish. (See Paragraph 21 of 1992 Panel's Report.)

This report of the 1992 Panel was "endorsed" by the General Assembly resolution 47/52 L. This resolution, together with the subsequent year's resolution 48/75 E requested the Secretary-General to prepare a report, with the assistance of a group of governmental experts, on the continuing operation of the Register in 1994. Naturally, "the continuing operation of the Register" was to include the question of the modalities for the expansion of the scope of the Register.

The deliberation of the expansion of the scope of the Register by the 1994 Group of Governmental Experts proved to be not quite a disaster, but an intractable frustration. Paradoxically, within less than two years of the establishment of the Register, the advocates and opponents of an early expansion of the Register appeared to have changed sides. By this time, most of the western nations were convinced that data on holdings and procurement should be included in the Register on the same basis as for transfers. As a matter of fact, they were already submitting most of such data in accordance with the CFE Treaty provisions which came into force quite recently. Therefore, many of them started to submit some information on holdings and procurement to the UN Register also.

For most of the Non-Aligned nations, the lowest common denominator that united them two years earlier in advocating an early expansion could no longer serve their interests once some of the western nations became enthusiastic about such an expansion. Ironically, however, there were some other Non-Aligned nations like Egypt, representing the interest of Arab states, who still advocated an early expansion for quite different reasons - in order to include transparency measures with respect to weapons of mass destruction.

It was under such circumstances that, during the debate in the 1994 Group of Governmental Experts, Japan and other middle-of-the-road nations came up with the suggestion that standardized forms might be introduced for the submission of information on holdings and procurement, without changing the voluntary nature for the submission of such information. Such standardized forms might be similar to the ones already agreed upon for the submission of data on transfers, covering only the seven categories of conventional weapons. The annual consolidated report on the Register might include, in addition to data on transfers, contents of such information on holdings and procurement, instead of just an "index of interrelated information" as was agreed two years earlier.

In fact, this suggestion appeared to be supported by quite a number of the members of the 1994 Group of Governmental Experts. In the end, however, this suggestion, like all other proposals including the one to submit information on holdings and procurement on the same basis as for transfers, could not command complete support from the members of the 1994 Group. This was perhaps because time was not yet ripe in 1994, with only two years' implementation of the Register, to fully evaluate the merits and demerits of the Register. Therefore, the General Assembly subsequently decided to request the Secretary-General to prepare a report on the continuing operation of the Register and its further development with the assistance of a group of governmental experts to be convened in 1997.

Whether or not this year's Group of Governmental Experts will arrive at any conclusion on the question of the expansion of the scope of the Register is of course entirely up to the governmental experts themselves. Unlike in 1994, five years' experience with the Register as well as data and information already accumulated should serve as favorable factors for the experts to deal with the question perhaps more competently and skilfully. Basically, Japan is in favor of expanding the Register to include data on holdings and procurement. This is because Japan believes that the security interests of nations can better be served by enhancing confidence among nations, and for this purpose the promotion of transparency in armaments can play an important role. In this age of information technology and satellite intelligence, the degree of transparency already introduced with respect to the transfers of major conventional arms might be extended to holdings and procurement not only without causing much harm to the security interests of nations, but also for the sake of greater benefits to be derived from the new relationship of trust, confidence and openness among nations.

However, we will have to see whether this way of thinking can command the support of the overwhelming majority of nations at this point in time. In case it proves that the time is still not ripe to expand the scope of the Register, then we will have to see what practical and incremental steps are there to be taken with the blessing of this overwhelming majority of nations in order to bring us closer to the goal agreed upon six years ago. In either case, Japan is ready to exert its utmost efforts so that some satisfactory arrangements will be worked out as a result of the deliberations now being held in this year's Group of Governmental Experts.

CHAPTER 6

UN Arms Register: Some Interpretations of Barriers to Transparency and Accountability

Ravinder Pal Singh

Introduction

An element of uncertainty surrounds the progress of the United Nations Register of Conventional Arms (UNROCA) in the 1997 review process. It is all the more essential that the current review is more successful than the last one held in 1994 if the momentum of the UNROCA is to be maintained. Failure to show progress in the review that is currently under way is likely to take the UNROCA onto a slow and painful path that could lead to another case of failure of good intentions.

The diverse range of objections to the expansion of the UNROCA are matched by an equally diverse group of countries raising those objections. `The challenges and crunch issues that confront the advocates of the UNROCA are threefold: (i) addressing its conceptual shortcomings that impair implementing its basic rationale of preventing the excessive accumulation of destabilizing arms, (ii) broadening the participation of countries in reporting their weapon holdings and domestic arms production, and (iii) the participation of countries or regions that are significant importers of arms but are still not reporting their conventional arms transfers. The UNROCA has perhaps laid more emphasis on expanding the participation rate than preparing the ground for tackling the major stumbling-blocks in the 1997 review process.

This paper will examine some of the difficulties in the expansion of the UNROCA which includes the following aspects: (i) interpretations of selected countries to transparency in conventional arms procurement indicating general objections to public reporting on arms acquisitions. In this context it will also analyse national security concerns aroused by demands for transparency in domestic defence production; (ii) the feasibility of transparency in domestic arms production by developing a database of export licences issued for assembling the seven categories of weapon systems; and (iii) acceptability and durability of recipient side arms procurement restraints as against supplier side arms control initiatives for transparency.

Interpretations of transparency and security concerns generated by public reporting on national arms procurement

Confidentiality in weapons acquisitions still remains an important security concern in almost all the countries. The security-related decisions and even arms acquisition processes are more or less closely guarded. Confidentiality concerns relating to arms acquisitions vary with the politico-military circumstances prevailing in different countries, and these may include the following:

- the military security threats perceived in those countries;

- the development and maturing of civil–military relations and public perceptions of the role of the military and its status in society;

- the autonomy of the military in the security decision-making processes;

- acceptance of public accountability norms as they relate to the military's decision making practices;

- public-interest monitoring and legislative oversight of the arms procurement processes.

More specifically, confidentiality classification of arms and technology acquisition depends on the levels of sophistication of the weapon systems available in the region. Among the reasons seen as critical from the security perspective of the military for maintaining secrecy in domestic arms production are the following :

- providing new military capabilities and superior performance;

- maintaining an element of technological surprise;

- strengthening the military technological base; and

- the prevailing assumption in some societies that anything to do with the military needs to be secret.

These criteria shape the confidentiality concerns in the arms development and acquisition processes of the major powers as well. As the major powers have much higher levels of critical conventional technologies, their concerns about confidentiality are of a lower order in the case of arms listed in the UNROCA. However, notwithstanding an understanding arrived between the five major arms exporters to exercise arms sales restraints, confidentiality in arms sales is driven by commercial consideration among the major arms suppliers.[1] In the absence of international norms on the interpretation of transparency in arms transfers, development and procurement, including the development of military technologies, production of weapons and arms sales, countries located within the regions of tension remain sceptical in their support for transparency in arms acquisitions as required by the UNROCA.

Among the general findings of SIPRI's project on arms procurement decision making, some of the objections to transparency in arms acquisitions evolve from the following characteristics of security policy making processes:

- Lack of broader representative character in the security threat assessment process. In many countries, the political threat assessment has either a weak or an insignificant influence on the military's security assessment process. Absence of integrated security policy making processes and structures results in different and often rigid positions taken by the military from its foreign policy process which leads to a minimal horizontal flow of information and interaction between them. Such a situation impedes growth of preventive action shaped from diplomatic initiatives.

- In countries where arms procurement decisions are dependent either on a single source or on a predominant arms supplier, the arms suppliers have better information of procurement decisions than the elected representatives of the recipient countries. The commercial confidentiality which surrounds such linkages leads to opportunities of waste, fraud and abuse of public resources, and consequently, develops attitudes that are normatively opposed to accountability.

- Allocations from the defence budget for arms procurement are not explicit. This could be due to either ambiguity, inefficiencies or archaic budget designs. In a number of cases the military budget allocations are made in equal proportions or without a clear input and output relationship, that is, the costs of weapon systems and their contribution to security.

- Legislative bodies responsible for security policy oversight have serious limitations in monitoring arms procurement issues for reasons such as lack of resources, professional capacities, weak constitutional provisions for demanding information, or indifference to defence policy issues as electoral concerns demand different constituency priorities.

- Statutory audit authorities in some cases are either not empowered to audit the military's arms procurement actions or lacking in interdisciplinary skills.

- The military's resistance to transparency in arms procurement decisions is possibly driven more by its institutional perception of the need to have a restrictive attitude towards confidentiality. Whereas, security concerns in the domestic defence industry and R&D establishments are driven as much by their resistance to industrial accountability as their need for commercial confidentiality. Consequently, a convergence of interests develops between the industry and the military's security rationale.

- Cultural attitudes towards security or social norms of bureaucratic élitism are deliberately manipulated to heighten military security concerns to create low levels of public accountability. As the general public has a poor understanding of security policy and decision making methods, the norms of a public right to information remain underdeveloped. Broader professional capacities in the civil society are generally excluded from generating an informed public debate on security policy making.

Although a varying quality of public information on domestic arms production is available in different countries through official organizations, public media and non-governmental organizations (NGOs), such information is available in a disaggregated manner. Besides the annual reports of the arms-manufacturing companies, there are reports by national audit authorities and to the parliaments. In some countries, the media have better access to information relating to arms production than in others. What is missing are comprehensive national statements on domestic arms production that could serve as the basis for initiating a international or a regional mechanism for arms procurement restraints.

Samples of transparency related security concerns

Among the objectives of the UNROCA, transparency in arms acquisitions aims to prevent excessive and destabilizing accumulation of conventional weapons. The general intention is to avoid a recurrence of situations which compelled the Coalition forces to the 1990 Persian Gulf War, and contributed to the decision on developing a UN Register on conventional arms.[2] Curiously, the security rationale against reporting domestic defence production overlooks the fact that national intelligence services have a fairly accurate assessment of the arms production capabilities of the countries in their region. The irony is that such reports cannot be made public to support the initiation of international arms procurement restraints, as ambiguity is required to be maintained regarding national intelligence sources, their capacities and limitations. The arguments of national security concerns made out against expansion of the UNROCA need to respond to the fact that such reports, in any case, do not form the basis of planning for intelligence channels. However, they do provide the basis for officially acceptable data for initiating a mechanism for arms procurement restraints through diplomatic channels. Therefore, it is equally important that UNROCA designs regional and international level processes to activate arms acquisition restraints, which will also serve as an effective Confidence Building Measure (CBM). Unless the transparency rationale of UNROCA is supplanted by a CBM rationale, its opponents will remain sceptical of its directions and objectives. In the absence of a comprehensive and transparent reporting mechanism which is backed up by an effective diplomatic process for initiating arms acquisition restraints, the difficulties in alerting the international community and preventing an excessive and destabilizing accumulation of conventional weapons remain unaddressed.

Opposition to UNROCA's expansion stems from diverse interpretations of its transparency requirements. According to one definition, transparency relating to conventional arms includes such measures as disclosing information on defence expenditure, military force levels and equipment acquisitions so that these are not perceived as surprising new threats that can upset the regional military balance.[3] Such interpretations suggest that the focus of UNROCA remain as an early-warning device for alerting the international community to initiate the arms control processes. On the other hand, broadening the objectives of UNROCA as an CBM instrument, and creating checks to restrain acquisition of destabilizing arms and related technologies, would give it a wider acceptability. The debate on the role of UNROCA thus far indicates that transparency for arms control concerns retains primacy over designing initiatives for encouraging arms procurement restraints or CBMs. Serious doubts remain among countries for which the listed arms are seen as critical to their military capabilities.

On the other hand, opposition to public reporting on arms production in the arms recipient countries has more to do with the security concepts being based on deterrence through military technological potential in the absence of developments in security norms based on mutual confidence and co-operative security. A South Korean view of requirements of confidentiality in military projects lays down the following criteria: (i) arms procurement of vital strategic weapon systems; (ii) high-technology projects which need confidentiality in the interests of diplomatic bargaining; and (iii) projects vital to national interests.[4] These criteria are indicative of the heightened national security concerns prevailing on the Korean peninsula.

One Chinese viewpoint on military transparency is that China will not make public its military-related information if it undermines Chinese political stability. Chinese inhibitions in allowing transparency in conventional arms are influenced by the following factors: the prevailing low levels of mutual trust; the absence of comparable technical verification capacities; inadequate understanding of the implications of military transparency among the Chinese leadership; and the leadership's sensitivity to issues which apparently question its sovereign right to information.[5] Chinese participation in the UNROCA has therefore been limited only to its arms transfer dimensions.

Israeli objections to the transparency required by the UN Register are based on the following: the failure of other countries in the region to participate in the Register; its need to maintain security and deterrence through an element of 'technological surprise and superiority'; and Israel's policy of deterrence based on 'deliberate ambiguity in the area of nuclear capability and ballistic missiles'. As long as there is a possibility of conventional or non-conventional attack, Israel will reject transparency in arms procurement.[6]

Notwithstanding Indian objections to transparency in domestic arms production suggesting it is not in the country's national security interests, public demands for transparency seek a greater accountability of arms procurement processes. Compared to other Asian countries, the Indian press enjoys relative access to the security establishment and freedom of reporting on security issues. Additionally, a certain amount of arms procurement data is available from the statutory audit reports, despite the mandatory requirements of disguising the details. However, absence of an official security policy statement and lack of transparent procurement procedures leads to administrative shortcomings such as ambiguity in arms procurement decisions, weak legislative oversight mechanisms, cost and time overruns. Besides elements of waste, fraud and misuse creep into the arms acquisition decision-making process.[7]

In a similar vein, demands are being made in Thailand for transparency in arms procurement decision making and for proposed procurement expenditures to be explained.[8] One opinion from the Thai military establishment informs that transparency in arms procurement is not so much concerned with 'what, why or how' *the weapon systems are being acquired* as with 'when and where' *such weapons are being employed.*[9]

In most of the countries the level of awareness and of public debate on the transparency requirements of the UNROCA is low. The communication and information flow between the security bureaucracies is not only rigidly channelled and restricted, but lacks transparency to generate creative ideas.[10] National representatives and experts at international meetings report from a narrow base of inputs, generally echoing the sentiment of their own office. Consequently such interpretations reflect a cautious opinion that should be acceptable to the community of security officials back home.[11] In most cases, evidence of a comprehensive decision- or opinion-forming process that encapsulates a broader public opinion and the opinion of the security bureaucracies is conspicuously absent. Even in Israel, military professional opinion on security issues eclipses broader national or even government opinion.[12]

The question of losing technological surprise or erosion of vital strategic interests through participation in the expansion of the UNROCA will have difficulties in standing a test of closer scrutiny because the reports to the UNROCA do not obligate any qualitative reporting. Although the Chinese objections on the basis of comparable technical verification could be addressed by designing a suitable process, that would go against the spirit of voluntary reporting for building mutual trust. Such values far outweigh possible gains in accuracy through verification. It is more likely that the real objections to expansion of UNROCA are inadequate understanding of the implications of military transparency on the part of the Chinese leadership and its sensitivity to questions of sovereign right to information. These conditions are not only true in the case of China, but for most of the countries objecting to the UNROCA's expansion. It seems that the supporters of UNROCA have not been able to focus their attention on specific problem areas and instead expected that these problems would somehow disappear of their own accord. The price of optimism is often failure where hard-nosed national security issues are concerned.

Lack of transparency in public reports on domestic arms production leads to reduced accountability, which has consistently resulted in allegations of misuse of public funds and scandals in India, Israel, Japan, South Korea and Thailand. The fact that reports on arms acquisition scandals are not being reported in the state-controlled Chinese media does not imply their absence.[13]

Alternatives to building transparency in domestic defence production

What are the alternative approaches that can be developed to address objections to transparency in domestic arms production? If such objections are seen in the context of high performance weapon systems and key technologies that are considered critical for maintaining operational superiority, the countries at the leading edge of military technology are willing to report only the non-critical weapons and technology.[14] In much the same way as development of high-technology military R&D is not transparent in the major powers because of its criticality to military effectiveness, transparency attitudes are similarly shaped in the middle-level powers regarding the seven categories of conventional arms listed in the UN Register as these are deemed critical to their military security.

The rationale for establishing the UNROCA was driven by concerns posed by an excessive and destabilising character of arms build up.[15] Should the UNROCA remain as a arms transfer register, it will address the problem partially, that is of 'excessive' accumulation of arms. The destabilising nature of weapons and technologies developed through national establishments remains unaddressed. UNROCA will not be able to mature into an acceptable CBM instrument unless it provides a level field by recording the 'destabilising' character of advanced weapons technology.[16] In order to tackle the broader challenges of transparency in conventional arms to prevent threats to international peace, there is a need to address potential threats posed by the destabilizing character of excessive developments in military high-technology R&D. As a military technology race characterises the motive force of arms acquisition spirals, absence of recording or restraints on military technology developments generates both push and pull factors that influence arms acquisition — and consequently instability.

A continual expansion of the UNROCA would help in addressing such questions in an ongoing manner. The immediate challenge is to find ways and means to broaden the participation on reporting domestic defence production.

Domestic arms production goes through several stages of R&D before going on to the manufacturing stage of systems and components to be finally assembled as a weapon ready for transfer or induction in the inventory of national armed forces. The transfer could be in the shape of a fully assembled weapon system or in the shape of completely or semi-knocked down kits for final assembly in the recipient countries. Technology transfers by the major arms suppliers for domestic arms production also take the form of feasibility studies or consultancy services for formulating project definition, etc. The arms procurement process from domestic arms production can be described as progressing in three broad stages as follows:

Research & development ------------> Manufacturing ------------> End use

Research & development stage

Includes the following steps:

1. Concept definition

2. Feasibility studies

3. Project definition

4. Project design

5. Systems integration and validation

6. Development and testing of full-scale engineering models

7. Prototype development

8. Trials for development, technical and maintenance evaluation, confirmatory and so on.

Manufacturing stage

On the basis of a study which describes nine levels of arms procurement autonomy,[17] it is possible to identify seven levels of arms production autonomy for the seven categories of arms listed in the UN Register. These capacities will of course vary considerably between countries producing these weapon systems.

1. Production based on indigenous design, raw materials, processed materials, domestic parts, components, integration of sub-systems and major sub-systems;

2. Domestic and imported components for an indigenous design and development;

3. Domestic and multiple source imported components for copy or redesigned imported system;

4. Domestic and single-source imported components for copy or redesigned imported system;

5. Domestic components for copy or redesigned imported system:

6. Domestic and multiple source component substitution for licensed assembly;

7. Licensed assembly from semi or completely knocked down kits.

End use stage

Involves induction in national armed forces or international transfers of either complete systems or components and kits for assembly in recipient countries.

Depending upon the complexity of weapon system being developed or sub-systems to be integrated, only a limited number of countries enjoy comparative production autonomy in respect of all the arms categories. In most cases countries producing weapons at their national facilities are primarily weapon system integrators. Particularly in the case of sophisticated weapon systems, many countries also need external assistance from the feasibility study stages onwards.

Considering the global national arms production capabilities, there are only four countries that can claim to have production autonomy levels 1 or 2 in all the seven categories of weapon systems listed in the UN Register.

Another six countries have significant R&D and manufacturing capabilities to achieve arms production autonomy levels 2 and 3 in all the seven categories of weapon systems, but have chosen not to do so for a variety of reasons.

The third group of countries have adequate R&D and production autonomy levels 3 and 4. They have some design capabilities for sub-assembly that could go into assembling major weapons platforms. This group of about 14–15 countries also licenses the largest group of arms-producing countries to manufacture components or assemble major sub-systems.

This largest group of countries has limited R&D and production capabilities (primarily assembly of weapons) in only a few of the seven categories of weapon systems. These countries have autonomy levels 4 to 7 which vary with the type of weapons platforms.

Based on the above categorisation of arms production autonomy, a grouping of countries could be developed as described below. It should be noted that this grouping is neither complete nor static but has been developed as a sample to show how such clusters could be developed and used in analysing domestic arms production.

Group A. Countries that have complete production autonomy in all the seven categories of weapon systems listed in the UN Register—France, Russia, the UK and the USA (4).

Group B. Countries which have significant autonomy in R&D and production capabilities in most of the categories of weapon systems and provide licences for manufacturing either complete systems, major assemblies or components—e.g., Canada, China, Germany, Italy, Japan and Sweden.

Group C. Countries with adequate R&D and manufacturing autonomy in only some of the seven categories of weapon systems—e.g., Australia, Austria, Belgium, Belarus, Brazil, the Czech Republic, Israel, the Netherlands, Poland, Slovakia, South Africa, Spain, Switzerland, Ukraine and the Federal Republic of Yugoslavia There are ca. 14–15 countries in this group which also issue licences for the manufacturing of major assemblies or components for the arms listed in the UN Register.

Group D. Countries with limited R&D and manufacturing autonomy in all or some of the seven categories of weapon systems. These countries are generally characterised by limitations in designing competitive weapon systems. Between 25 and 30 countries are in this group—e.g., Argentina, Bulgaria, Chile, Croatia, Egypt, Finland, Greece, Hungary, India,

Indonesia, Iran, Iraq, North Korea, South Korea, Malaysia, Norway, Pakistan, Romania, Singapore, Taiwan, Thailand and Turkey. Arms production autonomy capabilities vary considerably in this group.

Group E. Countries which manufacture arms other than the seven categories listed in the UN Register. These include countries such as Algeria, Burma, Peru, the Philippines, Slovenia, Syria, Viet Nam.

Group F. Countries that do not manufacture arms.

Production autonomy levels would have to be defined in the case of each of the listed arms, which would vary considerably between different systems.

It is possible for systematic research to capture data from the public domain on the types of arms under production in most of the countries in Groups A, B, and C that have production autonomy levels 1 to 4. It will not, however, be feasible to provide data on the volume of output. If these 25-odd countries agree to expansion of the UN Register to include reporting of their domestic defence production, as well as reporting the end users of the export licences issued to the arms-producing countries in Group D, the process would be able to capture a major proportion of global arms production. Domestic arms production of the seven arms categories is found in only about 50 countries. Such a data bank would help to provide the international community with a better assessment of domestic arms production than currently exists. The Wassenaar Arrangement already has provision for exchanging information on weapons and related technology between the member countries, however, as it is neither universal nor a transparent arrangement, it could serve as a basis for building a process for reporting the export licences to UNROCA.

 As data on these export licences issued are already available with national arms export control authorities, a significant proportion of arms production would become transparent, if it is reported to the UNROCA. If the supplying countries also agree to report consultancy contracts relating to the seven categories of arms, then all the three stages of the arms procurement process could also be mapped out, namely R&D, production and end use.

The implementation process

Such a process would require the following actions: one, a systematic identification of countries that either routinely issue or have capabilities to issue licences for production of arms. Two, it would involve identifying and categorising weapons components, subsystems and major sub-assemblies that go into major weapon platforms listed in the UNROCA.

In the third stage, it would involve building up a data bank of reports on national arms production and export licences issued, indicating the end use destinations of designated components.

An assessment could thereafter be developed of the domestic arms production of various countries from the collation of export licence data. Although there would be limitations in accurately identifying the scale of domestic production, a periodic review of such data would help in building a fair assessment of arms production in the remaining 25–30 countries. As this process matures, the recipient countries could be encouraged to make declarations of their own domestic arms production.

Arms (procurement) restraint or arms (sales) control?

It is equally essential that new avenues are explored for pursuing the broader objectives of preventing excessive accumulation of destabilizing arms. This requires a continual engagement of challenges posed by the interests that promote arms transfers and production. As national security is still primarily perceived in terms of building military capabilities for deterrence and exercising military options, creative ideas and methods are required to be continuously generated to form a family of initiatives to prevent accumulation of destabilizing arms and related technologies.

Arms procurement restraints is one such concept which could be defined in terms of harmonising the arms procurement requirements of the military with the broader priorities of society. In that sense, an arms restraint paradigm in major arms developing and exporting countries would also involve restraints on developing and producing new weapon systems and technologies, restraints on arms sales promotion in areas such as arms export financing, size and public resources available to the arms export promotion, and so on.[18]

Arms procurement restraints aim at building capacities in the public domain in both supplier and recipient countries to engage their governments, legislative and audit bodies and other related agencies to restrain the arms transfers and production rationale. More often than not, reasons of military technology competitiveness, creation of job opportunities or commercial reasons are advanced to promote arms production. Such rationale generates an atmosphere of information control in order to limit public criticism of national arms transfer policies or decisions.

Recipient side arms procurement restraints involves developing legislative oversight procedures, and audit and monitoring mechanisms to serve the domestic objectives of preventing waste, fraud or misuse in the national arms procurement processes. These initiatives for developing accountability in arms procurement would have greater acceptability and a more enduring quality than the transparency arguments advanced earlier on in this paper.[19] The arms acquisition data generated by such public-interest initiatives could be useful tools to press into use with international initiatives to prevent excessive accumulation of destabilizing technologies and weaponry.

Domestic criticism of lack of transparency that impairs public accountability in national arms procurement processes would have a stronger effect than international initiatives for transparency as undertaken by UNROCA, which in any case, is handicapped by its low profile in the national security debate. To begin with, the objectives of UNROCA could be well served by transparency in the processes of national opinion making. More often than not, national positions on issues like expansion of UNROCA are likely to be formulated within the confines of a small office.

It could be a profitable exercise to broaden participation in the formulating of national positions on the expansion of the UNROCA. Initiatives to raise its profile in national debates would be resisted by the arms procurement interest groups in the security establishment whose positions may feel threatened by attempts to seek related information. Nonetheless, public debate would provide a diversity of inputs in understanding the limitations, opportunities and threats to expansion of the UNROCA. Such an exercise would involve the participation of the security community, the NGOs, legislative bodies and media in countries which are the target audience of the opponents of the expansion of the Register.

Conclusion

The group of experts participating in the 1997 review process well recognises the fact that it is easier to resist the expansion of the Register on a security rationale, a line of argument which may subsume commercial as well as extra-constitutional interests as well. It is much more challenging to develop creative ideas which should maintain the momentum of building international norms for pursuing a stable peace. Such norms need to recognise that existing conceptual limitations of the UNROCA need to be addressed. Unless movement is seen in building overall restraints on arms acquisitions and advanced military technologies which can threaten stable peace, piecemeal arms control initiatives will remain of symbolic value only. Domestic criticism of lack of transparency primarily aims at building accountability in arms-procurement processes—an approach which is far more acceptable, insightful and robust enough to compete with the security arguments advanced in favour of confidentiality.

---

1   The Chinese refusal to notify prospective arms sales in advance is indicative of the commercial interests driving arms transfers. See Feldman, S., 'New arms control agenda' in Avi Becker, *Arms Control Without Glasnost: Building Confidence in the Middle East*, Israeli Council of Foreign Relations, Jerusalem, 1993, p. 40.

2   Edward J. Laurance , 'A conceptual framework for arms trade transparency in South East Asia' in Gill, B. and Mak J.N. *'Arms, Transparency and Security in South East Asia*, SIPRI Research Report No. 13, Oxford University Press, 1997, pp. 14 and 18.

3   Nelson, R., *Military Transparency in East Asia: Implications for the ASEAN Regional Forum*, Atlantic Council of the United States, vol. VII, no. 1 29 Jan. 1996.

4   Chin Soo Bae, Transparency in South Korea's Arms Procurement, Working Paper for the SIPRI Arms Procurement Project (unpublished), p. 13, referring to the Korean Ministry of Defence, *Report on the Yul Gok Project, Past, Present and Future* (in Korean).

5   Xue Tong Yan, China's Security and Military Transparency, Working Paper for the SIPRI Arms Procurement Project (unpublished), pp. 10–11.

6   The effect of the Gabrial surface-to-surface missile during the Yom Kippur War and the use of unmanned aerial vehicles (UAVs) for electronic countermeasures during the 1982 Lebanon campaign are seen as examples of successful technological surprise. Steinberg, G., The Influence of Foreign Policy and International Agreements

in Arms Procurement Decision Making in Israel, Working Paper for the SIPRI Arms Procurement Project (unpublished), pp. 5, 8–9.

7   'Defence deals lack transparency', *Hindustan Times* (New Delhi), 7 June 1996; and 'Need for transparency', *Hindustan Times*, 14 Oct. 1995)

8   'Military urged to clarify its arms purchases', *Bangkok Post*, 6 Feb. 1995.

9   My italics. Capt. Chumpol Srinavin, 'Perspectives on National Security, Military security and Military Capability', Working Paper for the SIPRI Arms Procurement Project (unpublished), 1 Mar. 1995.

10   For the purposes of this paper the term 'security bureaucracies' means the ministries of foreign affairs and defence, the military and the defence R&D and manufacturing establishments.

11   The concerns indicated by Russian officials are illustrative of the difficulties of the UN experts representing their countries' positions. Chalmers, M. and Greene, O., *The UN Register in its Fourth Year*, Bradford Working Paper 2, University of Bradford, Nov. 1996, p. 21.

12   Eva Etzioni Halevy, 'Civil-Military Elite Relations and Democratisation: The case of Connection between the Military and Political Elites in Israel,' Unpublished paper presented at the IPSA World Congress, Berlin, Aug. 1994.)

13   Ravinder Pal Singh, SIPRI, *Arms Procurement Decision Making: China, India, Israel, Japan, South Korea and Thailand* (Oxford University Press: forthcoming). The study describes the effects of lack of transparency in arms procurement in allowing opportunities for extra-constitutional practices, e.g., the Bofors affair in India, the Rami Dotan affair in Israel, the Amukdari system in Japan, the audit reports on the South Korean Yul Gok project, the recent allegations against the South Korean Minister for Defence on his relationships with arms brokers. *Korea Times* (Seoul), 21 and 22 Oct. 1996; comments on the defence budget secret funds by members of the Thai National Assembly, Piyanat Wadcharaporn, 11 Dec. 1986, cited from Chaiwat Sathanad,

'Defence Budgeting in Thailand', Unpublished paper for SIPRI Arms procurement project, Mar. 1995, p. 9; and 'Minister orders investigations of F-18 purchase', *Thailand Times*, 8 Nov. 1996, p. A2.

14   Comments by Jean-Paul Credeville, International Relations Division, Ministry of Defence, France at the Tokyo workshop on 'Transparency in Armamentsí: UN Register of Conventional Arms, 12-13 May 1997.

15   UN Resolution 46/36 L, 'Transparency in Armaments'.

16   Six characteristics of arms acquisitions and military build up have been described as destabilising by a definition. See Mussington, D. and Sislin, J.,' Defining destabilising arms acquisitions', *Jane's Intelligence Review*, vol. 17, no, 2 (February 1995), pp 88-90. These include the following: decreased warning time; provision of breakthrough capabilities; no effective defence against weapons; one side gaining insight into the other side's military preparations; a broadening of target sets, and engendering of hostile feelings.

17   Sperling, J., Louscher, D. and Salomene, M. A., 'Reconceptualization of the arms transfer problem', *Defence Analysis*, vol. 11, no. 3 (Dec. 1995), p. 295.

18   The US Government alone spends as much as $7.5 billion a year to support annual arms exports of $15 billion. It has 6500 employees promoting, servicing and lobbying for arms sales internationally, provides tax breaks to arms manufacturers, grants loans at favourable rates of interest to the recipients and often writes off bad loans. 'Arms sales galore', *International Herald Tribune*, 23 Apr. 1997, p. 8.

19   See reasons for transparency, Note 3.

CHAPTER 7

Military Holdings

Terence Taylor

Introduction

The perspective in this paper is from the point of view of an editor of an open source publication, *The Military Balance*, which provides information on the armed forces of 169 countries. The book, which is published annually, is produced by the International Institute for Strategic Studies, an independent research institute, which is funded privately. *The Military Balance* includes data information and analyses on military organisations, weapons, equipment and all aspects of defence economics including defence budgets, arms sales and the defence industry. The scope of weapons and equipment dealt with in the book is wider than the seven categories covered by the United Nations Register of Conventional Arms. It covers all types of weapon systems and their delivery means, including logistic support systems such as transport aircraft and support ships, down to light weapon systems (where this information is available).

Categorisation in The Military Balance

In *The Military Balance* the focus is on major weapon systems and military organisations since they give clear indications of the overall military capability of a state's armed forces. A change in the number of a major weapons system and its type is an obvious indication of a change in capability but that is not sufficient alone. Matched to organisations, the true significance of any changes can be more usefully assessed. Personnel numbers of ground forces and non-state armed groups give a good indication of numbers of light weapons and small arms. Light weapons are defined as those which are designed to be man-portable either completely assembled or in parts. In order to make a proper assessment of military holdings it is essential to use universal equipment definitions.

Equipment

The Military Balance uses the following definitions for the major weapon systems:

Ground Forces

Main Battle Tank (MBT). An armoured tracked combat vehicle weighing at least 16.5 metric tonnes unladen, that may be armed with a 360° traverse gun of at least 75mm calibre.

Armoured Combat Vehicles (ACV). A self-propelled vehicle with armoured protection and cross-country capability. ACVs include:

Armoured Personnel Carrier (APC). A lightly armoured combat vehicle designed and equipped to transport an infantry squad, armed with integral/organic weapons of less than 20mm calibre. Variants of APCs converted for other uses (such as weapons platforms, command posts and communications terminals) are included.

Armoured Infantry Fighting Vehicle (AIFV). An armoured combat vehicle designed and equipped to transport an infantry squad, armed with an integral/organic cannon of at least 20mm calibre. Variants of AIFV are also included .

Heavy Armoured Combat Vehicle (HACV). An armoured combat vehicle weighing more than six metric tonnes unladen, with an integral/organic direct-fire gun of at least 75mm (which does not fall within the definitions of APC, AIFV or MBT). *The Military Balance* does not list HACVs separately, but under their equipment type (light tank, reconnaissance or assault gun), and where appropriate annotates them as HACV.

Artillery. Guns howitzers or mortars with a calibre of 100mm and above, capable of engaging ground targets by delivering primarily indirect fire, namely guns, howitzers, gun/howitzers, multiple-rocket launchers and mortars. Where the information is available on weapons of a lower calibre, such as light mortars (e.g. down to 60mm in a few cases, but more commonly 81mm) and light anti-tank weapons, they are also included. Low level air defence guns down to below 20mm are also included where accurate information is available. Generally for the smaller countries a good indication of quantities of these smaller calibre weapons can be obtained. For the major countries it is very difficult to obtain accurate data on very large, and constantly fluctuating, numbers of light weapons

Military Formation Strengths

The manpower strength, equipment holdings and organisation of formations such as brigades and divisions differ widely from state to state. However the numbers of personnel in all military organisations is the best guide to the numbers of small arms likely to be held.

Naval Forces

Categorisation of warships is based on their operational role, weapon fit and displacement. Ship classes are identified by the name of the first ship of that class, except where a class is recognised by another name. Where the class is based on a foreign design or has been acquired from another country, the original class name is also shown. In *The Military Balance* the term 'ship' is used to refer to vessels with over 1,000 tonnes full-load displacement that are more than 60 metres in overall length; vessels of lesser displacement, but of 16m or more overall length, are termed 'craft'. Vessels of less than 16m overall length are not included. In making judgements on operational capabilities it is important to appreciate that the term 'commissioning' has different meanings in a number of navies. In *The Military Balance* the term is used to mean that a ship has completed fitting out, initial sea trials, and has a naval crew; operational training may not have been completed, but in all other respects the ship is available for service. 'Decommissioning' means that a ship has been removed from operational duty and the bulk of its naval crew transferred. Removing equipment and stores and dismantling weapons, however, may not have started. Where known, ships in long-term refit are shown as such.

Classifications and Definitions

To aid comparison between fleets, naval entries are subdivided into the following categories, which do not necessarily conform with national categorisations:

Submarines. All types of submarine are counted. Those with submarine-launched ballistic missiles are listed separately as 'Strategic Nuclear Forces'.

Principal Surface Combatants. These include all surface ships with both 1,000 tonnes full-load displacement and a weapons system other than for self-protection. All ships in this category are assumed to have an anti-surface ship capability. They comprise: aircraft carriers (defined below); cruisers (over 8,000 tonnes) and destroyers (less than 8,000 tonnes), both of which normally have an anti-air role and may also have an anti-submarine capability; frigates (less than 8,000 tonnes) which normally have an anti-submarine role. Only ships with a flight deck that extends beyond two-thirds of the vessel's length are classified as aircraft carriers. This distinguishes them from other classes that also carry significant weapon systems and are listed as helicopter cruisers.

Patrol and Coastal Combatants. These are ships and craft, the primary role of which relates to the protection of a state's sea approaches and coastline. Included are corvettes (600–1,000 tonnes carrying weapons systems other than for self-protection); missile craft (with permanently fitted missile-launcher ramps and control equipment); and torpedo craft (with an anti-surface-ship capability). Ships and craft that fall outside these definitions are classified as 'patrol'.

Mine Warfare. This category covers surface vessels configured primarily for mine-laying or mine countermeasures (which can be mine-hunters, mine-sweepers or dual-capable vessels). A further classification divides both coastal and patrol combatants and mine-warfare vessels into offshore (over 600 tonnes); coastal (300–600 tonnes); and inshore (less than 300 tonnes).

Amphibious. This includes ships specifically procured and employed to disembark troops and their equipment over unprepared beachheads or directly to support amphibious operations. The term 'Landing Ship' (as opposed to 'Landing Craft') refers to vessels capable of an open-ocean passage that can deliver their troops and equipment in a fit state to fight. Vessels with an amphibious capability, but which are known not to be assigned to amphibious duties, are not included. Amphibious craft are listed at the end of each entry.

Support and Miscellaneous. This category of essentially non-military vessels provides some indication of the sustainability and range of the naval forces concerned.

Weapons Systems. Weapons are listed in the order in which they contribute to the ship's primary operational role. Significant weapons relating to the ship's secondary role are added after the word 'plus'. Short-range self-defence weapons are not listed. To merit inclusion, a surface-to-air missile system must have an anti-missile range of 10 km or more, and guns must be of 100mm bore or greater. Exceptions may be made in the case of some minor combatants which have a primary gun armament of a lesser calibre.

Aircraft. All armed aircraft, including anti-submarine-warfare and some maritime-reconnaissance aircraft, are included as combat aircraft in naval inventories.

Organisations. Naval groupings such as fleets and squadrons are often temporary and changeable; organisation is only shown where it is meaningful.

Air Forces

The term combat aircraft is used to refer to aircraft normally equipped to deliver air-to-air or air-to-surface ordnance. The combat aircraft totals include aircraft in operational conversion units whose main role is weapons training, and training aircraft of the same type as those in front-line squadrons that are assumed to be available for operations at short notice. (Training aircraft considered to be combat-capable are separately identified). The number of aircraft categories used is kept to a minimum. 'Fighter' denotes aircraft with the capability (weapons, avionics, performance) for aerial combat. Multi-role aircraft are shown as fighter ground attack (FGA), fighter, reconnaissance and so on, according to the role in which they are deployed. Different countries often use the same basic aircraft in different roles; the key to determining these roles lies mainly in air-crew training. For bombers, 'long-range' means having an unrefuelled radius of action of over 5,000 kms, 'medium-range' 1,000–5,000km and 'short-range' less than 1,000 kms; light bombers are those with a payload of under 10,000 kgs (no greater than the payload of many FGA). For helicopters four types are defined and counted:

- Attack helicopters which are defined as those equipped to employ anti-armour, air-to-ground or air-to-air guided weapons by means of an integrated fire control and aiming system;

- Combat support which are defined as those which may be armed with self-defence or area-suppression weapons, but do not have an integrated control and guidance system, within this category are armed "assault" helicopters which are designed to deliver troops to the battlefield;

- Armed helicopters are those not falling in the above categories but which are designed to deliver some form of ordnance such as anti-submarine weapons;

- Unarmed transport helicopters.

Missiles

Missiles of all types are included in *The Military Balance* down to and including man-portable anti-tank and air defence systems. In general, only data on numbers of launchers are given as no reliable information is available, as is usually the case for ammunition, on the missiles themselves. This kind of information is, understandably, well-protected for security reasons to avoid revealing details of combat sustainability. For the small man portable systems generally only the type is specified as data on numbers is unreliable and fluctuating.

Definition of a Military Holding

To count a country's total military holdings for all the equipment defined above it is necessary to collect data on as wide a basis as possible. While organisations, whether regular or paramilitary, are a valuable qualitative guide to the state of readiness and operational role of weapons and equipment they can be changed quickly. Also, account has to be taken of equipment in storage, refit or repair. In arriving at a complete definition of a country's military holdings, equipment held at least by the following elements should be taken into consideration:

- regular or active forces;

- reserve forces;

- paramilitary forces;

- storage facilities in varying states of readiness;

- organisations conducting repair, overhaul, refit or modernisation;

- research and development prototypes.

For *The Military Balance* equipment held by production factories, whether state or privately owned is not counted. These figures tend to be relatively small and rapidly changing as equipment, once completed from production, with a few exceptions, is handed over to the buyer with little delay.

Use of Open Sources

An independent non-governmental organisation has to use a variety of approaches to assure the quality of data and information it publishes. Data is examined and assessed from all perspectives including:

- political objectives and alignments of governments;

- defence economics, including overall defence spending, arms production, sales and purchases;

- technological developments and research and development programmes including an analysis of the capabilities of individual countries;

- military and paramilitary organisations;

- military exercises and deployments.

The sources used include the following:

- governments through legislative procedures, parliamentary debates, answers to requests for information and declarations under international agreements such as the UN Register of Conventional Arms, the Conventional Armed Forces in Europe (CFE) treaty and other confidence building measures such as those associated with the Vienna Document (1994);

- other non-governmental organisations through their publications, meetings and contacts;

- all forms of public media including the press, television and radio as well as the Internet;

- IISS members world-wide who reside in more than 100 countries;

- visits and discussion around the world by IISS staff.

Challenges

The main challenge in obtaining accurate data and information is without doubt security concerns of particular states which vary widely depending on the particular circumstances faced by governments as well as the nature of their political systems. The most common security concern relates to protecting information on ammunition stocks, including missiles, in order to not reveal the period and intensity over which they could sustain combat operations. Another important difficulty in making assessments is the differing definitions of military organisations and how individual weapons are defined and counted. Different types of equipment present varying degrees of difficulty to the business of collecting accurate data. Major weapon systems are clearly more easily identified while the smaller systems, in particular light weapons and small arms, are difficult to count. In a number of instances governments themselves have difficulty in accounting accurately for the smaller weapon systems, particularly in cases of recent or current conflicts, and where substantial quantities are in the hands of non-state armed groups.

CHAPTER 8

Expanding the Register to include holdings and national procurement: issues and options

Malcolm Chalmers and Owen Greene

Introduction

The most important task for the 1997 Group of Experts is to find ways to extend the UN Register of Conventional Arms to cover more fully military holdings and procurement from national production, without provoking key states to withdraw from their participation in the Register. The importance of this task is widely recognised. So, too, are the difficulties of achieving satisfactory agreement. This chapter aims to identify and examine the main options for achieving progress in this area through the 1997 review process, on the basis of recent experience with the development of transparency in this area.[1]

It is important to recognise how central the expansion of the Register is to the legitimacy and usefulness of this transparency arrangement. As discussed in chapter 1, initial proposals in 1992 to establish a register of arms transfers were widely rejected as inequitable and inadequate. For example, it was widely argued that it was unfair to increase transparency of procurement by countries that are dependent on arms imports without also requiring arms-producing states to reveal their procurement from national production. Moreover, the status of, and trends in, countries' overall military holdings were of more direct relevance and concern than annual transfers or procurement in itself.

The United Nations Register of Conventional Arms was thus established by the UN General Assembly on the explicit understanding that it would be expanded to cover national procurement and military holdings as soon as possible. This aim was endorsed by the 1994 Group of Experts and repeatedly re-confirmed by the UN General Assembly. It is to this area, above all others, that those concerned with promoting conventional arms transparency and developing the Register will look for progress. The question is whether consensus can be achieved on any such expansion, given the failure of the 1994 Review in this area.

The next section examines the experience of the 1994 review, to provide lessons for 1997. The following section then reviews and analyses the submission of 'background information' on military holdings and procurement from national production by Register participants in its first four years of operation. Then, possible approaches to expanding the Register in this area in 1997 are discussed in some detail. Four key options are identified and examined. These are not exclusive, there are a range of other possible variations available. However, we believe that they do represent the major approaches on which negotiations could usefully focus. Whichever option may be adopted, technical questions will be raised on how to design appropriate reporting guidelines and definitions for implementing any expansion in the Register's scope. Such questions are addressed in the penultimate section. The chapter ends with a brief conclusion.

The 1994 Review

According to our understanding, more than half of the 23 states on the 1994 Group of Experts unreservedly supported the expansion of the Register to cover procurement from national production and military holdings on the same basis as for holdings.[2] This had been the policy of Australia, Argentina, Brazil, Canada, Netherlands, Germany and Japan for some time, and France, UK, USA and Finland had recently come to share their view. All these eleven states already provided data to the UN on their procurement and holdings through the provision for 'available background information'. Expansion was also supported by Egypt and Jordan, although they did not themselves provide the necessary data. On the other hand, China, India and Israel, supported for the most part by Cuba, were not ready to agree to provide reports on their military holdings or national procurement, and rejected any proposals to expand the Register in a way that would place them under an obligation to do so.

The Russian representative was prepared to support inclusion of holdings and procurement, but did not press strongly for this outcome, not least because of uncertainty about whether other elements in the Russian government would in practice be prepared to supply such data. Pakistan had argued strongly during 1992-3 for the inclusion of procurement from national production alongside transfers, and did not abandon this position in the Group of Experts. However, they were less enthusiastic about including military holdings, and their interest in gaining symmetry of transparency with India (which produces more of its arms domestically than Pakistan) was counterbalanced by their desire to maintain friendly relations with China. Finally, for various reasons, Ghana, Mexico, Singapore and Zimbabwe did not come down firmly on one side or the other in this debate.

A compromise was floated, by which states would be 'encouraged' to provide numerical data on their military holdings and procurement from national production on standardised forms, but would be under less obligation to do so than for transfers. Its advocates argued that such an arrangement would at least standardise and publish any submitted information. It might encourage some additional countries to make such submissions, and could gradually help to establish an international norm that countries should normally submit information on holdings and procurement.

This compromise was rejected by the representatives of France, UK, USA and Canada. They argued that such a compromise would be so weak that few countries that did not already voluntarily provide data on their holdings and procurement would feel under any pressure to do so in the future. By establishing multiple levels of obligations within an arrangement that was already voluntary, the compromise could encourage an attitude where states felt able to pick and choose what they would report. Moreover, they feared that accepting such a compromise could postpone a full expansion of the Register indefinitely, whereas failure to agree would ensure that the issue would remain at the top of the agenda for the next review process.

Thus, these western states appeared to adopt an 'all or nothing' approach to this issue in 1994. At the same time, although India, China and Israel were prepared to consider the compromise proposal, they continued to steadfastly refuse to accept full expansion, arguing that such disclosure could endanger their security. The combination of these two opposing positions ensured that the 1994 Group of Experts failed to agree on any development of the Register in this area.

Background Information: the reporting experience so far

In the existing Register, in addition to their submissions on arms transfers, states are invited to provide 'available background information' on their military holdings, procurement from national production, and relevant national arms transfer policies, legislation or administrative procedures. Every year since the Register came into operation, a significant number of states have provided background information including data on their military holdings and national procurement. This experience provides a basis for the future further expansion of scope of the Register in this area.

There is a lower level of obligation on participating states to provide such background information to the Register than there is to report on arms transfers. There are no standardised forms or guidelines governing what background information is required and how it should be presented. Moreover, background information submitted by states is not included in the annual Secretary-General's report on the Register, nor is it otherwise published by the UN. It is however available for consultation at the library of the Centre for Disarmament Affairs (CDA) in the UN in New York. Initially there was some doubt about the extent of public access to this data, but it is now firmly established that non-governmental groups may also have full access to this information at the CDA after the publication of the annual Secretary-General's report. The full data on military holdings and procurement from national production provided by states during the Register first four years has been published as part of the Bradford Arms Register Studies (BARS) series. [3]

Countries providing 'background information'

Some 42 countries have provided background information on holdings and/or national procurement at some time over the last four years (see Appendices 1 and 2). However, several of these states have only provided such data irregularly. Thus, after an initial increase between the first and second year, the number of countries providing background information on holdings and national procurement has now remained steady - at around 30 - for the last three years. For example, of the 94 states that had by spring 1997 submitted reports on their arms transfers for the fourth year of the Register, 31 also submitted 'available background information', and 28 included data on their military holdings. Table 1 summarises the numbers of countries providing background information during the last four years.

Table 1 UN Register submissions in 1993-1996

	1993	1994	1995	1996
Number of countries replying to the Register by November 14	82	85	87	92
of which, number of countries providing 'available background information'	33	36	33	31
of which: providing information on military holdings and/or national procurement	25	31	30	29
of which: providing information on military holdings	25	30	28	28
Number of countries providing information on procurement from national production	12	16	21	20

Note: Albania provided holdings data relating to 1992 in 1994. It is included in the 1994 figures.

Table 2: Countries submitting background information but not providing data on national procurement or holdings

Year data provided	Number	Countries
1993	9	Czech Republic, Finland, Israel, Norway, Panama, Qatar, Republic of Korea, Switzerland, Yugoslavia
1994	5	Hungary, Israel, Mexico, Republic of Korea, Switzerland
1995	3	Jamaica, Republic of Korea, South Africa
1996	3	Finland, Republic of Korea, South Africa

Note: Finland provided a copy of part of its Vienna submission in 1996, containing some relevant information.

Table 3 Provision of holdings or procurement data to the UN Register by region

	1993	1994	1995	1996	Countries in region
Europe	16	17	17	18	38
Asia & Oceania	3	3	4	2	33
America	5	6	7	5	35
Former Soviet Union	-	1	1	3	15
Sub-Saharan Africa	-	4	1	-	48
Middle East	-	-	-	-	18
Total	24	31	30	28	187

Some 21 countries have established themselves as regular providers of data, having submitted holdings or procurement information in at least three of the last four years. Twelve of the EU's 15 members do so on a regular basis, but provision of holdings data is by no means confined to Western Europe. Several important states in Asia & Oceania (Australia, Japan and New Zealand), Central & Eastern Europe (Bulgaria, Czech Republic and Poland), North America (Canada and the US) and South America (Argentina and Brazil) have provided holdings data in three or more of the last four years.

Despite the weak nature of the request for background information, provision of holdings or procurement data has now become the norm for OECD states. 22 of the OECD's 29 members provided data in 1996. Of the seven OECD members that did not, Norway's consistent policy of not providing data is perhaps the most surprising, given its membership in NATO and its participation in the CFE Treaty. Two countries - Iceland and Luxembourg - have very few armed forces to report, and may have felt there was little point in providing data (although both have consistently provided nil returns to the Register of transfers). Finland submitted sections of its Vienna document to the UN as background information, but, although some relevant information was included, the main sections relating to military holdings were omitted. Australia has been a strong supporter of the Register, and its failure to provide background information in 1996 appears to be a temporary lapse. Hungary supplied holdings data in 1993, but has not done so since. South Korea provides background information on its export policies, but not on its holdings or procurement.

Several non-OECD members also provided holdings or procurement data in 1996. Argentina, Brazil and Bulgaria have been consistent providers of holdings data since 1992 (or 1993 in the case of Argentina). Significantly, Armenia, Azerbaijan and Belarus decided to provide such data in 1996 - Azerbaijan for the first time. This encourages hopes that other states in the area of the former Soviet Union, including Russia and Ukraine, may follow this lead (see discussion in chapter 15).

Each year, the number of countries providing information on their military holdings has been greater than the number providing procurement from national production (See Table 1). Although most countries reporting their holdings also provide data on national procurement, several typically do not - perhaps because they are not arms producers. For example in 1996, of the 28 states providing holdings data in 1996, 20 provided data on procurement through national production. So far it has been relatively rare for a state to provide a report on its national procurement but not on its military holdings. However, it does happen: for instance by Malta and South Africa in the third year of reporting.

The submitted information

The lack of UN guidelines or standardised forms for submitting holdings or procurement data has meant that countries have provided such information in a wide variety of forms and with differing scopes and definitions. This creates problems for interpreting or comparing the reported data.

Nevertheless, during the last four years there has been a clear trend towards countries providing data on their holdings and national procurement using the same categories as for exports and imports. In 1996, 26 out of the 28 countries providing holdings data used the seven Register titles to present them.[4] Thus, over time, almost all governments providing holdings data have decided to do so in a way that requires a separate data-gathering effort.

Register definitions may not always have been rigorously applied - as is also the case with reports on transfers - but where this is the case it is often because of a tendency to include more, rather than less, information (though with the significant exception of missiles and missiles launchers, which we discuss separately below). Moreover, as countries have adhered more strictly to the seven Register categories, they have sometimes reduced the scope of the information they provided in early years. For example, Canada, Japan, and the Netherlands initially reported holdings of a wider range of weapons, such as including smaller warships and helicopters falling outside the 'attack helicopters' definition. As they moved towards a stricter use of the Register categories, the number of items reported was significantly reduced.

A substantial proportion of countries submitting information on holdings or national procurement provide qualitative information on weapons types or models, as well as numerical data. For example, out of 28 countries providing information on holdings in 1996, about half (13) provided information on the types or models of the weapons reported. Such countries, at least, have decided that providing qualitative information on their military holding is consistent with their security.

Nevertheless, most countries appear to have been more cautious about providing types data for their military holdings than for their arms transfers. Governments appear particularly concerned about revealing any information on their holdings of missiles and missile launchers (MML). Of the 28 states reporting holdings in 1996, nine declined to provide any information on MML holdings. These included Czech Republic, France, Germany, Mexico and Turkey. A further seven states reported nil holdings of MML, and two states (Argentina and Brazil) reported holdings of missile launchers, but not missiles. Only ten states with missile stocks reported any information on their existing arsenals of MML: Bulgaria, Canada, Greece, Italy, Netherlands, Poland, Portugal, Spain, the UK and the US. No country was willing to provide information on the types/models of the missiles in its possession.

Information on withdrawals and other innovations

One of the main goals of the Register is to facilitate the identification of trends, worrying or otherwise, in the accumulation of conventional arms. In order to identify such trends, it is not only useful to have information on new procurement, whether it comes from abroad or from domestic production. It is also useful to know whether new items are replacing items of equipment that are being retired from service, or whether they constitute net additions to holdings.[5]

Thus, it is to be welcomed that five countries (Austria, Brazil, Canada, the Netherlands, and Portugal) now include a detailed explanation each year of why reported holdings have changed. In addition to including information on imports and on exports of equipment from national holdings, these countries also include information on:

- Withdrawals from service. This is often accompanied by a short explanation, such as 'crashed', 'scrapped', 'added to historical collection' or simply 'decrease in inventory'.

- Changes in reported holdings as a result of correction of previous data or recategorisation of equipment. Inevitably, experience with the Register has led countries to refine data collection and/or re-examine previous interpretations of the seven Register definitions.

This information is of considerable value in the interpretation of trends in military inventories, and could provide a useful precedent for the development of reporting of holdings by others. If applied to US submissions, for example, it would have greatly increased the value of the information provided. The three most recent US reports on military holdings have all included a footnote to the effect that 'more inclusive definitions' and 'more accurate accounting procedures' have contributed to changes in reported inventories. Yet there is no information provided as to the size of the adjustment made as a result of this correction and recategorisation. Nor is information provided on numbers of systems withdrawn from service, or on the types of weapons in military holdings. As a result, even after four years of reporting, the US's Register report on military holdings remains relatively difficult to interpret.

In a quite separate innovation, Bulgaria has provided data each year on equipment 'awaiting or being refurbished for export'. In 1996, reported equipment in this category included 244 battle tanks, 478 large calibre artillery and 39 combat aircraft. The clear implication is that these systems are not included in reported military holdings.

Approaches to expanding the Register in 1997

The experience with reporting 'background information' on military holdings and procurement from national production to the Register during its first four years has been useful and instructive. Despite the weakness of the existing invitation to provide such data, a significant number of states have done so. Moreover, over time, an increasing number of such countries have provided such data in a reasonably standardised form: providing information according to the Register's weapon categories involving a dedicated national compilation process. A substantial number have also provided information on weapon types, at least for categories other than 'missile and missile launchers'. Moreover, useful precedents have been set, such as providing information on withdrawals or changes in holdings, and separately reporting equipment awaiting export.

However, it is also clear that present arrangements are inadequate, and that they need to be strengthened if transparency in this area is to develop further. The number of states that provide 'background information' on holdings or national procurement has stabilised over the last three years, and seems unlikely to increase significantly without further measures. The problems of interpreting and comparing submitted data cannot be solved without establishing standardised reporting forms and common guidelines and definitions. Furthermore, it is unsatisfactory that the data submitted is only disseminated through non-governmental sources (primarily in the Bradford Arms Register Studies (BARS) series) rather than officially - for example through the annual UN Secretary-General's report.

Most importantly, the UN General Assembly and virtually all member states have repeatedly endorsed the expansion of the Register to include procurement from national production and military holdings as well as transfers. The existing transfers Register does not cover major parts of many countries' arms procurement processes and tends to discriminate against countries that are relatively dependent on arms imports. The Register cannot begin to achieve its full potential in contributing to international security until it fully covers military holdings and procurement from national production as well as arms transfers.

Unfortunately, the full expansion of the Register to include procurement and holdings on the same basis as for transfers may be unnegotiable in 1997, on anything approaching a consensus basis. Although each year about 28 states now provide such data, this still represents a minority of participants in the Register. Moreover, although they appear to have become more comfortable with participation in the Register and other military transparency arrangements, there is no reason to think that countries such as India, China or Israel have so changed their position that they would be willing to accept full expansion in 1997, where they refused to do so in 1994.

If this is the case, this situation is unfortunate. The possibility of moving towards full expansion should be carefully explored by the 1997 Group of

Experts. It is important to continue to make it clear that full expansion of the Register remains a central objective. However, a negotiating strategy entirely focused on achieving full expansion of the Register in 1997 has a high risk of failure. It is necessary to balance the risks involved in accepting a more gradual attainment of the long term objective with the risks that would follow from the failure of the 1997 review to achieve any significant advance at all. In this context, it is important to explore whether agreement could be usefully achieved on some intermediate proposal, that would at least mean taking a step towards full expansion.

In line with this, we identify below four possible options which could form the basis for useful agreement in the 1997 Group of Experts. Clearly, many detailed variations on these options are possible. Our aim in presenting them is to focus on distinctive approaches, rather than to be fully comprehensive. Moreover, each acceptable option must to some extent be considered as a 'package'. It is particularly important that any compromise deal is a useful transitional step towards the agreed long term goal of full expansion, and therefore contains elements that ensure that compromises do not undermine the prospects for achieving this goal through a future review.

Option 1: Full expansion to include military holdings and procurement from national production

Our preferred option is to achieve agreement to expand the Register so that participants should report information on their procurement from national production and military holdings with the same level of obligation as for transfers. This would enable the Register to achieve its full potential and contribute to international security more effectively than any of the compromise options. For example, any international body aiming to use the Register to identify and prevent 'excessive and destabilising accumulations of arms' would need all three of these categories of information.

For this option, guidelines for reporting on procurement from national production should be directly equivalent to those applying to transfer. However, in principle, there is no compelling reason why guidelines and standardised forms for reporting on military holdings should not be different from these. It could be decided, for example, that participants would be under less obligation to provide detailed qualitative information (for example, on weapon types or models) on their military holdings than for transfers or procurement from national production.

Option 2: Revisiting the 1994 compromise proposal

If full expansion of the Register proves to be unnegotiable in 1997, one option would be to seek a compromise along the lines of that supported by Australia, Germany, Japan and the Netherlands in the 1994 Group of Experts. In such an approach, states would be under a lesser obligation to report their military holdings and procurement from national production than their annual arms transfers. This would accommodate the present refusal of states such as China, India and Israel to provide such data, since they could decide against providing such information and yet remain a participant in the Register. For this very reason, however, it would raise all of the problems raised by France, Canada, USA and UK in the 1994 review.

This compromise option could be slightly redesigned to make it more attractive. For example, it could be explicitly recommended by the Group of Experts only as a transitional arrangement, which should be reviewed and revised at the next opportunity. Moreover, the wording of the request to states to provide data on their holdings and procurement from national production could reflect the fact that the UN General Assembly has repeatedly and overwhelmingly agreed that reporting such data to the Register should become the international norm. Thus, states should at least be 'encouraged' to provide such reports, and preferably 'called upon to do so unless special circumstances mean that such submissions would damage national security at the present time'.[6]

This approach would provide a 'let out' for countries that were definitely not ready to provide such data. Though necessary to achieve consensus, this would be a pity since these countries would probably include Register participants whose procurement activities are of particular interest to the international community. At the same time, however, such an approach would establish that submitting data on holdings and procurement from national production on standardised forms was part of the normal practice of participating in the Register. It would facilitate and re-inforce efforts by promoters of the Register to encourage more states to participate in the transparency regime and regularly provide information on their holdings, procurement and transfers. In such circumstances, it seems likely that the number of states regularly providing such information could increase significantly beyond the present thirty or so countries. Moreover, the use of standardised forms would make submitted data more comparable and systematic. It could also contribute to regional measures to promote transparency and build confidence, such as those developing within the ASEAN Regional Forum (ARF).

However, a substantially weaker recommendation, which was not clearly transitional or which merely 'invited' countries to submit information on holdings and procurement from national production on standardised forms where they deemed it useful, would contribute relatively little and might even undermine future efforts to expand the Register.

Option 3: Expand to include procurement from national production on same basis as transfers

An alternative compromise approach would involve expanding the Register to include procurement from national production on exactly the same basis as for transfers, but *not* military holdings.[7] Some countries that are currently unwilling to provide detailed information on their military holdings might be willing to submit information on procurement from national production. Adoption of this option would recognise that the security and accountability issues, as well as the reporting demands, raised by transparency measures in these two areas are different.

Such an approach should also be explicitly regarded as a transitional step towards full expansion of the Register. However, as noted above, even in a fully expanded Register it may not be desirable for reporting requirements for military holdings to be identical to those for transfers or procurement from national production. In contrast, the case for equivalent transparency requirements for transfers and for procurement from national production is particularly strong. They complement each other, providing balanced information on national arms procurement, whether through imports or domestic production. Procurement by arms producing countries would become subject to the same transparency requirements as arms importers participating in the Register already face. The Register would be able to track the increasingly important development of licensed production (especially evident in the rapidly industrialising states of East Asia).[8] Changes in countries' military holdings, and thus trends in their accumulation of major conventional weapons, would become more transparent.

Accurate Register replies on both imports and national procurement, submitted over a period of 10-20 years, would eventually allow a good picture of participating countries' military holdings to be obtained (particularly if they were supplemented by information on withdrawals from holdings). However, such a picture would only develop gradually, and countries would at every stage have the possibility of withdrawal, should they become uncomfortable with their transparency commitments.

This may make the expansion of the Register to include procurement from national production much more negotiable than an immediate disclosure of military holdings. Similarly, if such an expansion were to be agreed by the countries represented in the 1997 Group of Experts, there would be a relatively good chance that all other existing participants in the Register would continue to participate after the scope of the Register had been expanded.

If the Register was expanded to cover procurement from national production on the same basis as transfers, measures to increase reporting requirements for military holdings could be weaker (along the lines of the compromise approach discussed above in Option 2) or deferred until the next review. Such an outcome would probably be better than the Option 2 compromise approach outlined above. Although members of the 1994 Group of Experts were aware of this possible approach,[9] it was hardly discussed in the 1994 negotiating process. This was mainly because potential advocates saw it as a distraction from attempts to achieve full expansion. It should be explored more fully this time.

Some countries represented in the Group of Experts might still be reluctant to agree to provide data on their procurement from national production. However, they are unlikely to oppose such expansion as strongly as they opposed full expansion of the Register to include military holdings. Moreover, they would find it harder to justify such opposition, either in terms of national security or in terms of international equity between arms importing and arms producing countries. At the very least, there might be a significant reduction in the size of the group of countries in the 1997 Group of Experts that were strongly opposed to such expansion.

The national data-collection requirements for reporting on annual procurement from national production would usually be relatively modest. Information on their arms procurement through national production is more likely already to be centrally available to governments than data on annual transfers (because the latter often only involve the government at the licensing stage). Moreover, the volume of annual procurement from national production is typically likely to be less than or roughly equal to that of transfers.[10]

If this approach were to be pursued, the new UN transparency regime would be expanded to cover national procurement as well as transfers of major conventional arms. In this context, the question of reporting on how states deal with 'surplus weapons' withdrawn from holdings is naturally raised, to provide a more complete picture of changes in countries' military holdings.[11] Systems are permanently withdrawn from military holdings due to: accidents; war; scrapping of 'surplus' weapons; or export. It would thus be consistent to include a 'withdrawals' section in the Register.[12] However, detailed discussion on introducing such a 'withdrawals' section should probably be deferred to a future review: it may distract attention from higher priority issues in 1997.

The main advantage of this option over Option 2 is that there would be greater chance of moving towards greater transparency, in relation to procurement, in states which do not currently provide such information (such as India, Pakistan, China, Indonesia or Russia). In any discussions on this option, therefore, it would have to be made clear that its acceptance would require all Register participants to provide procurement data on the same basis as the current Register does for imports and exports. Such a recognition would be a necessary quid pro quo for a further delay in moving towards fuller transparency on military holdings themselves.

Option 4: Compromise expansion to include procurement from national production

If full expansion of the Register is rejected by key states like China and India, and neither of the two compromise options outlined above prove to be negotiable, the 1997 Group of Experts will be faced with a choice between complete failure in this area or trying to find an even more limited step forward. In this undesirable situation, it is worth exploring the possibility of adopting the 'compromise' approach discussed above in Option 2 in relation to including procurement from national production only.

This would imply agreeing, *as a transitional step* to be reviewed at the next opportunity, that states be 'called upon to submit data on procurement from national production (on standardised forms), unless special circumstances mean that this would damage their national security'. This would establish a clear norm, while still providing a let out clause for any participating country that has determined that it is not ready to provide such data. In this context, no weak compromise would be agreed on military holdings, but instead this issue would remain unresolved for the next review.

There is no doubt that this option would be disappointing. The question here is whether it would be better than nothing. It could make real progress towards expanding the Register to cover procurement as well as transfers. The arrangement would clearly be transitional, and so it would not appear to undermine the prospects for further expansion or strengthening after the next review. The strong wording of the compromise would induce many participating states to provide data on national procurement where they did not do so before. Moreover, disentangling transparency arrangements for military holdings from those for procurement from national production would do no long term harm. As discussed above, a fully expanded Register could involve reporting requirements for military holdings that are different to those for transfers and national procurement. The key long term principle is that transparency arrangements for procurement from national production should be the same as those for transfers, and this approach would not profoundly compromise this.

The key to the viability of such an option would be whether or not a significant number of additional states were ready to use the opportunity provided to supply national procurement data. If, for example, Russia or the ASEAN states were willing to provide procurement data under such an arrangement, it might be worthwhile to go ahead even if China were not. But this option would barely improve on the status quo unless it induced a significant increase in the number of countries providing such data, or at least some additional regional or global powers.

Implementing an expanded reporting system

Implementing any of the approaches outlined above for expanding the Register would require adopting standardised reporting forms and agreed guidelines and definitions. This will require addressing technical challenges. However, in practice these have already been substantially tackled, by the 1992 UN Panel of Technical Experts and by work done in the context of the 1994 review process (by non-governmental analysts and UN consultants as well as governmental experts).[13] Although choices would have to be made, if the political will exists to expand the scope of the Register to include military holdings and/or procurement from national production, there is no reason why the technical guidelines and definitions could not be satisfactorily settled quite rapidly.

In establishing agreed definitions and guidelines, it is important to take full account of the fact that the UN Register is based on a political agreement, and is a confidence-building measure. It is not an international treaty, for which full compatibility with the domestic law must be established, or for which water-tight obligations must be negotiated in full detail. The priority therefore is simply to establish the most straightforward and effective common guidelines and definitions required for the purposes of the Register itself. In the spirit of a voluntary transparency arrangement, if the minimum reporting guidelines are not sufficient to provide appropriate transparency, states should voluntarily provide additional information to prevent misunderstandings. Moreover, guidelines can be revised and developed as appropriate, as participants gain experience in implementing them.

In this spirit, we now briefly consider guidelines and definitions for reporting on procurement from national production and military holdings.

Procurement from national production

As discussed above, if the Register is expanded to cover procurement from national production, the reporting requirements for national procurement should be directly equivalent to those for arms transfers. The same weapons categories would therefore be used, and the same guidelines relating to the provision of information on weapons types would apply.

For the purposes of the UN Register, production of a weapons system would be defined as:

> 'any process by which components, systems and equipment
> items are changed in such a way as to create an item covered
> by the Register where an item in the same category did not
> exist before'.

This would therefore cover all licensed production and final assembly processes as well as fully indigenous production. It would only be necessary to report if they involved changing a system so that it came into one of the Register's weapons categories when it did not before.

On the basis of this, it is possible to define what is meant by 'procurement from national production' as follows:

> 'procurement from national production takes place when a
> system in one of the categories in the Register is procured by
> the state authorities from suppliers located within the
> territorial jurisdiction of a state .'

This appears to accord with the definitions already used by those countries who already provide information on procurement through national production to the Register. For example, the UK defines procurement through national production as 'complete weapon systems in each of the seven categories ...purchased by the Government during the relevant calendar year from suppliers within the UK or from programmes in which the UK is a collaborative partner.'

This approach would directly complement the reporting of imports and military holdings. Adding reported imports to reported procurement through national production would provide total procurement by a particular government. If military holdings are also reported, it would be possible to explain the change in military holdings between two years by the formula: Holdings (end year 2) = Holdings (end year 1) + imports (year 2) + procurement through national production (year 2) - withdrawals from service (year 2).

Military holdings

As already emphasised, it is not necessary in principle that reporting requirements and guidelines for military holdings should be directly equivalent to those for procurement from national production and transfers. For example, any guidelines requesting data on types of weapons transferred or nationally produced need not fully apply to some or all categories of military holdings. As a first step, for example, the standardised reporting form for military holdings could simply be modelled on the format that has been widely adopted by states already providing background information. Thus, the aggregate number of weapons held by a state could simply be requested for each of the seven categories covered by the Register.

The question of how to define a state's military holdings raises potentially difficult issues about what to include. However, as with national procurement, we believe that in practice one approach is clearly the most sensible and straightforward at this stage. To begin with, it is clear from the 1992 UN Panel of Technical Experts' discussion of the definition of transfers that military holdings should exclude systems held by other states' armed forces on one's own territory but include weapons held outside national territory by one's own forces.

On this basis, questions could be raised about whether to include holdings by state forces other than regular armed forces, such as paramilitary, internal security or reserve forces or the coast-guard. However, organisational distinctions between different parts of states' armed forces vary between countries and over time. Any attempt to agree distinctions between them is almost certain either to prove unnegotiable or to undermine the value of the Register. In the first instance, countries are concerned about the overall arsenals of other states. Thus all of the weapons systems owned by the government of a state should be included in the definition of military holdings.

It is important to clarify whether military holdings include weapons that are within a state's territorial jurisdiction but are not in the government's possession, such as weapon systems that are held by non-governmental rebels, held by private arms companies (for example awaiting export), or in historical museum collections. It is probably best to exclude these from the agreed definition of military holdings, not least because of the difficulty involved in gathering information. Governments should, however, be invited to add an explanatory note when significant numbers of weapons in the seven categories are held on national territory outside the control of either itself or another national government acting with its agreement. As experience is gained with reporting military holdings, reporting guidelines and definitions could be revised and developed through future UN reviews of the Register.

Conclusions

The most important task of the 1997 Group of Experts is to find agreement on ways to expand the Register's coverage of military holdings and procurement from national production. After four years of merely inviting participating states to submit 'available background information' on their holdings and national procurement, it is time to expand and strengthen the reporting system in this area.

If at all possible, recommendations to achieve the full coverage of holdings and procurement on the same basis as transfers should be agreed (Option 1). But it seems probable that the states that blocked full expansion in 1994 will do so again in 1997. If this is the case, it is important to explore more negotiable intermediate measures, to avoid repeating the failure of the 1994 review. These should explicitly be regarded as transitional steps, to be reviewed and revised at the next opportunity, and carefully designed to promote rather than undermine the medium-term prospects for achieving full expansion.

Three potentially useful and relatively negotiable compromise approaches are identified. Of these, perhaps the most desirable would be Option 3: full inclusion of procurement from national production on the same basis as for transfers, with the more sensitive issue of including military holdings being either deferred to the next review or included on the basis of a weaker reporting obligation. This would mean that the Register would be extended to cover national procurement as well as transfers. Perhaps the second most desirable compromise would be Option 2: expand the Register to cover military holdings and procurement from national production on the same basis as transfers, but with a 'let-out' clause to accommodate participating states that are unwilling as yet to submit such additional data. The formulation of such a recommendation would be a delicate task, but it should be such that provision of national data on holdings or procurement from national production should clearly become the norm for participating states. If neither of these intermediate positions are negotiable, then Option 4 should be considered in which the compromise approach of Option 2 is at least adopted for procurement from national production.

Appendix 1: Summary table on military holdings data provided during 1993-1996

Country	Provided during 1993	Provided during 1994	Provided during 1995	Provided during 1996
EUROPEAN UNION				
Austria	*	*	*	*
Belgium	*	*	*	*
Denmark	*	*	*	*
Finland		*		
France	*	*	*	*
Germany	*	*	*	*
Greece	*	*	*	*
Ireland				*
Italy	*	*	*	*
Netherlands	*	*	*	*
Portugal	*	*	*	*
Spain	*	*	*	*
Sweden	*	*	*	*
UK	*	*	*	*
OTHER EUROPE				
Albania		*		
Bulgaria	*	*	*	*
Czech Republic		*	*	*
Hungary	*			
Poland	*	*	*	*

Switzerland			*	*
Turkey	*			*
ASIA AND OCEANIA				
Australia	*	*	*	
Japan	*	*	*	*
Marshall Islands			*	
New Zealand	*	*	*	*
AMERICA				
Argentina		*	*	*
Brazil	*	*	*	*
Canada	*	*	*	*
Chile	*	*		
El Salvador			*	
Mexico			*	*
Nicaragua	*			
Paraguay		*	*	
US	*	*	*	*
FORMER SOVIET UNION				
Armenia			*	*
Azerbaijan				*
Belarus		*		*
SUB-SAHARAN AFRICA				
Comoros		*		
Cote D'Ivoire		*		
Niger		*	*	

Sierra Leone		*		
TOTAL	24	31	29	28

Appendix 2: Summary table on national procurement data provided during 1993-1996

Country	Provided during 1993	Provided during 1994	Provided during 1995	Provided during 1996
EUROPEAN UNION				
Austria	*	*	*	*
Denmark	*	*	*	*
France	*	*	*	*
Germany	*	*	*	*
Greece	*	*	*	*
Italy	*	*	*	*
Netherlands	*	*	*	*
Portugal	*	*	*	*
Spain	*	*	*	*
UK	*	*	*	*
OTHER EUROPE				
Bulgaria	*			
Czech Republic		*	*	*
Hungary	*			
Malta			*	
Poland		*	*	*
Switzerland			*	*
Turkey				*
ASIA AND OCEANIA				

Japan	*	*	*	*
New Zealand		*	*	*
AMERICA				
Brazil	*	*	*	*
Canada	*	*	*	*
Mexico			*	*
US	*	*	*	*
TOTAL	16	17	20	20

1   This chapter is a revised and developed version of a paper
        presented at the Tokyo workshop on Transparency in Armaments
        on 12 May 1997, which itself drew extensively on the discussion of
        this issue in Malcolm Chalmers and Owen Greene, *The UN
        Register in its Fourth Year, Part B: Priorities for the 1997 Review*,
        Bradford Arms Register Studies (BARS) Working Paper No 2,
        Bradford University, November 1996.

2   For further details, see the discussion in Malcolm Chalmers and
        Owen Greene, *Taking Stock: the UN Register after Two Years*,
        Westview Press/Bradford University, 1995, especially pp 223 - 226;
        or in E. Laurance and H. Wulf, 'The 1994 Review of the United
        Nations Register of Conventional Arms', *SIPRI Yearbook 1995*,
        Oxford University Press/SIPRI, Oxford, 1995, pp 223 - 266.

3   Malcolm Chalmers and Owen Greene, *In the Background:
        reporting national procurement and military holdings to the
        Register 1993 - 1996*, Bradford Arms Register Studies (BARS)
        Working Paper No 3, University of Bradford, March 1997. Earlier
        publications in the BARS series providing data submitted as
        background information helped to establish the precedent of public
        access: Malcolm Chalmers and Owen Greene, *Background
        Information: an analysis of information provided to the UN on
        military holdings and procurement from national production in the
        first year of the United Nations Register of Conventional Arms*,
        BARS 3, Bradford University/Westview Press, March 1994;
        Malcolm Chalmers and Owen Greene, *Taking Stock: the UN
        Register after two years*, Westview Press, London, 1995, Appendix
        7 ('Background Information on military holdings and procurement
        from national production (1993)').

4   That is: Battle tanks, armoured combat vehicles, large calibre
        artillery systems, combat aircraft, attack helicopters, warships, and
        missiles and missile launchers. The two countries that have not
        done, used these UN Register categories - Denmark and Sweden -
        provided data from their Vienna declarations, prepared as part of
        their participation in the CFE Treaty and OSCE confidence-
        building agreements. In the first three years of reporting, Australia
        provided a copy of its annual defence report: a document which,

although informative and detailed in other respects, fails to provide all of the holdings data that other OECD states typically include. In 1996, for some reason, Australia omitted to provide even this document.

5   For further discussion, see Malcolm Chalmers and Owen Greene, 'Expanding the Register to include procurement through national production and military holdings' in Malcolm Chalmers, Owen Greene, Edward J. Laurance and Herbert Wulf, (eds.) *Developing the United Nations Register of Conventional Arms,* Bradford Arms Register Studies, Number 4, Westview Press, 1994, pp. 170-171.

6   For the present, there should probably be no attempt to define what is meant by 'special circumstances' in this context, in order to avoid getting bogged down on this issue. The main aim is to establish the principle that reporting on military holdings and procurement from national production as well as transfers should be the international norm.

7   This option was identified and explored in detail in the informal workshop for the 1994 Group of Experts in Monterey, (April 1994). See M. Chalmers and O. Greene, 'Expanding the Register to include procurement from national production and military holdings', in M. Chalmers, O. Greene, E. Laurance, and H. Wulf (eds.), *Developing the UN Register of Conventional Arms,* Bradford Arms Register Studies No 4, Westview Press, Oxford, 1994, pp 153 - 175. Others have also suggested this general approach, such as P. Turner, 'Asia-Pacific Approaches to the 1997 Experts Review', papers presented to UN Workshop, Kathmandu, 24 February 1996.

8   The transfers Register covers only complete weapon systems, and thus excludes transfers of technology or arms production equipment. Where such transfers result in domestic arms production, this would be reported as procurement from national production. Note that, to the extent that it stimulated more countries to provide information on procurement from national production, Option 2 above would also contribute to improving transparency on issues such as transfers associated with licensed production.

9   For example, it had been identified and explored in detail by the
     present authors in an informal workshop attended by most
     members of the 1994 Group of Experts in April 1994: see M.
     Chalmers and O. Greene, 'Expanding the Register to include
     procurement from national production and military holdings', in
     M. Chalmers, O. Greene, E. Laurance, and H. Wulf (eds.), 1994,
     op cit.

10   By comparison, levels of military holdings might typically be
     between 20 - 40 times those of average annual procurement, and
     governments often do not have accurate data on their holdings of
     major weapons outside active units (i.e. in storage).

11   See E. Laurance and H. Wulf (eds.), *Coping with Surplus
     Weapons: A Priority for Conversion Research and Policy*, Bonn
     International Conversion Centre, 1995.

12   Malcolm Chalmers and Owen Greene, 1994, *op cit*., pp 170-171.

13   See, for example, UN Panel of Technical Experts, *Report on the
     Register of Conventional Arms*, UN General Assembly A/47/342,
     14 August 1992; Malcolm Chalmers and Owen Greene, 1994, *op
     cit*., pp 153 - 175.

Part C: Strengthening the Register

CHAPTER 9

Remarks on Strengthening the UN Conventional Arms Register

Giovanni Snidle

Introduction

In this chapter, I aim to share with my fellow members of the Group of Governmental Experts and other interested supporters of the Register some thoughts I have on how to strengthen the Register. I will focus on some practical measures which can be taken unilaterally, bilaterally, and by the UN.

Country western music is very popular in the United States. One famous country western song is entitled 'When you leave walk out backwards, so they will think you are walking in'. I hope I can succeed in following this advice with the suggestions I am about to make.

I will briefly address five potential areas of strengthening the register.

Five Steps to Strengthen the Register

1. Holdings and Procurement through National Production

The first step concerns how to expand the Register to include military holdings and procurement through national production, on the same basis as transfers. I begin here, at the Register's fifth anniversary, by quoting the unfulfilled mandate of General Assembly resolution 46/36L

> 'to prepare a report on the modalities for early expansion of the scope of the Register by the addition of further categories of equipment and inclusion of data on military holdings and procurement through national production.'

The register as currently constructed is discriminatory between those countries that indigenously produce and those that import. Providing background information on military holdings and procurement through national production would present a more complete and balanced picture of conventional arms, holdings and procurement. It would be among one of the best measures to strengthen the Register.

2. Tighter Definitions

A second step to strengthen the Register would be better definitions of some of the categories of weapons.

As a result of the past five years' experience, I believe that while the seven categories used for reporting equipment on conventional arms transfers are not ideal for every situation, they represent the best fit for global reporting of conventional arms imports and exports. Some, however, are in need of better definitions or technical adjustments.

Category seven is the best example of this. Missiles and missile launchers need to be separated. Lowering warships' displacement tonnage and lowering the calibre of artillery are two other examples. Changes to these categories would capture more trade in conventional arms. These technical changes would contribute to greater transparency and confidence in the arms trade.

Likewise, another area of possible clearer definitions that deserve attention is the definition of transfers. There are, and will continue to be, some inconsistencies in the number of transfers reported by some importing and exporting states due to differences in transfer dates, and in the manner in which transfers are defined by different states with different regulatory and legislative authorities. While it may be ambitious to expect to achieve a universal definition of transfers, at a minimum, each country should be required to make explicit the definition it employs with its submission.

3. Raising the Profile of the Register

Another practical improvement that would strengthen the UN Register is to raise its profile.

The effort here would be to achieve better distribution and dissemination of the Register. It would also involve beginning a process of using the exchanged information.

In these areas, I have the following suggestions:

I. Improve public and Governmental access to the information

Outside of UN circles, the UN Register is a little known global confidence building measure. I would also venture to say that outside of New York, many governments do not have other countries' submissions of past years. Thus, two immediate improvements would be:

- Annually send to each capital a complete package (a computer disk) of submissions and

- Establish a separate home page on UN CSBMs to highlight the register and military expenditures

II. National Points of Contact

A second recommendation is to identify National Points of Contact for the UN Register (in each country's national submission). This would be either a person or office which should be contacted regarding a country's Register submission. Automatically, this would increase countries' continuity in participation, open an avenue for consultations both before and after submission of data, and perhaps increase accuracy.

III. Conferences

A third suggestion which immediately comes to mind is the holding of further regional conferences. The practice of holding regional conferences sponsored by regional organizations or the UN Disarmament Center have proven to be useful, both for the instructions they provided and for the opportunity they offer for exchanges of views among representatives on a wide range of issues relevant to the submissions and to national import/export policies.

4. Encourage Complementary Regional Registers

A fourth area of strengthening the Register concerns regional registers. The former UN Secretary General in his foreword to the 1994 Group of Governmental Experts acknowledged their importance in the following words:

> 'I welcome the observations of the Group concerning the steps that might be taken in applicable forums to encourage regional approaches based on specific local conditions. At the same time, I fully concur that such approaches should complement and not detract from the universal instrument.'

The UN Register has stimulated interest in the possible utility of establishing regional registers. We should recognise that in order to include the most threatening weapons in particular regions, in some cases regional registers maybe needed to facilitate achieving fuller transparency. For example, how often does a nation in the Caribbean acquire combat aircraft? Once in thirty years? Never? How often would they acquire small arms? Regional registers could more readily capture the transfers more relevant to subregions. Regional registers are an especially valuable adjunct to the global UN Register. I welcome the efforts by West Africa to develop a moratorium and register of small arms. I hope they succeed in their endeavours.

5. Moving from Transparency to Confidence Building

Lastly, one of the best ways of strengthening the Register is using it. With five years of experience behind us, I believe it is time to focus some attention on how the information that is exchanged can be used to build confidence on a bilateral, sub-regional, and regional basis. I applaud the efforts of the Organization of American States, the Organization on Security and Cooperation in Europe, and the ASEAN Regional Forum in this area.

My own country has taken an important step in this direction. Last October, at the Defense Ministerial of the Americas, Former Secretary of Defense William Perry announced that,

> 'The United States will give advance notice to all 33 democracies of the hemisphere of our acquisition of significant weapons covered by the UN Register of Conventional Arms."

More diplomatic policy activity needs to be devoted to encouraging bilateral, multilateral, regional, and sub-regional consultations to discuss individual submissions of the data. This would truly establish the Register as a transparency arrangement and, more importantly, as a confidence building measure.

If participation in the Register is an indication of a willingness to enter into a security dialogue, I hope we see the blossoming of more security dialogues among neighbors, friends and foes. With this, I conclude my remarks.

CHAPTER 10

Strengthening the Register

Malcolm Chalmers and Owen Greene

Introduction

This chapter seeks to explore some of the ways in which the Register might be strengthened in order to increase transparency and provide additional information. Part of the strength of the Register is that it provides both framework and flexibility: setting out a clear structure for the provision of information, but allowing individual governments some latitude for increasing transparency at a pace with which they feel comfortable. Consequently, strengthening the information provided in Register submissions is a process that takes place at both a national and international level. The purpose of the Group of Experts is to assess whether a broad consensus can be found for the basic framework of the Register to be strengthened in some respects. But individual countries also have a responsibility for assessing whether they could individually make more use of the facilities the Register provides for additional information to be included (for example, on types and model data, national procurement and military holdings).

Because of the continuing opportunities for developing transparency through action at both a multilateral and a national level, this chapter makes suggestion for progress on both levels.

Qualitative information

Participants in the Register are 'called upon' and 'requested' to provide numerical information on transfers with each trading partner, but are only 'invited' to provide qualitative information specifying model, type or intended role of the transferred arms. To symbolise the fact that provision of qualitative information is at the discretion of each participating state, a small gap is included in the standardised reporting form between the first five columns and the additional 'remarks' column, which is subdivided into sections for 'description of item' and 'comments on transfer'.

A strong case can be made for deepening the Register's reporting system by strengthening the obligation to provide qualitative data on weapon types or intended roles for the weapons concerned. It would give a much more complete picture of the significance of the reported transfer: it makes a big difference whether a reported transfer of a tank or warship relates to a new M1 Abrams or an old T-54 tank, or to an aircraft carrier or a frigate. It would highlight those, quite frequent, cases in which states have chosen to include transfers in their reports that strictly fall outside the seven Register categories. It would help to identify and clarify discrepancies between submission from importing or exporting states, and those between information reported to the Register and data from other sources. It would therefore do much to help to improve the reliability of the Register and confidence in it.

Since the establishment of the Register, a number of states have overcome their initial caution on this issue and have included weapon descriptions in their reply. Only six of the 13 states which did not provide types data in 1993 (the Register's first year) were still declining to do so in 1996: China, India, Japan, Russia, the UK and the US. Not all the replies due in 1997 have yet been received. The UK has now decided to provide types data for the first time[1], but the US and Japan have not done so.[2] Information on the content of India's reply is not yet available. To our knowledge, replies for the Register's fifth year have not yet been submitted by China and Russia.

The willingness of key countries to supply additional information in this regard is a welcome symbol of commitment to the Register at a time when there is concern that some states may no longer take the Register sufficiently seriously. Especially important in this regard are:

- The decisions of France and the UK (in 1996 and 1997 respectively) to provide types data. All EU members now provide such data to the Register.

- The decisions of Singapore, Thailand and Vietnam to provide types data for the first time in 1996. All ASEAN participants in the Register now provide types data.

With most states in Europe, South America, the former Soviet Union and ASEAN already providing types data, China, India, Russia, and the US should review their position on this issue as a matter of some priority. The failure to provide types data is particularly puzzling in the case of the US, which already provides detailed information to Congress on its exports of major conventional arms, much of which then becomes publicly available. It is not clear why similar details cannot also be provided to the UN.

Even if these four countries (all of whom are represented on the Group of Experts) are not willing to provide types data unilaterally, some of them may be willing to join others in supporting a revision that increases the degree of obligation attached to the provision of such data by the UN. Once a consensus in principle on the desirability of providing types data had been established, specific guidelines could be agreed on the format in which that information should, where possible, be provided. We have discussed elsewhere ways in which such guidelines could be developed.[3]

In the past, one source of resistance to the inclusion of types data appears to have come from exporters' concerns about the possible reaction of customer states, particularly in the Middle East, who prefer confidentiality and do not participate in the Register. The decision by France, Germany, the UK and other smaller suppliers to take a lead in this area suggests, however, that this argument should not be overstated. Moreover, if the major suppliers were now to decide to join together in providing qualitative information, none would suffer competitive disadvantage against the others. Even if some recipient states would still prefer not to have details of their purchases available publicly, this should not be the decisive factor in determining the extent to which suppliers participate in the Register. It does suggest, however, that much stronger efforts are needed in order to convince the Gulf states to take part in the Register themselves.

The question of whether and how to strengthen the obligation to provide qualitative data to the Register is perhaps second only in importance to the question of expanding its scope to include holdings and national procurement. In fact, the two issues are linked. If the Register is expanded to include procurement from national production and military holdings, then obligations to include qualitative information on transfers should presumably be applied across the board. Whereas transparency rules should be the same for transfers and procurement from national production, they could differ (and perhaps be less stringent or comprehensive) for military holdings.

Other qualitative information

The immediate priority in relation to the provision of qualitative data is to continue the trend towards universal provision of information on the types and models of items being transferred. But the facility for providing qualitative information can also be used to provide 'other ... explanatory remarks as Member States see fit'. In this regard, the Group of Experts should consider whether there are other categories of information that might contribute to a better understanding of developments in force structures, and thus contribute to a process of security dialogue. For example, the column headed 'comments on the transfer' could be used to include information on whether equipment being imported is an addition to existing holdings or a replacement for items being retired from service. It could also be used to summarise the role(s) - reconnaissance, air defence, training, etc. - for which the equipment is intended.

Missiles

The one area where providing information on weapons types appears to raise real security concerns relates to the 'missiles and missile launchers' category. Some missiles can be considered as a form of ammunition, and some states are particularly sensitive to providing information that could be used by potential adversaries to calculate their missile stocks. Knowledge about ammunition or missiles shortages might be of strategic importance in a war. Some countries' particular sensitivities about revealing missile stocks may mean that the 'missiles and missile launchers' category would need to be treated somewhat less stringently than the other six weapons categories in this context. It could be subject to less stringent reporting rules on types and models than the other six categories, or could even be exempted entirely from any obligations to provide qualitative information.

Yet providing type and model information on annual imports of missiles and missile launchers is very different from providing data on total stocks. And security concerns have not prevented a number of, normally cautious, states from providing types data on missile imports. In 1996, Singapore reported the import of 11 Harpoon missiles, Greece 16 Harpoons, Korea 31 Harpoons and 88 AMRAAM's, and Peru 28 Javelins. France, for its part, reported the export of 8 Exocets to Chile, together with 1 ITL70 to Oman and 2 ITL70 to Qatar. The Group of Experts should, at a minimum, build on the transparency that has already been achieved in these examples. It would be highly desirable if it were also to agree a general norm that type and model data should (except in unusual circumstances) be provided for all seven categories.

In summary, we believe that the 1997 Group of Experts should prioritise negotiations on the strengthening of obligations to provide qualitative information on transfers (and on procurement from national procurement, if the Register is expanded). If full reporting on weapons types and roles proves unnegotiable at this stage, intermediate arrangements are available to allow more limited progress to be made.

Discrepancies and definitions

As we have discussed elsewhere, there continues to be a significant number of discrepancies between the transfers reported to the Register by the importer and the exporter.[4] In the first four years of the Register, discrepancies between the exports reported by the US and imports reported by its recipient countries have been particularly frequent, with only 15% of the exports to other Register participants reported by the US matched by identical reports from the importing state. By comparison, 52% of the exports reported by other exporting states were matched in this way.[5]

It would not be realistic, or even perhaps desirable, to expect 100% matching in the replies of exporting and importing states. Yet such high levels of discrepancy, even after four years of experience of operating the Register, suggest the need for the Group of Experts to look seriously at measures that could improve the situation. For example:

- There should be a fresh effort to move towards a convergence of definitions what is meant by transfers. Some countries take the time of transfer as being the date when transfer of title takes place, while others use the point of departure from (or entry into) national territory. Some use both 'transfer of title' and 'control' as criteria. This variation in practice contributes to the problem of discrepancies.

- There should be a re-examination of the issue of whether weapons that are leased to the armed forces of another country should be included in the Register. The level of exports from some countries are significantly underrecorded because of the practice of excluding leased equipment from Register replies.

For example, the failure of the US to report the export of a Knox-class warship to Thailand in 1994 (which was reported by Thailand) may be the result of the US's practice of using 'transfer of title' as the criterion for transfer. The US has interpreted this criterion to exclude the lease of military equipment to foreign armed forces. This helps to explain why four countries reported imports of warships from the US in 1995, but the US did not report the export of any warships during the same year. Taking a longer period, obligatory reports to Congress show US exports of 5 destroyers, 34 frigates and 13 tank-landing ships over the four years since the Register began in 1992. But only four exports of warships were reported to the Register by the US during this same period.[6]

In order to address this problem, which significantly reduces the level of transparency in an important part of the arms trade, we propose that the Group of Experts agree that, in future, equipment transferred to the control of another state on a lease basis should be included in the Register. States may wish to add a 'remark' to the report of the transfer to indicate that the equipment is being supplied on lease. If the equipment is subsequently returned on expiration of the lease, this too should be recorded.

One of the biggest contributions towards reducing the significance, if not the level, of discrepancies would be for all governments to agree to provide types and model data for transfers. One of the most common explanations for discrepancies appears to be differing judgements as to whether or not a particular system should be included. Inclusion of types data allows the rapid identification of such problems.

Revising existing categories of weapons covered by the Register

The existing seven categories of weapons covered by the Register exclude several systems of potential significance for regional security, and could usefully be expanded. In the past, there has been concern that the expansion of existing categories to include systems of rather less significance might tend to 'dilute' the categories, obscuring important transfers within larger numbers. Thus, for example, a lowering of the missile range threshold for inclusion in the Register from 25 km to 5 km might appear, at first sight, to constitute an increase in transparency. But this would in fact only be clearly the case if enough data was included to make clear what type of missiles are being transferred. Without such information, the transfer of, say, 100 Harpoon missiles could be hidden within a much larger transaction (for example of short-range anti-tank missiles).

Simply expanding weapons categories will not necessarily increase transparency for those countries that do not provide information on weapons types in their submissions. The issue of expanding categories is therefore integrally linked with the issue of the provision of qualitative data. If the three major exporters (China, Russia, US) who currently refuse to provide such data were to agree to do so, however, this argument would no longer be of any significance.

One set of proposals for revising existing categories consists of ideas for lowering the thresholds for inclusion in the Register. For example, the calibre threshold for inclusion in the 'large calibre artillery systems' category could be reduced from 100 mm to 70 mm to cover a wider range of mortars. It could even be lowered as far as 12.5mm: the threshold used by NATO in February 1994 in establishing a zone free of 'heavy weapons' around Sarajevo[7]. The 25 km range threshold for missiles could be lowered also, as could the 750 tonnes threshold on the 'warships' category.

A second set of proposals suggests the addition of major categories of military equipment whose primary role is not as weapons platforms. For example, the 'helicopters' category could be extended beyond attack helicopters to include combat support and unarmed transport helicopters specifically fitted for military use. Similarly, there is a case for covering specialised military support aircraft, designed for reconnaissance, aerial refuelling, airborne early warning, or electronic warfare. The definition of warships could be revised from those 'armed <u>and</u> equipped for military use' to those 'armed <u>or</u> equipped for military use'.

A widening of categories in this way might, in some cases, lead to a blurring of the distinction between systems provided for military and civilian use. Provided that revised definitions included clauses making clear that the systems were specifically designed for military use, however, this may not be an insuperable problem.

The existing 'missiles and missile launchers' category requires revision. There is no logical case for aggregating missiles and missile-launchers into a single category, particularly as long as only numerical information needs to be provided on transfers in this category. They should be disaggregated. In addition, the present exclusion of ground-to-air missile systems should be ended as soon as possible: such systems can clearly be of significance for regional and indeed global security.

It is important to recognise that attempts to revise existing categories are prone to become rapidly bogged down. In 1994, the Group of Experts spent substantial time on this issue, revisiting the debates involved in the initial negotiations to establish the Register. The experience demonstrated how difficult such seemingly modest revisions of categories can be to negotiate. The existing categories are the result of protracted negotiations in 1992, and a complex of national interests and concerns are embedded in them. Attempts to open debates about one definition tend to stimulate other countries to raise questions about every other category.

Nevertheless, it is worthwhile to devote some effort to address the obvious problems under this heading. Where useful expansion or revision seems widely acceptable, it should be done. Where key countries seriously object to proposed changes, however, negotiators should avoid spending much valuable time in the Group of Experts trying to press the issue.

Institutional Strengthening of the Register

The problem of discrepancies highlights the need to develop systems to clarify and resolve apparent discrepancies or problems, to promote confidence in the reliability of the Register.

The most obvious first step towards achieving this would be to allow the UN Secretariat at the Centre for Disarmament Affairs to play a more active role in maintaining the Register. At present, the Secretariat has a very restrictive mandate. It is to receive, collate and publish information submitted to it. In practice, it is allowed to clarify basic ambiguities by asking questions of member states (such as 'to what year does the submission relate?'; 'can you confirm that this is a nil return?', or 'we cannot read this submission, please resend'). It can provide technical advice on request. However, it has no remit to draw participating states' attention to apparent errors or discrepancies in their submissions, so that the states involved can review and, if necessary, revise, their submission before the Register is published by the UN. It would seem a small procedural step to allow them to do so, yet the 1994 Group of Experts failed to recommend this - a situation that the 1997 Group of Experts should consider rectifying.

A second way in which the Register could be strengthened in this context is to further develop systems for encouraging, helping and reminding states to compile and submit annual submissions for the Register. At present, the Secretariat plays a useful but limited role in reminding states to respond to the UN Secretary-General's annual request for submissions to the Register. Informally, OECD and other states that support the Register have occasionally co-ordinated bilateral diplomatic efforts to encourage wider participation. For example, Japan has played an important role in promoting participation by developing East Asia states, and states of the EU, Canada and the USA have helped to promote participation in Africa, Central America and other regions. However these efforts need to be strengthened and developed. The Secretariat could be mandated to play an active role in promoting participation, through direct reminders and assistance and indirectly by helping to stimulate and co-ordinate bilateral encouragement and assistance.

Workshops

The organisation of national and regional workshops could help substantially to promote awareness amongst relevant government officials and train them to participate in the Register. Several such workshops were organised in 1992 and early 1993 at a regional level, and there have subsequently been two more small workshops for officials from Central Africa and the Asia-Pacific. However, much more could be done in this area. If the Register is significantly extended or developed as a result of the 1997 review, it will be vital to organise such workshops, in order to ensure wide implementation. However, the case for organising further workshops to promote implementation of the Register is strong in any event. States that support the Register should allocate further resources to sponsor such workshops, to be organised in cooperation with the UN Centre for Disarmament Affairs.

Conclusions: priorities for the 1997 review process

The UN Register has established itself as an important global transparency regime, yet it is still far from achieving its full potential. It is important that the 1997 review of the operation and further development of the Register achieve substantially more than the 1994 review, which failed to achieve anything substantial. Although the initial political impetus behind its establishment in 1992, in the immediate aftermath of the Gulf War and the end of the Cold War, has somewhat dissipated, a wide range of states continue to support the further development of the Register. It is important that they devote the resources and high-level political attention to the 1997 negotiations that are necessary if this goal is to be achieved.

The issues on the agenda remain much the same as in 1994, and much the same set of states will be involved. Therefore, unless the key states involved carefully review their policy positions, there is a real danger that the negotiations will proceed along the same lines as in 1994, with the same disappointing results. Important opportunities would be missed usefully to promote transparency, confidence-building and security.

One of the most important issues for the 1997 review relates to measures to strengthen obligations to provide qualitative data on weapons types and roles alongside the numerical data already reported. If agreed, this would greatly strengthen the Register. If the Register is expanded in scope, any revised reporting rules for transfers should also apply to procurement from national production. But if necessary, the transparency rules could differ for military holdings.

The issue of whether and how to add or revise weapons categories will also need to be addressed in the 1997 review. It should be recognised that, for better or worse, negotiations in the 1997 Group of Experts to add new categories of arms are unlikely to be productive. Similarly, a good case can be made for expanding some of the existing categories and revising the unsatisfactory 'missiles and missile-launchers' category. However, this is an area where negotiations could become unnecessarily bogged-down. The prospects for agreement on each proposed revision should be explored at an early stage. Where the prospects are good, (and there are several revisions for which the prospects for agreement do appear good), useful expansions or revisions of existing categories should be recommended. But the issues at stake are not of the first importance to the Register at this stage of its development.

---

1   The UK still declines to provide types data on transfers of missiles and missile launchers.

2   Japan reported no exports in 1996. The only import reported was 70 missiles and missile launchers from the US. In its submission of 'available background information', Japan did provide types data on national procurement and military holdings for the first six Register categories. It is not clear whether Japan would now be willing to provide types data for imports in the first six categories if such imports were to take place.

3   See, for example, Malcolm Chalmers and Owen Greene, 'Further development of the Register reporting system', in M. Chalmers, O. Greene, E.J. Laurance and H. Wulf (eds.) *Developing the United Nations Register of Conventional Arms*, Westview, 1994, particularly pp 56 - 63.

4   Malcolm Chalmers and Owen Greene, *The UN Register in its Fourth Year*, November 1996.

5   *Ibid*, p. 13.

6   Paul Pineo and Lora Lumpe, *Recycled Weapons: American Exports of Surplus Arms 1990-1995*, Federation of American Scientists, 1996. Our thanks to Lora Lumpe for her help on this issue.

7   For further discussion, see Malcolm Chalmers, Owen Greene, Edward J Laurance and Herbert Wulf (eds), 1994, *op cit,* p. 73.

CHAPTER 11

The UN Register: Transparency and the Promotion of Conflict Prevention and Restraint

Jasjit Singh

In principle, greater transparency in military postures and policies is necessary and an important element in building confidence among states. However, it is important also to take note of the assets and limitations of transparency and of divergent motives for support or opposition to transparency by many states. At the outset it also needs to be noted that the very focus on arms transfers tends to provide only a partial picture of military capabilities. The Register covers only seven major weapon systems, and while it aims to include military holdings and national production of such weapons, the institution of such a step is not likely in the near future. By the very nature of industrial development, it is the developing countries that account for the bulk of arms imports. But if the intention is to promote conflict prevention and restraint, then total procurement of arms by states needs to be taken as the basic parameter. This is, after all, the reason for demands to include holdings and national production in the UN Register. However, this starts to raise many questions and issues, direct and indirect, about the implications on national security and foreign policy of states. At the root are the conflicting parameters of the need for greater transparency in military affairs on one side, and considerations of national security (which promotes secrecy) on the other. This creates a chicken-and-egg problem. The central issue is that measures have to be mutually acceptable and honoured, including those at the regional/bilateral framework.

This raises a more fundamental point: that of the conceptual base of inter-state security. The Westphalian sovereign state system has produced a paradigm that is essentially competitive. Other aspects of human endeavour, like the free market principle of trade and economic activity, and democratic political systems have reinforced the competitive framework of the goals and functions of the sovereign state. For a century, the world has sought to evolve a paradigm that could manage this competition at lower levels of militarisation and conflict. Some progress towards a more co-operative basis of inter-state security has been witnessed in recent years, mostly at bilateral levels. But we are a long way from the paradigm shift from competitive to co-operative security that will provide the requisite framework for greater transparency in armaments without states being nervous about their security. At the global level what is, therefore, needed is a universally-accepted conceptual base for inter-state security based on the principle of *co-operative security* which would seek to establish 'mutual and equal" security, such as forms the basis for the relationship that India and China are developing across their borders. [1]

There is need for clarity in the approach to the issue of transparency and the UN Register. The Register at present provides a very limited amount of transparency which relates only to inter-state transfers of seven categories of major weapon systems. Even this information suffers from limits on transparency because of many ambiguities in the Register's design and functioning. For example, some countries only report those transfers which involve a change of legal title, whereas arms continue to be transferred to states on a lease or loan basis. [2] Significant quantities of arms (in categories covered by the Register) have thus been transferred between states but not reported in the Register since no transfer of legal title took place. There is also, of course, the unique phenomenon of over 100 combat aircraft landing up as transfers from Iraq to Iran during the 1991 Gulf War. But transparency for purpose of confidence building requires that all physical transfers get reflected in the Register. There is an obvious contradiction in the demands for including national production and military holdings and poor support for including all physical arms transfers in the Register.

The Register has only been in operation for five years. With the passage of time some of the existing ambiguities and anomalies will, no doubt, get removed. Meanwhile, it is essential to bear the limitations in mind so that expectations from the transparency provided from the Register do not outpace its capabilities and potential.

Transparency in Armaments

In order to examine how the Register should be strengthened and what role it can play in enhancing transparency and promotion of conflict prevention and restraint, it is important to define some basic issues. It is necessary to be clear on the purpose and goals in the use of data submitted to the Register. Studies have already indicated that the bulk of the information that is included in the Register is already available in the public domain. However, the Register performs an important function in that the information is authentic and authoritative since it is provided to the UN by governments.

Although the Register provides more accurate and authentic information, little purpose would be served if the goals of transparency were restricted to only the accumulation of information. On the other hand, the Register has great potential in respect of the function and purpose which it can, and must, perform. This relates to the commitment of states to transparency as the central function, and the information emerging from this providing the expectation that a great deal would be possible in the areas of conflict prevention and restraint based on such a commitment.

Goals and Implications of Transparency

The basic elements and dynamics of transparency need to be examined in some detail if we are to use it to a greater degree in dealing with armaments. Transparency could be introduced for a general purpose or for more specific goals, at the broader global level or in regional/bilateral framework. At the same time, the implications of transparency in military postures are far more complex than what is generally believed.

Transparency, of course, is not an end in itself but rather the means to the ends sought. There is a need for clarity and transparency in establishing the ends sought through transparency. The basis of seeking transparency through the UN Register has been to enhance confidence among states and through that process, promote conflict prevention. But there are concerns among many developing countries that this may not be the full picture, and that there may be other, even if unstated, goals. At the same time, lack of clarity about the stated goals complicates matters. One of such goals, for example, is to prevent excessive and destabilising accumulation of armaments by a state which could threaten international peace and security. But as long as clear and transparent criteria of what constitutes 'excessive" accumulation of arms is not devised and universally accepted, there will remain the risk of arbitrary application of the objective to specific situations. This is most likely in pursuit of foreign policy goals of states rather than on the basis of a detached approach to the arms acquisition process.

Ad-hoc non-transparent cartels are already functioning which seek to deny technology (tightened under the label of dual-use) and the building of national capabilities for legitimate defence. The Wassenaar Arrangement has been established to control the flow of technology (including dual-use items). Its stated goals include control of supply of arms. It is inevitable, therefore, that while states will continue to have reservations about specific measures seeking greater transparency because of national security concerns, this is compounded by concerns about how and why the information supplied would be used in relation to their national interests.

There is a need to recognise that transparency may mean different things to different states, and serve different purposes for different states. An otherwise desirable step may be seen by some as pressures by a section or all of the international community that operates against perceived national interests. Transparency in military capabilities would serve the interests and advantages of a powerful state to a greater extent since it adds to the credibility of deterrence and the value of 'compellence" with superior military capability. In fact, this itself becomes a strong reason for unilateral transparency measures by some states. For the militarily weaker states, on the other hand, ambiguity provides a degree of advantage in security terms since it would add to the strategic uncertainties. However this has to be weighed against the risk of miscalculation by either party to a potential conflict, and the contribution transparency may make to stability.

Transparency and National Security
Transparency measures are more readily accepted by states that do not perceive direct threats to their national security and territorial integrity. The United States is representative of this category at one level, especially since it needs to display transparent military capability and posture if it has to play a global military role. Countries like Australia, New Zealand, and France are representative of this category at another level. The winding down of the Cold War, and the instruments (like the Conventional Forces in Europe (CFE) Treaty) that accompanied and reinforced the process, introduced much higher levels of transparency in military postures of NATO and WTO countries than had either existed earlier or had been possible in the conflictual relationship over the previous four decades. The end of the Cold War and the collapse of WTO (and USSR) completely altered the needs for secrecy and the dynamics of transparency in Europe. The disappearance of the traditional threat to the homeland territories in Europe made it easier to expand transparency measures. But a similar situation is not universally applicable.

Transparency in military postures, including armaments, does not stand isolated from other factors. In fact, the most important linkage is the relationship of transparency in public affairs inside a state, transparency in overall military posture, and transparency in arms acquisition processes which are derived from the transparency paradigm that a state follows. It would be unrealistic to expect a state which does not practice even a modicum of transparency in its public affairs, to introduce transparency in arms acquisition policies and practices.

States with well established democratic polities are, by definition, committed to greater transparency in public affairs and may be expected to support transparency measures in military affairs too. India, for example, practices substantive transparency in its military matters, although it is unlikely to go as far as some countries that do not face a real-life challenge/threat to national security and territorial defence. Greater progress in India's approach to transparency in military affairs will, of course, be possible if countries like China and Pakistan introduce even elementary transparency in their military postures.

On the other hand, closed authoritarian states with little or no transparency in public affairs and governance are, not surprisingly, extremely sensitive to even limited measures of transparency in military matters. Most such states do not even share the information with their own people. China, Pakistan, Saudi Arabia, Syria, the former Soviet Union, and a number of other countries fall into this category.

Low Visibility Systems
One of the greatest challenges to instituting transparency in armaments comes from the process of the technological change. The US has already termed the changes, or at least some aspects of them, as the 'revolution in military affairs". Current trends indicate that technology will continue to enhance military capability, especially for offensive employment, through use of force-multiplication rather than the traditional reliance on improvements of weapon platforms alone. Weapon platforms, especially the major systems in the categories included in the Register, will continue to play a crucial role. But software (rather than hardware), electronics, and sensor technologies are increasingly the essence of superior military potential enhancing the real capabilities relevant for warfighting.

There is unlikely to be a one-to-one replacement of weapons in the force modernisation process, and military forces are likely to see further downsizing. But the weapon systems promise to be more capable in range, accuracy, and lethality. More significantly, combat support and combat-enhancement (mostly referred to as 'force-multiplier") systems are likely to tilt the balance of military capabilities in future. Such systems have low visibility to start with. Present processes and mechanisms for generating transparency in armaments are not designed to provide the requisite levels of transparency in such systems.

A great deal will depend not only on the technological quality of such systems, but also on the operational tactics and doctrines employed by a particular country in relation to the likely adversary. A classical example is that of the use of airborne early warning system, electronic intelligence systems, and precision guided munitions in an integrated manner by Israel in its operations in the Beqa'a valley in June 1982, which resulted in a devastating defeat for the Syrians. The point is that the type and number of systems (such as the E-2C) in the inventory of Israeli military were known world wide even from open sources. But not many could have foreseen the way in which they were used, or adequately assessed the impact of their use. It is quite evident that, nearly a decade later, Saddam Hussein had not imbibed the key lessons of the 1982 campaign, with consequences which are now a landmark in military history. The low visibility of new technology systems and their method of employment introduces a qualitatively different set of dynamics into assessment of military capability (and hence, the framework of transparency) than the traditional one which relied heavily on quantities of hardware, especially capital stocks.

Commitment to Transparency?
The Register has started to provide information regarding transfers of the specified seven categories of major weapon systems. Although a large number of countries that import arms do not participate in the Register, the exporting countries have almost invariably reported the transfer (at least of legal title). Thus a level of authentic information is available about arms transfers covered by the Register. But this is not necessarily co-terminus with enhanced transparency.

The Register has achieved remarkable success in the past four years. But it has a long way to go before universal participation becomes a reality, and many reasons for this can be identified. The overall commitment to the goals of the Register will need to be based on the record of participation over the period of four years, as well as the trends in participation as visible during this period. While an average of 88 countries (out of 187) have been participating in the Register, only 31 percent (58 countries) of the total reported for all four years, and 37 countries reported only once. Some of the major arms importing countries have consistently stayed out of participation. This supports a conclusion that the commitment to the goals and objectives of the Register is low among the international community.

The importance and relevance of transparency is the greatest in a regional and bilateral context. If we look at participation from a broadly-defined regional perspective, serious discrepancies and deficiencies become apparent. Europe has been consistent with a high percentage of countries regularly participating in the Register. But only 19 out of 55 countries of (geographic) Asia and Oceania participated in the Register for all the four years. As regards the Americas, only 10 out of 35 countries have participated consistently. While participation by states of the former Soviet Union improved markedly in 1996, only three (out of 15) states participated for all four years. The record of participation by countries in the Middle East (which is a major arms importing region in the world) and Africa has been disappointing. Only one country (Israel) out of 18 in the Middle East has participated for all the four years, and only one other (Iran) has participated for three years. Similarly, only one country (Tanzania) out of 48 countries of Sub-Saharan Africa participated in the Register for all the four years.

But what is more significant and requires attention is the fact that a large number of important states seem to have opted out of the Register after making submissions in the first year. Out of the 83 countries that reported for 1992, 12 countries (over 14 percent) never reported again. Five of these belong to the Middle East region, which has been one of the biggest importing regions during the past three decades. In fact, only three countries of the Middle East, Iran, Libya and Israel, have reported for three or more years. Two of these are generally described as irresponsible and 'rogue" states. Important and responsible countries like Egypt and Saudi Arabia have either not participated or have dropped out of participation. Lack of participation and withdrawal from participation leaves a serious gap and constitutes a substantive weakness in the functioning of the Register.

Most of the transfers taking place are being reported by exporting countries even though the importing countries are not participants. Participation by the importing country, therefore, is significant not so much from the point of information regarding transfers, but rather from the point of the commitment of the non-participant country to the principle and practice of transparency accepted by the international community. If countries of Europe and North America (who are committed to greater transparency both because of greater transparency in public affairs and the CFE agreements which require transparency related to holdings of the categories of weapons included in the Register) are excluded from the list of countries that have participated in the Register for all four years, less than 18 percent of the remaining 149 countries have been participating for all four years.

States are likely to see the Register becoming less relevant without wider commitment to transparency and participation of key countries in each region. The 1997 Group of Experts will have to take a view whether to press for expansion of participation by countries or to move ahead with further development of the Register. Pressing ahead with expansion and further development of the Register without ensuring greater participation on a regular basis runs the risk that participation of relevant countries may actually *decrease*, since an increasing number of states may see the Register as failing to fulfil the central purpose as a transparency regime for which it was established. This will be particularly so among countries that currently participate in the Register, but continue to have reservations on some aspects.

The UN Register plays an important role in enhancing transparency. However, as the participation record of the past four years indicates, the commitment of a large number of states to greater transparency appears well below that needed to sustain and expand an international transparency regime. It will be necessary to listen carefully to the reasons for non-participation by the vast majority of countries and to take measures to reassure them whereever possible.

Promotion of Conflict Prevention

There are diverse causes of armed conflicts between states. But there is little empirical evidence to prove that excessive accumulation of armaments has led to wars. It also can be argued that transparency may, in fact, encourage aggression since it will expose the military weaknesses of another state. This is one reason why the majority of states are extremely shy of transparency in armaments and military postures. For many countries, ambiguity, rather than transparency offers a more attractive approach to national security. As it is, the UN Register has a rather limited goal. There is need for caution in expanding our expectations from it if we are to ensure that a workhorse is not over-flogged in making it run the Ascot.

Changing Nature of War

The ultimate objective of enhancing transparency and promoting conflict prevention and restraint is to reduce the probability of (essentially inter-state, military-to-military) war and its effects. The trend in war over the past five decades indicates a definite transmutation process in which regular war has substantively given way to irregular warfare and armed conflict. The transmutation of armed conflict has already reached a situation where the probability of a regular inter-state military-to-military war is now remote. Even with a low probability, steps to institute measures for war prevention and transparency/restraint in accumulation of armaments and systems used in wars will have to be promoted. On the other hand, what is happening, and is likely to be the dominant pattern is the 'small war" variety which is essentially fought with light weapons and non-military and non-state actors (except when the military is used by a state to respond to such threats).

Transparency and restraint in transfers of small arms requires a significantly different approach than that for major categories of weapons covered by the UN Register, and the international community is only beginning to address the problem. It is not possible to go into detail here. But it is clear that the issue of small arms and light weapons should not be juxtaposed onto the current Register without the risk of jeopardising the purpose and the progress of the Register. Transparency (and accountability) will play a crucial role in control of proliferation and diffusion of small arms and light weapons, and should form the core principle of all efforts to deal with them.

Conflict Prevention

According to conventional wisdom, there is a strong linkage between arms build-ups and the occurrence of war, and that such build-up would almost inevitably lead to war. There is also an implicit judgement that countries that acquire large quantities of armament are more prone to destabilise the environment by initiating aggressive military action. But the weight of empirical evidence indicates that there is no real correlation between military build-ups and incidence of war. Consistently high quantities of modern high quality arms acquisitions like those by Saudi Arabia, and even Iran (between 1973-80) have not led these states to initiate any war. If anything, they were either threatened by aggression (as in the case of the former in 1990-91), or actually attacked, as in latter's case (in 1980). The role of restraint in arms transfers in conflict prevention is, therefore, likely to remain open to question. Enhancing transparency in this context would also play an uncertain role in spite of the apparent logic that it should somehow be able to make an important contribution.

Transparency in armaments is a useful element in building confidence and knowledge about military capabilities and postures. But it also needs to be recognised that transparency will not, by itself, prevent conflicts. Perhaps the classic case is that of Pakistan and India in 1947-48. Almost total transparency existed about each other's military holdings and reserve stocks since a joint commission undertook the task of dividing the military assets of the erstwhile British India when the country was partitioned. In any case, the personnel had served in the British Indian military through the Second World War till August 15, 1947 and thus were even conversant with the professional capabilities of each other. The division of military assets had also been defined to be in a proportion of 2:1 between India and Pakistan, the two newly independent countries. But this did not prevent Pakistan from launching a war a few weeks later. Remarkably, the Indo-Pakistan Military Commission, charged with dividing the assets, continued its work through the early weeks of the war.

Promoting Restraint
Many measures to introduce restraint in the transfer of weapons have been attempted in the past. The most notable was the attempt of the permanent members of the UN Security Council to evolve co-ordination in introducing restraints just after the Gulf War. If the experience of those attempts is any yardstick, it is unlikely that the main suppliers (which are mainly the industrialised developed countries and especially the five permanent members of the UN Security Council) would institute any durable and effective measures. In fact, the US and Russia have already made it clear that their arms export policy will also be guided by techno-economic considerations.

On the other hand, it is also necessary to note that weapons acquisitions are likely to increase in the coming decade. Soviet/Russian arms production had declined dramatically because of the disintegration of the erstwhile USSR and socio-economic crises that emerged at the same time. But it was already cutting back production rates since 1985 because of the shift toward higher technology weapon systems. The end of the Cold War also marked the end of supplies to a large number of states by the two super powers. Chinese production rates also declined, as the Chinese defence industry started to adjust to military modernisation. The 1990-91 Gulf War placed a high premium on high technology weapon systems and force-multipliers. The immediate reaction, accelerated by contraction of military budgets and defence industry, was to rely on upgrades as an interim solution to shorter term needs of military capability. This process has, by and large, peaked. Significant quantities of equipment world-wide will soon start coming up against end of their design life even after extensions.

Existing problems with increasing the transparency in armaments should not, however, be interpreted to mean that accumulation of armaments, especially to high levels, would not create problems or should not be addressed. Possession of armaments and the capability that they represent provide the state with the means to engage in armed conflict. There are also issues of allocation of resources to arms accumulation which could be better utilised for human development and welfare, especially in countries which require such attention, whether they fall in the category of developed or developing states. It is, therefore, necessary to maximise restraint in the accumulation of armaments by states and their use. If the issue that needs to be addressed here is formulated as, what can be done to enhance transparency, especially through the UN Register, in order to promote conflict prevention, then the answer objectively would be that the limitations of this process and mechanism for this purpose must be recognised.

It is necessary, therefore, to develop norms and guidelines for restraint in arms transfers in the future. The UN Register is unlikely to be a suitable vehicle for this purpose. Nor should the international community rely mainly on the five permanent members of the UN Security Council, although the primary responsibility for international peace and security rests with the Council. Since techno-economic national interests of these five powers are deeply involved in arms exports, the initiative for instituting norms and co-ordination for restraint measures must be taken by the international community at large, and some key states in particular.

Concurrent Measures

The UN resolution establishing the Register also requires that attention is given to measures relating to other 'relevant issues" in fulfilling the aims and objectives of the resolution. It appears that little or no attention has been devoted so far to this aspect of the issue. Such measures would mostly relate to confidence-building and to the role countries perceive for their military power.

Politico-military Doctrines

Mere strengthening of the Register through technical changes and expansion to include national production and holding will not really improve transparency in armaments as it relates to the final objectives of making the world safer and (if possible) devoid of military aggression and wars. Other steps are required, including transforming national strategic-military doctrines towards a more co-operative paradigm and defensive or 'non-offensive" defence doctrines (a process which the UN had initiated, but has apparently abandoned with the end of the Cold War) and their harmonisation among states. Such steps working in tandem with the UN Register, and other measures to build a more co-operative basis for international security, may provide the real solutions rather than overloading the UN Register.

It is in this context that the issue of 'excessive accumulation" of armaments has to be situated, since the very term implies accumulation of weapons beyond the needs of legitimate self-defence (enshrined in Article 51 of the UN Charter). So far, no progress has been possible in working toward some sort of co-ordinated approach by the international community on this issue. This is essentially because of the difficulties of evolving the criteria for what constitutes excessive and de-stabilising in terms of levels of armaments held by a country. The approach to define national military doctrine should provide the conceptual base for arriving at objective criteria for levels and types of armament held by states. In the absence of such criteria, there is a risk that the concept of controlling 'excessive accumulation" and 'de-stabilising" weapons acquisitions is more likely to be used as an instrument of foreign policy of particular states, or as a means of denying legitimate self-defence capabilities to states. The linkage of the impetus to the Register with Iraq's military power also conveys the signal that the concern about 'excessive" armaments may well be driven by calculations of future scenarios of Western military interventions in the developing world.

Trust Building

A clear direction on the use of transparency in military postures (and, hence, also the information in the Register) is necessary if it is to serve the purpose of reducing mistrust and enhancing mutual confidence. This makes transparency an integral element of concerted and co-ordinated measures to promote conflict prevention and restraint. Merely increasing transparency in military posture without corresponding measures to build trust could have counter-productive results.

For example, during the mid-1980s, there were strong internal pressures in India for enhancing transparency about military matters. As a consequence of these demands, many measures were introduced, including greater availability of information in the public domain regarding a major military exercise (code-named 'Brasstacks") planned for the winter of 1986-87 in Western India. Such exercises had been held, with some variations, frequently in the past, but without information about them being released to the public before or during the exercises. A direct consequence of the attempt at transparency was that serious concern, bordering on alarm, was generated in Pakistan, although Pakistan's military was also holding its own military exercise. Pakistan decided to respond by mobilising its armour strike forces. Fortunately the potential crisis was defused in time. But this episode certainly emphasised the necessity of concurrent measures to increase mutual trust if unilateral transparency measures are not allowed to become the problem rather than a solution!

Increasing the Register's Efficiency

There have been suggestions for revising the existing categories of weapons included in the Register. While the intention of such revisions is no doubt to enhance the scope and utility of the Register, the first question that must be asked is whether such steps serve the goals and objectives of the Register as originally sought when it was established. The fact that five of the seven weapon categories in the Register had already been accepted as the most threatening and destabilising, and hence earmarked for mutually agreed reductions under the CFE Treaty, no doubt made it easier to accept the same categories for the UN Register. Any significant changes (especially those which tend to include weapons which have greater orientation and role for defensive military purposes, as a 100-ton warship would) that cannot be justified on the basic principles on which the Register was established are hardly likely to be accepted. Any effort to press for expansion of the Register in violation of this principle, on the other hand, is likely to reduce the already low level of support for participation in the Register.

Weapon Categories: the case of missiles

This does not, however, mean that no changes should be sought to the existing framework. In fact, there seems to be a necessity to elaborate the reporting of missile transfers in a manner that strengthens contribution to the goals and objectives of the Register in a more meaningful way. The Register already includes missiles as a category of weapons whose transfer is to be reported. But the aggregate quantity-based reporting as currently adopted is not very helpful. For example, a total of 14,447 missiles and missile launchers were reported as transferred in 1994 alone. This does not provide even a reasonable degree of transparency about the nature of such missiles. Firstly, the Register requires reporting of missile launchers and the number of missiles as a single aggregate figure. There is a need for disaggregation of these as separate items within the same category of weapon system being reported.

Secondly, it is the surface-to-surface missiles (especially ballistic missiles) which are the most destabilising because they fundamentally constitute weapon systems against which there is no credible defence available at present. Their short time of flight, high terminal velocities, and ability to carry a variety of warheads including weapons of mass destruction, make them attractive to many countries in enhancing their strike capabilities. Mobile missiles pose serious difficulties in even locating them. Their neutralisation through counter air operations in the past has not proved successful. On the other hand, over 26,000 surface to surface missiles have been fired in wars since they were first used in World War II. All these missiles were armed with conventional high explosive warheads. But nevertheless, they invariably had a profound impact in political and psychological terms even where the direct military effect was limited. The intrinsic destabilising characteristics of ballistic missiles had led to the INF Treaty between the superpowers in 1987.

Missile proliferation is considered to be a major threat to international peace and security. No clear steps to deal with it that could be adopted universally are yet in sight. Ad-hoc regimes like the MTCR (Missile Technology Control Regime) are, at best, an attempt by a US-led cartel to control technology for missiles and missile transfers above 300-km range and 500-kg payload. But the overwhelming majority of ballistic missiles out of the total of around 5,000 missiles in the world are below the 300-km range. They are no less destabilising for that reason.

The principle followed in identifying the seven categories of weapon systems for reporting in the UN Register was undoubtedly to focus on the most threatening offensive weapons, and bring about transparency in the transfer of the most destabilising weapon systems. Aggregate reporting of missiles in the present form gives no idea of the type of missiles involved. In the absence of authentic knowledge about transfers of ballistic and cruise missiles, countries tend to operate on the basis of worse case scenarios. It would, therefore, be desirable to introduce a sub-category under missiles to specifically report transfer of surface to surface missiles. Such reporting should include the range/payload of the missiles. This would add greatly to confidence-building. Such elaboration would be in keeping with the definition and categorisation under the UN resolutions (46/36L and 48/75E) establishing the Register which specifically mentions ballistic and cruise missiles (and launchers) to be reported.

Reporting Schedule

The Register requires states to submit reports by 30th April each year for transfers during the previous calendar year. The submission of these reports is voluntary, and often countries submit their data fairly late. For example, even by August 1, 1993, only 71 countries had made submissions to the Register for 1992; and the figure for 1993 by August 1, 1994 was 77. The ultimate number of submissions for 1992 was 93, while for 1993 it was 91. Over a length of time, delays in submissions would even out and should not be cause for concern. Late submissions would be in the spirit of the arrangement even though they may not be in keeping with the letter of the resolution establishing the Register. But in the short term, late submissions do not contribute to the objectives of the Register, which clearly require submissions of transfers of 'weapons indispensable for surprise attack and large scale offensive military operations.' As much as two years could elapse without transfers getting reported if they take place at the beginning of a calendar year and are reported up to 9-12 months after the due date. The period could be much longer, and the very purpose of the Register could be defeated if a state stops reporting for a year or more. It would be desirable, therefore, if transfers were reported by states as and when they take place, or at the maximum, every quarter. The UN could continue to issue an annual report, possibly by April 30, every year.

Conclusion

In the final analysis, we need to recognise that the Register is a very useful instrument in enhancing transparency, especially if it carries with it a commitment to transparency. But it is also necessary to bear in mind the limitations of a linear approach that focuses only on the Register and does not seek to integrate other aspects of relevance. The low commitment to transparency in military affairs by an overwhelming majority of states requires serious examination. The limitations of the Register in providing transparency are fairly clear. It is sobering to acknowledge that few, if any, governments are likely to be using the information currently contained (or which may be introduced even by adding holdings and national production) for concrete defence planning purposes.

The Register needs to be sustained and strengthened. But the expansion process needs to be undertaken on a step by step basis. Total procurement (including those from national and multinational production) of arms of specified categories by states needs to be brought into the framework of the Register. But at the same time, greater trust needs to be established and sustained between the developed industrialised countries (especially the major arms producers) and the developing countries that these processes would not merely provide additional instruments to deny legitimate defence needs or technologies required for legitimate developmental purposes. This requires that priority be given to discussion and harmonisation of strategic politico-military doctrines of states, with the goal of vectoring them toward a more defensive orientation within a paradigm of co-operative security.

Transparency in armaments is not a panacea for conflict prevention, especially on its own. In fact it has complex dynamics where transparency could easily be a factor promoting aggression and offensive action. The contradiction between needs of national security which requires secrecy, and transparency for greater trust and confidence can be resolved only through a broader approach that seeks to integrate the principles of the UN Register with other collateral measures. Restraint in arms transfers has little chance of success without a fundamental re-orientation of the inter-state security paradigm toward a co-operative security framework, rather than the competitive one that has characterised the security relationship between states for four centuries. Transparency would have a greater role to play in this transformation if its elements were not based on narrow national interests and foreign policy goals.

---

1   For one approach to the co-operative peace and security paradigm, see *Towards a New Asia*, Report of the Commission for a New Asia, 1994, which outlined fourteen principles on which to base it (pp. 13-14).

2   For example, the US exported 5 destroyers, 34 frigates and 13 tank-landing ships over the four years since the Register has been in

existence. These were not included in the submissions by the United States on the basis that the legal title had not been transferred. However, such transfers could make a significant difference in the actual military capabilities of the recipient country, as indeed the transfer on lease of 8 destroyer/frigates had doubled the surface combatant strength of the Pakistani Navy within a year in the late 1980s.

CHAPTER 12

The Register as an Instrument for Promoting Restraint and Preventing Conflict

Herbert Wulf

The value of transparency in armaments

Promoting greater openness and transparency in the field of international arms transfers is an uncontroversial issue - at least at the declaratory policy level. The extent to which this widely accepted goal of the international community has been put into practice is a different matter. Transparency in armaments is the primary objective of the UN Register, as underlined by the title of the 1991 General Assembly resolution establishing the Register (which was 'Transparency in Armaments').

An objective observer of present day international relations will recognize the gap between the proclaimed policy, expressed by an overwhelming majority of UN members in voting to support the 1991 resolution, and the quantity and quality of actual participation in the Register as it exists in 1997.

Transparency is not an aim in itself. Transparency in armaments - as it is conceptualized in many arms control and disarmament forums - is supposed to prevent excessive and destabilizing accumulation of arms and to create confidence. Furthermore, it is assumed to be a key part of the effort to reduce mistrust and miscalculation in military security. Transparency can help to build security communities, whose function it is to prevent conflict and to play a role in bringing about peace and security. Transparency can be a tool of preventive diplomacy and should - at least indirectly -contribute to the reduction of armaments. The Register is not an arms control regime *per se*. However, proponents note that transparency is intended as a step towards the goal of limiting or reducing the number of weapons.[1]

The foundation stone for the creation of transparency is *information*. Without relevant, appropriate and precise information it is difficult to generate the openness required for confidence and trust.

In this chapter I will examine the extent to which the Register in its present form provides at least the basic and minimum quantity and quality of information to make it a useful transparency tool for the international community. Furthermore, I will look at which avenues could realistically be pursued to improve the transparency function of the Register for the sake of promoting restraint in arms build-ups and conflict prevention. Since the Register was heralded as an important practical step by the United Nations 'to create operational instruments of transparency at the global level' [2] I will try to find answers to the following questions:

- Does the Register report comprehensive information?

- Is the data accumulated in the Register accurate?

- Does the Register provide meaningful information?

- Is the submitted information adequately and effectively used by the member states?

- How can inadequacies in the Register system be corrected or overcome?

- Is a consultative mechanism a tool for improving the usefulness of the Register?

- Is there sufficient political will for restraint?

- How are transparency measures and security concerns related?

How much transparency is sufficient - what kind of information is essential?

Many governments find themselves in a paradoxical situation when requested to provide detailed information on arms transfers, production of weapons and military holdings to the Register. On the one hand, military thinking has traditionally emphasized restraint on information and concealment of military capabilities. A secrecy screen shrouds military structures and defense strategies. Threat-oriented military doctrines stress the need to hide or camouflage the military capabilities so that an actual or perceived adversary only has minimum knowledge on the armed forces, the number and quality of weapons, military doctrines, and so on. [3] This military-specific quest for secrecy, which led to partially paranoid reactions during the cold war is, of course, the enemy of transparency.

On the other hand, by participating in the Register exercise, governments are asked to open the secrecy curtain - at least a little bit. This requires that the military be convinced of the usefulness of such a policy. Transparency and openness are almost a contradiction to nationally-based concepts of military security since a certain amount of information-sharing is needed. The Register - as designed by its architects - is an instrument which will hopefully promote the transparency process by persuading like-minded (and eventually all) member states to take part.[4]

How much knowledge on the three key categories of information on weapons - arms transfers, procurement through national production, and military holdings - is transparent in the records of the Register? Figure 1 aims to illustrate the still-limited scope of transparency of the present Register (without claiming to represent the actual empirical quantitative shares).

As Figure 1 indicates, the major portion of global armaments is not transparent in the Register records. It was never the intention to include all arms in the Register and is probably unlikely to happen. The architects of the Register never aimed to create a comprehensive register encompassing the totality of military capacities or all weapon categories. It is a matter of temperament and judgment whether one regards the glass as half full or as half empty, considering that close to (or only) half of all states participate each year in a new and historic exercise in an area which takes this mode of commerce out of the largely unknown into the domain of the United Nations.

Figure 1: The Scope of Transparency

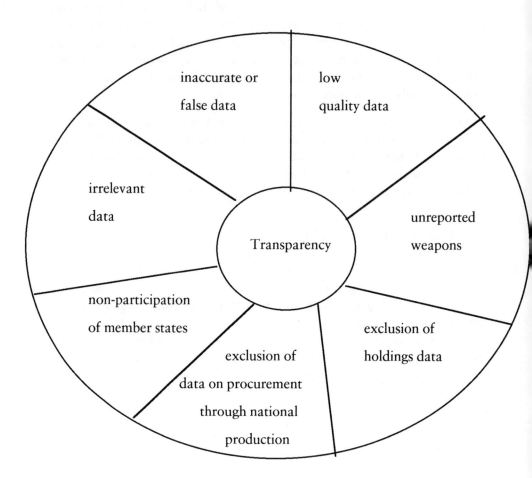

However, the questions raised above, on how useful is the collected data in the Register, remain. I will illustrate, with one example for each of the six key areas, the flaws and potentially contentious issues and what is still missing or lacking in the Register:

Categories of weapons and comprehensiveness of data
The seven categories of major conventional weapons can be considered the core of military hardware in most armed forces. It has been estimated that more than 90 percent of the actual transfers taking place (in the seven

Register categories) are covered by the Register.[5] But how much of all military procurement (both imported and procured nationally) is covered? The weapons covered in the Register are a long way from depicting a comprehensive or systematic overview of weapon stocks. A whole array of military equipment which is particularly relevant for military operations - reaching from small arms to C3I systems - is not even included in the scope of the Register at present.

Furthermore, even the limited seven categories of the Register are not fully covered in practice. The controversial debates during the deliberations for establishing the Register, which are still on-going, illustrate this point. Ground-to-air missiles are excluded on the insistence of one government, nuclear weapons are not included despite the insistence of another government, ships below a certain tonnage are excluded, and so on.

The 17 members of the Panel of Technical Experts who established the Register in 1992 had to compromise to accommodate a wide variety of views on the inclusion or exclusion of certain types of weapons. The final session of the Panel in 1992 resembled a bazaar where reconnaissance aircraft were traded against calibre of artillery, missile ranges bartered against cluster bombs, and airborne electronic equipment given away for air-breathing vehicles. The result is a political compromise on the categories of weapons in the Register, and not necessarily a blue print for openness and transparency.[6]

Universal participation of member states and comprehensiveness of reporting
The Register was developed as a universal and non-discriminatory process, which was global in scope. A majority of the key states in the arms trade did participate. Detracting from the achievement of the goal of universality, is the fact that each year roughly half of the UN members did not participate--among them several major weapons' importers. However, reviewing participation over the whole four years of operation of the Register somewhat improves this picture, due to high 'turnover' in participation in some regions. A total of 134 countries participated in the Register in at least one of the first four years of its operation (1992 to 1996).[7]

Information on procurement through national production and information on holdings

The United Nations Register is not called a 'transfer register' since the majority of members insisted in the original General Assembly resolution to include (eventually) procurement of national production and holdings of weapons in the armed forces in the Register. For as long as the Register has been discussed, this issue has been a contentious one, and it still is. The Register was originally intended to prevent an Iraq-like situation, by preventing the excessive and destabilizing accumulation of weapons.

However, the *de facto* construction of the Register as a transfer register does not allow for comprehensive appraisal of arms build-ups. For an adequate assessment of potentially excessive and destabilizing accumulation of arms or regional arms races, the total acquisitions of each party during the year in question is required - not only their imported weapons. Furthermore, it is unlikely that data on procurement of weapons for a limited number of years can provide clues about their stabilizing or destabilizing nature. Systematic data on military holdings would, however, get to the heart of a nation's national security. Many countries are therefore not prepared to provide any or detailed information on their holdings. The perceived sensitivity and the voluntary nature of reporting these two types of data has led to unsatisfactory results. Several non-official publications by expert institutions supply much more comprehensive and reliable data than the UN Register does.

Accuracy of data and reliability of reporting

A key issue for the further development of the Register is the quality and accuracy of the reported data. There is no institutionalized mechanism to verify the data supplied by member states. However, the extensive differences between exporters' and importers' submissions, if both governments report on the same transfer of weapon, illustrate that governments have not got their export or import statistics right, or are using different definitions of what constitutes a transfer in a certain category, or might even purposely have supplied wrong data. Often these discrepancies are not particularly troublesome, especially if the discrepancies are small, since they can be explained away by time-lags during transfers or inappropriate or unsynchronized accounting statistics. When, however, differences between an exporter and an importer of as many as 1000 combat tanks transferred emerged, as was the case in the past, one needs to ask whether the provision of obviously incorrect data is a contribution to transparency or if such reports add to the build-up of mistrust or confusion.

Relevance of data

Reporting information on transfers or production of weapons or supplying data on weapons holdings will contribute to transparency only if this information is meaningful. The Register category VII 'missiles and missile launchers' is - I gather from the debates during the 1992 Panel of Experts deliberations - purposely designed to obscure data on a particularly sensitive category of weapons. In contrast to all of the other weapon categories the missile and missile launcher category is designed to be imprecise, since it adds missiles (which are sometimes transferred in large numbers) and missile launchers (usually transferred in limited numbers) into a single figure. Furthermore, governments tend to refrain from giving information on weapons types and models, particularly in this weapon category. Since missiles are considered by most military planners as decisive for their war-fighting capability, certain governments did not want to disclose their missile imports or holdings. They insisted on - and got away with - the obviously anti-transparency measure of aggregating missiles and missile launchers into one category. To make the reporting in this category more meaningful, one could disaggregate missiles and launchers into two subcategories, add the types and models of the systems, or abstain from reporting the numbers of launchers completely.

Qualitative data, not just numbers

The reporting of just a number in any of the seven weapon categories is of limited (if any) value in transparency generation. As has been widely discussed, qualitative information on the type and models of weapons would greatly improve the utility of the Register and contribute to transparency.

Transparency improvement mechanisms

The concept of improving transparency in order to make the Register a better practical disarmament tool is not a complicated one. It is easy to identify *what* needs to be changed and improved, but difficult to propose realistic means of *how* it can be done. The difficulty is to find a political consensus on improvements to the present reporting system and expansion of the Register which is acceptable to governments.

Improving the system of reporting

Part of what needs to be done can be directly identified from the six deficiencies of the present Register discussed above. Figure 2 schematically illustrates this task:

- adding additional categories and restricting possibilities for excluding items within the already existing seven categories;

- . improving participation of member states;

- reporting adequately on procurement through national production and military holdings (with the same or similar reporting guidelines and with the same level of obligation as for transfers);[8]

- reporting accurately and reliably;

- reporting relevant and meaningful data, and withdrawing irrelevant and meaningless information;

- reporting qualitative information, such as the type and model of weapons, not just numbers on the weapons transferred, produced or in stock.

If this were done, the scope of transparency would be broadened. A larger portion of global armaments would be transparent, and information sharing would be improved. Thus, the Register would provide more useful data on military capabilities on arms build-ups, and be more able to achieve its overall aims.

Figure 2: Improvement and Expansion of Transparency

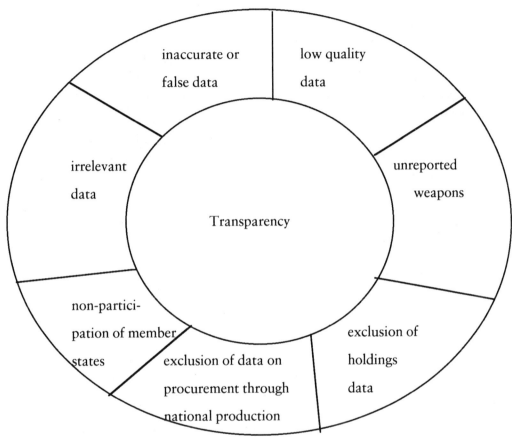

Improving the Register by using it

To make the Register a genuine transparency instrument for practical disarmament, promoting restraint in arms transfers and procurement, prevention of excessive and destabilizing accumulations of arms and conflict prevention, more is required than simply the collection of data and their improvement. The Register is a cooperative security arrangement, not an intelligence exercise. To achieve the objectives of the Register there has to be some follow-up to the pure collection and reporting of data.

The need for a consultative mechanism

In order to develop the Register into an instrument of cooperative security it is necessary to make full use of it. Since the Register's data is publicly available, the information can be used today by member states, academics, journalist, arms producers or merchants of death. However, it seems that the providers of the data, the governments of the member states, do not fully utilize the potential of the Register. To inform the public how many and which weapons have been purchased can only be a first step. Raw data does not explain the motives to buy and does not necessarily allow for evaluation and analysis.

The process of exchange, evaluation and analysis is itself important, as has been widely discussed in the literature on confidence-building, since it contributes to changing perceptions of security.[9] This is also the case for transparency and openness in the UN Register. Information on a certain transfer or procurement policy alone does not give the full picture of the reasoning behind that weapons build-up. A combination of access to precise information *and* a consultative mechanism [10] - a political dialogue to analyze the reasons or causes for certain actions - is required to make full use of the Register's potential. Consultation and dialogue enable concerned parties to 'explain their views, discuss their positions, expose their goals and motives, and uncover each other's perceptions and interpretations.'[11]

The Register's function as an early warning instrument against arms races would require active management and a consultative forum, neither of which are presently available as part of the UN Register. At present, data are reported (with flaws and faults) and are published by the UN Secretariat, irrespective of their relevance and accuracy. At best, these data indicate what the intentions of participants are. They might serve for bilateral discussions between governments concerned, or might be perceived as a symbolic act of political good will on the part of the participants. For many areas or participants, however, the Register is presently not much more than a collection of data, and at worst the reported data may sometimes be taken as evidence of the neighboring countries' bad intentions.

To make use of the Register as a cooperative instrument it is essential to *routinely* examine and discuss the reports of governments in a forum where questions on exports, imports, procurement through national production or military holdings can be raised without pushing this to a level where it might easily be perceived as a political affair or a diplomatic incident.

There are several possible forums which could function as facilitators of a consultative mechanism process, within existing institutions or established bodies or in addition to them:[12]

- Bilateral consultations could be expanded into a regional forum.[13]

- Ad-hoc multilateral groups or annual panels could be tasked with evaluation of the data.

- The UN Secretariat (the UN Center for Disarmament Affairs), in consultation with member states, could be entrusted with a more active role, beyond its present data collection and dissemination function, in order to improve the quality of data reporting and to rectify some of the obvious mistakes in states' reports. Furthermore, the Secretariat could be given a mandate to call for a regular review of the reports.

- The Conference of Disarmament, the UN Disarmament Commission, the First Committee of the General Assembly, the General Assembly itself or even the Security Council could function as a forum for a thorough and regular review process.

Thus, consultations on the Register should go beyond occasional reviews of expert groups charged with analyzing the experience and proposing expansions of the scope of the Register. Consultations should complement traditional diplomacy and provide a forum for debate, for policy review, interpretation, and dispute settlement. In short, what is needed is an established body which would meet regularly to address the data in the Register. Eventually such a forum could develop into a true security community which also discusses a range of other information (such as doctrines, joint exercises, maneuvers, arms reduction, and disarmament treaties).

The political will for restraint
The UN Register of Conventional Arms is an ex-post register, not a multilateral or universal control instrument. The Register cannot substitute or override national arms export or import control policy. If it promotes confidence, reduces mistrust and prevents miscalculation, the Register can then indirectly contribute to restraining the flow and procurement of arms. Unless there is the political will for restraint, these indirect measures have no chance.

A prominent example in which the Register generated transparency but failed to bring about restraint - an example of a regional arms race which had an impact on the military strategic balance and became quite apparent from the Register - is the arms build-up in the Aegean between Greece and Turkey. The supplies to Turkey and in similar quantities to Greece seem to be fanning the regional rivalries, as weapons are sent to both sides. The Greek-Turkish animosities in relation to Cyprus, which have led in the past to war, in addition to disputed areas in the Aegean, are far from being resolved, despite NATO pressure on the two members. Both Greece and Turkey are affecting the naval balance in the Aegean by acquiring a modernized surface force from the United States and Germany with additional equipment delivered by other NATO countries. Although both governments have fulfilled their CFE-related obligations by remaining below the stipulated maximum level in the five CFE weapon categories[14] (which the Greek government emphasized several times in its report to the United Nations Register of Conventional Arms), a qualitative arms race has nevertheless been induced. The effect of this regional arms race prompted neighboring countries, such as Bulgaria, to reconsider its own military posture and to import equipment from Russia. If suppliers and recipients in this particular case continue to pursue their past policies, the Register will remain an instrument of transparency without being able to prevent excessive and destabilizing accumulations of arms.

Figure 3: Regional arms race: imports of weapons by Turkey and Greece, 1992-95
number of items imported

	Turkey	suppliers	Greece	suppliers
Battle tanks	1,028	USA, Germany	940	USA, Germany, Netherlands
Armoured combat vehicles	773	USA, Germany, Italy, Russia	1,284	USA, Germany, Netherlands
Large calibre artillery systems	203	USA, Germany	243	USA, Germany
Combat aircraft	60	USA, Germany	98	USA, Germany
Attack helicopters	32	USA	20	USA
Warships	10	USA, Germany	12	USA, Germany, Netherlands
Missiles and missile launchers	34	USA	49	USA, France

Note: All Information taken from the Turkish and Greek reports to the United Nations. Not all figures match those given by exporter countries, nor those given by other public sources.

The supplies to the Aegean regional arms race also illustrate that security considerations (building a strong defense) are not the only reasons for purchasing or selling arms. A range of economic, political and psychological factors can play an important - sometimes decisive - role in arms transfers and procurement decision making, such as: jobs in the defense industry, the balance of payment of a country, company profits, saving the cost of scrapping surplus weapons, corruption and kickbacks, prestige and favoritism, or securing influence in a particular region or country. The business of purchasing and selling arms is less rational in security terms than military security rationales suggest.

In a situation where such considerations have priority, the Register will hardly be able to alter policies, unless both suppliers and recipients are forced into a regular consultation forum to reconsider or justify their policies.

The chicken and egg question: security or transparency first?

Can transparency (or other confidence-building measures) bring about restraint, arms control, disarmament and facilitate conflict resolution among potential adversaries? Is transparency of value without pre-existing security or détente? Or is an improved security situation between potential enemies or in a volatile region a precondition for engaging in transparency measures? More concretely in relation to the UN Register of conventional arms: can countries in the Middle East or South Asia afford to go ahead with increased transparency actions before solving their conflicts? What comes first: security and conflict resolution or transparency?

'Good fences make good neighbours', said the poet Robert Frost. It is doubtful, however, whether strong defense postures without intensive political relations are conducive to good neighborly relations. Traditional military-based concepts of security tend to focus on military strength, and neglect, ignore or even oppose confidence-building measures. At the conceptual level there is a certain degree of dissonance of military-based or threat-oriented security concepts versus transparency demands for common security. Thus, it is not surprising, in conflict-prone regions, to find limited enthusiasm for, or resistance to, participation in the UN Register.

The UN Register is intended to be more than a fair weather instrument and it is not an end in itself. The Register and the promotion of transparency is intended to build trust especially between rival states or potential adversaries. It has the potential to reduce the risk of war and can open or strengthen the channels of communication and break deadlocks. Access to accurate information, especially if evaluated in a consultation forum, can provide reliable evidence that certain behaviors and actions do not constitute a threat.

The goal is to improve understanding between states and to contribute to reducing misperceptions. The primary focus of transparency is not to resolve disputes between states, since this would be overestimating the potential of transparency measures. The argument in this paper is that transparency should be given due consideration by governments, which would require only a minimum of political will. It is unrealistic to expect a far reaching creation of transparency unless a minimum of trust and confidence exists. If properly applied, transparency could increase trust and this in turn would create opportunities for additional transparency measures; they would be mutually reinforcing. Thus, this chapter advocates the utility of transparency without underestimating the difficulties and structural impediments in implementing it between adversaries.

---

1   For an early description of the function and the aims of transparency in international arms transfers see the collection of papers in *Transparency in International Arms Transfers*, United Nations Disarmament Topical Papers 3, New York 1990.

2   Hendrik Wagenmakers, 'Transparency in Armaments: the United Nations Register of Conventional Arms as a proud member of a family of efforts', in Malcolm Chalmers, Owen Greene, Edward Laurance and Herbert Wulf (eds.), *Developing the UN Register of Conventional Arms*, (Bradford Arms Register Studies No. 4), Westview Press, London 1994, p. 22. Ambassador Hendrik Wagenmakers of the Netherlands was the Chairman of the Panel of Experts implementing the Register in 1992 and Chairman of the Group of Experts reviewing the operations of the Register in 1994.

3   Although, deterrence policy also requires impressing on an adversary that their own military capabilities are credible. Thus, a minimum of information needs to be made public or at least with the adversary's intelligence agencies.

4   On the philosophy of the Register see for example Hendrik Wagenmakers, 'The UN Register of Conventional Arms: A New Instrument for Cooperative Security', *Arms Control Today*, April 1993, pp. 17-19; Malcolm Chalmers and Owen Greene, *Implementing and Developing the United Nations Register of Conventional Arms* (Bradford Arms Register Studies No. 1), Peace Research Report No 32, Department of Peace Studies, Bradford University, May 1993; Edward Laurance, Siemon T. Wezeman and Herbert Wulf, *Arms Watch SIPRI Report on the First Year of the UN Register of Conventional Arms*, Oxford University Press, New York, 1993.

5   An estimate based, for example, on a comparison with the SIPRI arms transfer register.

6   For a review of this process see Herbert Wulf, 'The UN Arms Register' in *SIPRI Yearbook 1993*, Oxford University Press, Oxford, 1993, p. 539.

7   See analysis by Malcolm Chalmers and Owen Greene in chapter 2 of this book, and also: Malcolm Chalmers and Owen Greene, *The UN Register in its Fourth Year*, BARS Working Paper No 2, Bradford University, November 1996. By June 1997, this total number had increased to 137.

8   On these proposals see chapter 8 of this book, and also: Malcolm Chalmers and Owen Greene, *Taking Stock: The UN Register after two years* (Bradford Arms Register Studies No. 5), Westview Press, London, 1995; Malcolm Chalmers and Owen Greene, 'Expanding the Register to include procurement from national production and military holdings', in M. Chalmers, O. Greene, E. Laurence, and H. Wulf (eds), *Developing the UN Register of Conventional Arms*, Bradford Arms Register Studies No 4, Westview Press, 1994.

9   Marie-France Desjardins, *Rethinking Confidence-Building Measures*, Adelphi Paper 307, IISS/Oxford University Press, London, 1996.

10   Antonia Handler Chayes and Abram Chayes, "The UN Register, transparency and cooperative security", in: M. Chalmers, O. Greene, E. Laurance and H. Wulf (eds.) op. cit., pp. 197- 223. Edward J. Laurance, "The United Nations Register of Conventional Arms: Option and Proposals for Enhancement and Further Development", in: Steven Mataija (ed.) *Non-proliferation and multilateral verification: the comprehensive nuclear test ban treaty* (Centre for International and Strategic Studies, York University) Toronto, 1994, pp. 153-186.

11   M.-F. Desjardins, op. cit., p. 18.

12   For some of these models see Edward J. Laurance, op. cit., pp. 182-184.

13   Such forums have, for example, been discussed for Latin America and Asia. See chapters 13, 14 and 15 of this book, and also, for example, Ralph A.Cossa (ed), *Toward a Regional Arms Register in*

the Asia Pacific, Pacific Forum CSIS Occasional Papers, Honolulu, August 1995.

14 Ships and missiles are not included in the CFE-reduction agreement.

Part D: Regional Developments

Confidence-Building Measures in the Asia-Pacific: Their Relevance to the UN Conventional Arms Register

Amitav Acharya

Introduction

This paper reviews the progress in the confidence-building process in the Asia Pacific region since the establishment of the ASEAN Regional Forum in 1994. The ARF was inaugurated in 1994 with 18 initial members: Brunei, Malaysia, Indonesia, Thailand, Singapore, the Philippines, Vietnam, Laos, the US, Canada, South Korea, Australia, Japan, New Zealand, the European Union, Russia, China and Papua New Guinea. Cambodia joined a year later, while India and Myanmar were accepted as members in 1996. The ARF is a loose consultative grouping of Asia Pacific countries devoted to promoting a multilateral dialogue on security issues. Confidence-Building Measures (CBMs) have been an important part of its agenda since inception. But CBMs in the Asia Pacific region have also been developed on a bilateral basis, most notably the April 1996 agreement between China and Russia (along with Kazakhstan, Kyrgyz Republic and Tajikistan) called the Shanghai Agreement, and the December 1996 agreement between India and China. What follows is an examination of both multilateral and bilateral CBMs in the Asia Pacific, with a specific aim of highlighting those measures that are relevant to the development of the UN Register.

The ARF and the UN Conventional Arms Register

During its first year of operation, 10 of the 17 Asian countries who were to become members of the ARF by 1996 participated in the UN Register.[1] The number increased subsequently with Thailand participating for the first time in February 1995, and Vietnam's following suit in April 1995. In 1996, the fourth year of the register's operation, 13 out of 17 Asian members of the ARF participated in the register.[2] The three ARF members who have never participated are Cambodia, Myanmar, and Laos. It is noteworthy that in 1996, out of 34 countries located in Asia (eastward from

Afghanistan) and Oceania region, 21 countries have participated in the register. Out of this, 17 were ARF members. Conversely, of the 13 regional countries who did not participate in the Register, only 4 were ARF members.

The participation of the ARF-Asian countries in the Register has increased steadily, reflecting a similar trend at the global level. Moreover, unlike at the global level, there has been no 'turnover' in participation, in the sense that no ARF-Asia country who has once participated in the Register has failed to do so in subsequent years. On the negative side, ARF-Asian participants in the Register have consistently failed to provide information on national holdings and procurement from domestic sources.

It appears that the ARF's decision to encourage its members to participate in the UN Register has played a role in improving participation. Non-participation by some ARF members can be explained as the result of internal political problems (in the case of Cambodia and Myanmar) as well as lack of resources (in the case of Laos). Brunei was the only ASEAN member in 1995 not to have reported to the Register, but it did make a return for the first time in 1997.

The ARF and the Multilateral CBM Agenda

Participation in the Register is one of several measures being discussed and promoted through the ARF framework. The establishment of the ARF has done much to advance the multilateral CBM process in the Asia Pacific region. One of the major developments in this regard was the release of a 'Concept Paper' prepared by ASEAN for consideration by the ARF in 1995. The paper envisaged three stages of security co-operation: confidence-building, preventive diplomacy, and conflict resolution (later changed to 'elaboration of approaches to conflicts' as a concession to China which had warned against rapid institutionalisation of the ARF).[3] The list of measures outlined by the Concept Paper fell into two categories. The first category included measures which could be carried out in the short-term, while the second category contained measures which required longer-term consideration and approach.

The Concept Paper advanced two important declaratory CBMs: (1) the development of a set of basic principles to ensure a common understanding and approach to interstate relations in the region; and (2) adoption of comprehensive approaches to security. The drafting of the basic principles was to incorporate those found in ASEAN's Treaty of Amity and Cooperation, but it was apparent that other ideas and principles would have to be considered as well. (This was done subsequently at a meeting organised by Russia in Moscow in 1996). The notion of comprehensive security was already commonplace in the security discourse in the Asia Pacific region, with countries such as Japan, Malaysia, and Indonesia having developed security doctrines based on this notion.

The short-term measures envisaged by the Concept Paper consisted of dialogues on security perceptions, including voluntary statements of defence policy positions, and publication of defence white papers or equivalent documents. Measures in the long-term implementation category ranged from simple transparency measures (including information and communication CBMs) to somewhat more ambitious CBMs including prior notification of military deployments that have region-wide significance.

The Concept Paper sought to make use of existing global CBMs such as the UN Register of Conventional Arms by calling for the exploration of a regional version of the Register. Reflecting its emphasis on comprehensive security, the Concept Paper adopted a broad view of CBMs aimed at dealing with both military and non-military issues. Indicative of this are its proposals concerning information exchanges and training on drug trafficking and development of a mechanism to mobilise relief assistance in the event of natural disasters. The Paper paid particular attention to maritime issues, with ideas such as the establishment of a zone of co-operation in the South China Sea, the development of maritime data bases, and the development of co-operative approaches to sea lines of communications, beginning with information exchanges and training in such as areas as search and rescue and piracy. A relatively novel and interesting proposal contained in the Paper was the call to arms manufacturers and suppliers to reveal the destination of their arms exports. The Paper was strong on information CBMs; its proposals in this regard included co-ordination of existing security studies activities and the establishment of a regional security studies centre.

The 1995 meeting of the ASEAN Regional Forum, held in Brunei on 1 August 1995, selected the following items from the list of proposals contained in the ASEAN Concept Paper: exchanging annual defence postures on a voluntary basis, increasing dialogues on security issues on a bilateral, sub-regional and regional basis, maintaining senior-level contacts and exchanges among military institutions and encouraging participation of the ARF members in the UN Conventional Arms Register.

Following a decision by the 1995 ARF ministerial meeting to create an inter-governmental inter-sessional support group (ISG) on confidence-building, two meetings of the ISG held in 1996. These meetings stressed the importance of increasing defence contacts and exchanges. The recommendations of this ISG process illustrate the kind of incrementalism which has been evident in the process of developing CBMs in the ARF. These recommendations clearly build upon the measures adopted in Brunei in 1995. The very holding of the ISGs provides an additional avenue for dialogues on security perceptions, which itself is recognised as a CBM by the ARF. Furthermore, the ISG provided a venue for member countries who had not yet published defence policy/white papers or other relevant information briefed each other on their defence policies. The ISG also recommended that the scope of defence policy papers submitted voluntarily by ARF members should be expanded to include their defence contacts and exchange programmes. It encouraged discussion of the information provided in such statements in the ARF. It called for opening up of the ARF-SOM to defence representatives and encouraged their greater participation in inter-sessional activities. Contact CBMs were to be augmented by exchanges and meetings among national defence colleges and by compiling a list of ARF contact points. The process of instituting notification CBMs was advanced slightly as well, with the ISG recommending exchange of information on a voluntary basis on some of the on-going observer participation in and notification of military exercises among participants. (It should be noted that the participants are only asked to exchange information on their current practices in this regard; they are not accepting any new obligation to provide advance notification of exercises as a result of the ISG's recommendation.)

One of the important features of the ARF CBM agenda is the voluntary submission of defence posture statements to the ARF. These statements have varied in size and detail. In 1996, for example, Thailand submitted a one page summary on 'Thailand's Defence Policy', (an extract from Defence of Thailand 1996), while Singapore made a 5-page submission entitled 'Defence Policy Statement', providing broad outlines of its defence philosophy, organisation of the Singapore Armed Forces, overseas training, peacekeeping activities, and confidence-building activities. Australia's submission was far more detailed, a 16-page submission entitled 'Defence Policy Statement to the ASEAN Regional Forum, 1996', with sections on Australian Defence Policy, the structure of Australian Defence Forces, personnel strength, regional and international security relations, alliances, exercises, defence budget, defence science and industry, UN support operations, participation in defence exchanges and security dialogues, and order of battle. Japan, too, made a detailed submission, which included the full text of its submission to the UN Register of Conventional Arms for the year 1996, including arms transfers, military holdings, procurement through national production, and policy on the control of arms exports and imports.

It appears that the submission by the ARF members are derived largely from their defence white papers or periodic defence statements (for example, the 'Defence of Singapore' which is issued once every two years). Until now, the ARF process has not generated any information which is not available from published official sources of their member states.

Cautious incrementalism, rather than a broad-brush initiative, therefore appears to be the hallmark of the ARF's approach to CBMs. A second feature of this process is continued adherence to the principle of soft institutionalism which implies, that for the time being at least, the ARF will continue to emphasise the process rather than the product. The ARF has thus far avoided considering constraining measures of any kind, choosing instead to focus on principles, and transparency measures, particularly information and communication CBMs.

The Proposal for a Regional Arms Register

Malaysia's former Defence Minister, Najib Razak, was one of the first Asia Pacific leaders to call for the creation of a regional arms register. Perhaps the most detailed proposal for such a register was made by the Philippines at the Special ASEAN Senior Officials Meeting held in Bangkok in March 1994. The Philippine proposal envisaged a Southeast Asian Register of Conventional Arms and Military Expenditure (RCAME) to be modelled after the UN conventional arms register. The aim of the regional arms register was to prevent the arms modernisation programs of Southeast Asian states from turning into an arms race.

But the idea of a regional arms register found limited support among the regional governments. Four main reasons account for this. The first is the view that a regional arms register may compromise the national security of states by revealing the true operational status of their forces and weapons systems to adversaries. States with insufficient hardware and low levels of military preparedness may be worried that transparency created by a regional register will undermine their ability to deter attack. This argument remains surprisingly widespread, notwithstanding the fact that creating a regional register is mainly a political process without much military significance. While important as an exercise in preventive diplomacy, information obtained through a register is likely to be of limited military value, adding little to what may already be known to government intelligence agencies.

A second and related factor working against a regional arms register is the concern that it could undermine the domestic and international prestige of governments who are found to possess relatively less-sophisticated weapons systems. Third, a regional register is seen within the region as an idea whose time has not yet come. The Asia Pacific region has practically no previous experience in multilateral security co-operation. A register may be too big a leap in faith for countries who are just beginning to grow comfortable with the idea of discussing their security concerns with one another on a regular multilateral basis.

Last, but not the least, the proposal for a regional arms register fits uneasily within the region's preferred approach to conflict management. For example, part of what is called the 'ASEAN Way' of political co-operation includes a desire to conduct all diplomatic negotiations away from the public eye, and to avoid any open discussion of sensitive and contentious issues. Against this backdrop, a regional arms register requires governments to accept a degree of transparency and openness unprecedented in the history of regional diplomacy. In addition, the ASEAN countries believe that any regional transparency or confidence-building measure should be more than just that, i.e. it should offer some tangible benefit to the concerned actors. Thus, steps such as joint military exercises, exchange of training facilities, and defence industrial co-operation, contribute to the defence capabilities of those involved while at the same time serving as useful confidence-building measures between states. Such measures are preferable to those which are exclusively transparency-oriented, such as a regional arms register.

Bilateral Transparency Measures Among the ARF Members

Here, the most noteworthy developments are the Shanghai Agreement and the Sino-Indian Agreement, both concluded in 1996. The Shanghai Agreement (which as China insists, is a bilateral agreement between China and its neighbours) signed between Russia, China, Kazakhstan, Tajikistan and the Kyrgyz Republic in April 1996 is the culmination of the decade-long process of rapprochement in Sino-Soviet/Russian relations that began with the advent of former Soviet President Mikhail Gorbachev's new thinking on foreign relations. As the Sino-Russian rapprochement gathered steam, negotiations in arms control and CBMs were held alternately in each capital, leading eventually to the Shanghai Agreement.

The key provisions of the Shanghai Agreement are summarised under Article 1. These include:

- annual exchange of military information;

- prohibition on military exercises directed against any other party/parties;

- restrictions on the scale, geographic scope and number troop exercises;

- prior notification of large-scale military activities and troop movements causes by emergency situations;

- prior notification of any border-crossing activities by forces and armaments;

- mutual observation of troop exercises;

- prior notification of entry of river battle ships into the 100 km geographical area on both sides of the line of the Eastern part of the Russian-Chinese border;

- prevention of dangerous military activities;

- enquiries concerning unclear situations; and

- increased contacts between military personnel in the border area and other confidence measures agreed on by the parties.

Several provisions of the Shanghai Agreement are similar to those found in the 1994 Vienna Document on CBMs adopted by the Organisation for Security and Co-operation in Europe (OSCE). It is worth noting that negotiations on this document were proceeding parallel to those that resulted in the Shanghai Document. Perhaps the main difference between the two is that the former is primarily a border agreement whose provisions are specifically tailored to ensure peace and stability in the land border regions.[4] The latter is a more general and comprehensive instrument that applies to military developments anywhere in the territories of the parties. Moreover, with some exceptions, the provisions of the former are much less elaborate and specific than the Vienna Document. The latter is more ambitious in scope. For example, the Vienna Document provides for various kinds of 'military co-operation' including joint exercises on a voluntary basis. These provisions are not found in the Shanghai Agreement. In addition, the constraining measures contained in the Shanghai Agreement are rudimentary when compared to the Vienna Document.

Finally, the Shanghai agreement provides for no compliance and verification provisions.[5] While the Vienna Document provides for challenge inspections, and requires every party to accept a quota of one 'evaluation' of information exchanged on military forces per calendar year, the Shanghai Agreement's compliance mechanisms are limited to voluntary hosting of visits to clarify developments considered ambiguous by the other party.

In December 1996, China and India signed an accord called the 'Agreement on Confidence-Building Measures in the Military Field Along the Line of Actual Control in the India-China Border Areas". The Agreement is based on three important principles: the non-use of force, peaceful co-existence (especially the five principles of co-existence first enunciated in the 1950s), and 'mutual and equal security'. The latter is especially important, since it is to form the basis for deciding ceilings on troops and armaments along the LAC. The CBMs created by the Agreement include the following:[6]

Article I: Stipulates that 'neither side shall use its military capability against the other side'

Article II: Expresses the determination of the two sides to seek a fair, reasonable and mutually acceptable settlement of the boundary question and to respect the Line of Actual Control until then.

Article III: The two sides are to reduce or limit their respective military forces within mutually-agreed geographical zones along the LAC to mutually-agreed ceilings.

Article IV: The two sides shall avoid large-scale military exercises involving more than one division (approximately 15,000 troops) in close proximity of the LAC Exercises involving 5000 troops or more will be subject to prior notification

Article V: Prohibits flights by combat aircraft (not including transport aircraft, survey aircraft, and helicopters) within 10 km of the LAC except with prior notification

Article VI: Prohibits blasting, hunting and other related activities within two km of the LAC. Patrols coming face-to-face are expected to exercise self-restraint and the two sides will consult on such incidents.

Article VII: Provides for maintenance and expansion of scheduled and flag meetings between border commanders at designated points, telecommunications links between border meeting points and medium- and high-level contacts between border forces.

Article VIII: Provides for exchange of information on natural disasters, epidemics in border areas. It also lays down procedures for dealing with personnel straying across the LAC.

Article IX: Provides for a party to seek clarifications regarding doubtful situations in border areas or suspicions regarding the compliance by the other party to the agreement

Article X: Notes that the full development of some of the provisions of the agreement will depend on the two sides arriving at a common understanding of the LAC. The modalities to implement the CBMs, and measures to expedite the LAC clarification exercise, including exchange of maps are to be worked out by the two sides. Notes that the agreement will be implemented without prejudice to the position of the countries on the boundary question.

Article XI: Stipulates that detailed implementation measures are to be decided by the Joint Working Group and an Experts Group.

Like the Shanghai Agreement, the Sino-Indian Border Agreement focuses on land boundaries, although the terrain conditions are very different in the two cases. Some of the CBMs contained in the Sino-Indian Agreement, such as those relating to troop reductions and prior notification of exercises are similar to those found in the Shanghai Agreement, although details such as the size of exercises that are to be subject to notification, differ. But the Sino-Indian Border Agreement does not provide for exchange of military information or prohibition on 'dangerous' military activities. Its provisions regarding contact CBMs are less elaborate. The Sino-Indian Agreement places more emphasis on preventing air intrusions. Like the Shanghai Agreement, it avoids verification and compliance measures beyond provisions regarding the right of a party to seek 'clarification' of doubtful situations on the border region.

Next Steps: Maritime CBMs

The Shanghai Agreement and Sino-Indian agreements represent an useful advance in the area of land-based CBMs in the Asia Pacific region. But can the bilateral land CBMs be considered as a model for multilateral CBMs in a predominantly maritime region such as the Asia Pacific? A Chinese position paper on the ARF circulated in April 1996 stated:

> the Chinese side would like to call on the attention of the ARF members to the Agreement on the Build-up of Confidence in the Military Field in Border Areas, signed by the leaders of China, Russian Federation, Republic of Kazakhstan, Republic of Kyrghyzstan and Republic of Tajikistan on April 26 in Shanghai. This agreement will surely have a positive and profound impact on maintaining and further strengthening peace and stability in the Asia-Pacific region. It is also a practical action taken by the Asia-Pacific countries to enhance mutual trust and develop the good-neighbourly relations.[7]

Despite these encouraging words, Chinese commentators remain sceptical about regionalising the Shanghai Agreement through the ARF. They point to the fact that the ARF is too new and untested, it is yet to agree on common principles and is still at the stage of exchanging views. They insist that though technically multilateral, the Shanghai Agreement is actually the successor to a bilateral agreement between China and the former Soviet Union, and it was initially conceived as such, until the break-up of the Soviet Union made it necessary to include the three newly-independent Central Asian states sharing common borders with China. Thus, it is not easily duplicated within a multilateral context. Moreover, the Asia Pacific is a much larger and strategically different arena than the land border regions of China. The former is marked by the existence of a number of military alliances, and a host of unresolved security problems such as the Korean Peninsula and the Taiwan Straits which need to be addressed before the ARF can seriously consider a similar agreement among its members. Furthermore, as some Chinese scholars see it, CBMs are more complex and more difficult to negotiate in the maritime arena than in land.

The ARF Inter-sessional Support Group on Confidence Building Measures, co-chaired by the Philippines and China, held a meeting in Beijing on 6-8 March 1997. Some participants at the meeting 'voluntarily' circulated their submissions to the UN Conventional Arms Register to other ARF members. However, the meeting failed to make any breakthrough on the controversial question of observation and prior notification of joint exercises. A Chinese proposal concerning advance notification of joint exercises involving 'two or more countries' was not acceptable to the US, who saw this proposal as self-serving (since it would not affect China which, unlike the US, does not conduct joint exercises).[8]

The rationale behind China's interest in border agreements remains unclear. Official Chinese thinking asserts that these agreements are part of China's efforts to create a peaceful regional environment which will enable it to concentrate on its internal matters, including economic development. But it is also possible to take a more complex view of the matter.[9] Border agreements may reflect a shift in Chinese military doctrine and force modernisation strategy. This effort follows the revision of China's military strategy in 1985 in response to the perceived decline of the Soviet threat.[10] The focus of China's earlier strategic doctrine had been to defend against a massive Soviet invasion deep into Northern China's industrial and political heartland by conducting a war of attrition based on total mobilisation of society. The new doctrine, in contrast, replaces Maoist belief in 'defence in depth' against the superpower enemy (i.e. luring the aggressor deep into Chinese territory and then surrounding and attacking him), with a 'forward defence' orientation geared towards smaller-scale but intense regional conflicts in China's periphery, especially maritime conflicts in the South China Sea. As Sino-Soviet border tensions diminished, territorial disputes in the South China Sea emerged as the most important operational priority in China's military planning. This shift was reflected in China's intensified efforts to develop the PLA into a more technology-intensive force structure capable of fighting modern wars in the maritime arena. Border peace with Russia and India certainly releases resources that could be used for building up China's naval and power projection capabilities.

Moreover, bilateral agreements provide China with some justification to resist or dilute some of the proposals for more intrusive multilateral CBMs in the Asia Pacific region. China has been, and remains, wary of such efforts, despite recent indications of a more positive attitude toward the ARF. This concern is aggravated by the fact that multilateral CBMs may constrain China's military options in the Taiwan Straits and the South China Sea, both cases in which China maintains a hard-line position.

It should be noted that China has not been supportive of maritime CBMs proposed within the framework of the South China Workshops organised by Indonesia and funded by Canada since 1990. These workshops have discussed a number of specific CBMs, including: (1) non-expansion of military presence in the disputed areas, and (2) exchange of visits by military commanders in the disputes areas. Neither of these have been adopted thus far. But China has held the view that since the Workshop process as a whole is a CBM in itself, it was not necessary to discuss other, more specific, CBMs. Discussion of military CBMs should be left to the ARF process.

Concluding Remarks

The Asia Pacific region has made discernible progress toward greater transparency, but much remains to be done. The UN Register has proved to be an important vehicle in the process of confidence-building within the region, given the fact that participation in the Register is one of the first steps promoted by the ARF. Moreover, there are indications that some of the initial inhibitions of the ARF members toward greater transparency are being overcome. For example, the close parallels between the Shanghai Agreement and the Sino-Indian Agreement suggests that Asian countries do not reject 'imported' models of transparency blindly, but are willing to consider them with appropriate adjustments.

The ARF can and should do more to promote transparency with the help of the UN Register. One obvious goal would be to achieve 100% participation by ARF members in the UN Register, perhaps by the Year 2000. Such a move would be powerful symbol of its role as a new and important actor at the international stage and its commitment to regional and global stability. Accomplishing this goal will also create new momentum for the grouping to advance its CBM agenda in other respects, including further exploration of the idea of a regional arms register as envisaged by the Concept Paper.

The UN and the ARF can take collaborative steps to encourage greater participation by the ARF members in the UN register. Technical support should be provided to Laos and Cambodia to secure their participation in the register. Myanmar should also be queried about its non-participation. At a time when the regime in Burma faces international isolation and ASEAN is facing criticism of its decision to grant Burma full membership, encouraging Myanmar's participation in the Register and other transparency mechanisms would be helpful to ASEAN's image and role.

While the idea of a regional arms register has not progressed, some aspects of the confidence-building process in the Asia Pacific region are clearly designed to enhance transparency. For example, Article 3 of the Shanghai Agreement provides for annual exchange of military information including personnel strength and the quantity of main types of armaments and military equipment. Another important measure is the ARF's adoption of exchange of annual defence posture statement on a voluntary basis among members. Although these statements do not provide any specific information on arms transfers, national procurement or holdings, they do provide an useful overview of the security perceptions and policies of member states, and contribute to the goal of transparency and confidence-building.

The ARF needs to encourage its members to be more forthcoming in providing information on national holdings and domestic procurement on a voluntary basis. The meetings of the ARF, which discussed global arms control and disarmament issues such as the CTBT in 1996, should also devote some attention to exploring ways of improving the UN Register and providing inputs to the UN Group of Experts. For its part, the UN should consider expanding the Register to include the submission, on a voluntary basis, of a defence posture statement (as in the case of the ARF), accompanying the data on weapons transfers.

---

1   See appendix 2 of Malcolm Chalmers and Owen Greene, *The UN Register in its Fourth Year*, Working Paper 2, Bradford Arms Register Studies, University of Bradford, UK, November 1996.

2   Malcolm Chalmers, *Confidence-Building In South-East Asia*, Westview Press, 1996, pp. 171-172.

3   *The ASEAN Concept Paper*, Annex A and B, pp. 8-11.

4   It is worth noting that the Vienna Document resulted from a long process of (almost 25 years since 1975) building confidence. Perhaps it is more appropriate to compare the Shanghai Agreement with the Helsinki Document of 1975. Some of the provisions of the latter dealt with border issues. In fact, one of the main Soviet objectives in the Helsinki process was to get NATO's recognition of borders in Central and Eastern Europe. The price the Soviet Union had to pay for this recognition was to agree on NATO positions on CBMs and human rights.

5   When asked about this, one Chinese scholar argued that military CBMs depend on political will and there is no need for verification.

6   John Cherian, 'Strengthening Relations: India, China, After Jiang
         Zemin's Visit', *Frontline,* December 27, 1996, pp. 40-41.

7   'Chinese Position on Issues Relating to the Third ARF Meeting',
         Beijing, April 1996, p.3.

8   Source: Summary Report of the ARF Inter Sessional Group on
         Confidence-Building Measures, 6-8 March, Beijing, China.

9   One Asian diplomat in Beijing suggested that China may be using
         these agreements to 'buy time' to build up its economic and
         military strength vis-à-vis its neighbours.

10   Paul H.B. Godwin, 'Changing Concepts of Doctrine, Strategy and
         Operations in the Chinese People's Liberation Army 1978-1987',
         China Quarterly, no. 112 (December 1987), pp. 578-581.

CHAPTER 14

Arms Transparency in the Inter-American

Security System

Ricardo Mario Rodriguez

This chapter examines the role of the conventional arms transparency, and particularly the United Nations Register of Conventional Arms, in the contemporary Inter-American security system. It discusses participation in the Register by member countries of the Organisation of American States, and offers an explanation of why some of these countries are not participating in this mechanism. Further, it suggests adjustments to the Register which in my view will transform it into an even more useful instrument for the enhancement of peace in Latin America.

The evolution of the Inter-American security system

The collective security system of the Americas, based on the Inter-American Treaty of Reciprocal Assistance or TIAR, is presently undergoing a profound transformation.

This transformation is due to changes of political, economic and military order which are affecting the Western Hemisphere. In the political order, the great change is the consolidation of democracy in all the Organisation of American States (OAS) member countries. In the economic order, the great transformation is the dramatic increase of regional integration and trade among Latin American countries. The disappearance of the Soviet Union and communism, together with the appearance of new types of threats to hemispheric security, constitute the other great change in the hemispheric environment.

The consolidation of democratic regimes

All of the member countries of the OAS are presently governed by democratic systems. They all have governments which have been elected in reasonably secret, free and fair elections. Sharing the same political-democratic system facilitates dialogue between governments. It favours mutual support and fosters approaches to problems from a similar perspective. Throughout the history of the OAS, it has never happened before now that all Latin American countries are democratic. A consequence of the Continent's democratisation is the political concentration and high level of communication that exists today among the Hemisphere's heads of government. Democratisation of the Western Hemisphere has encouraged political consultation and cooperation among governments, and has obviously facilitated dialogue on collective security.

The development of trade and regional integration
Since the beginning of the 1990s in particular, there has been a dramatic increase in intra-regional trade within Latin America.

What is the impact of regional integration, particularly the increase in trade, on regional security? Prior to regional integration, many Latin American countries had a friendly, but to some degree competitive, relationship with their neighbours, characterised by some distrust in the area of security relations. Integration, with its tremendous increases in sub-regional trade, movements of capital and expansion of joint-ventures, is demanding a more cooperative relationship and the development of trust among the countries of the region. Before the dramatic increase in trade and integration, several Latin American countries viewed their neighbours as potential enemies. Now, neighbours are deemed as business partners, and as markets for national products.

The disappearance of the Soviet Union and the appearance of new threats to regional security
The disappearance of the Soviet Union and the Warsaw Pact had two consequences for Latin America. The first was that it deprived the Inter-American Treaty on Reciprocal Assistance, or TIAR, from an extra-continental adversary. For many, without a credible adversary, TIAR loses one of its principal *raisons d'etre*. The other consequence of the Soviet Union's disappearance for Latin America has been the end of the East-West confrontation in the Hemisphere, particularly in Central America. Along with the Soviet Union, one of the two elements of support to Central American conflicts also disappeared, thus making possible the pacification of the region.

New threats to regional security

In Latin America, the appearance of new types of non-state threats, such as drug trafficking, terrorism, illegal arms trafficking, car theft and transnational car trafficking, and kidnapping are all demanding new responses, whose fundamental element and common factor is regional cooperation.

The new threats also demand new attitudes in civilian decision-makers and in the military. In Latin America, before the nineties, there was an apprehensive attitude towards transparency in security matters. There was a clear tendency toward isolationism. Governments tended to believe that the less that was revealed to foreigners about security arrangements, the better. In the recent past, attitudes favouring transparency and cooperation were unpopular in Latin American military establishments. When speaking on international security issues, the language was one of confrontation.

In the meantime, new security problems were developing. Illegal drug production, trafficking, and related crimes evolved from traditional nuisances into major regional security threats. In a few years, the drug lords created criminal networks controlling thousands of members, billions of dollars, and their tentacles extended to most Latin American countries, Europe, the United States, and Asia. However, the threat posed by the drug traffic has taken an even more ominous turn in Latin America during the last three or four years. As a result of money laundering, there was already a penetration of drug money in the market. Most recently, in order to protect the illegal production of drugs and drug trafficking, the cartels are expending enormous resources in pressuring or corrupting judges, members of parliament, military and police officers, and government officials. The very fabric of society is in jeopardy.

A question, posed last October in Barbados, during a Regional Conference on Peace and Security in the Western hemisphere, is appropriate and relevant in this context. The question is, what will happen if a representative of a drug trafficking organisation is elected head of government in a Caribbean country, or for that matter in Latin America? The question is pertinent, because the presence of drug money is a new phenomenon in electoral campaigns. The conclusion is that a new, immense, multidimensional challenge of international character is threatening the security of the Western Hemisphere, and in consequence demanding an Inter-American response.

Parallel to drug traffic, illegal arms trafficking has also become a major regional problem, involving international cartels. Recently, Mexican authorities revealed that several freight cars with Chinese assault rifles, rocket launchers, and other infantry weapons had successfully reached local insurgents. This is yet another example of the scope, and sophistication of global illegal arms trafficking. In Central America, this problem is aggravated by one of the sequels of the internal conflicts of the 1980s and 1990s: the wide availability of a large number of infantry weapons. There are thousands of such weapons, either in the hands of individuals or, worse, stockpiled in secret places by former guerrillas or paramilitary forces. Many of these arms eventually find their way to the illegal weapons market.

These new threats reveal the weakening of the regional system in force in the Western Hemisphere up to a few years ago. This system did not include mechanisms to face the new types of threats now prevalent in the region.

The new circumstances, fifty years after signing of TIAR, are demanding a more comprehensive regional security system to replace it: a regional security system which is capable of meeting new threats and which gives greater priority to cooperation among its members than to confrontation with third parties.

The new threats are demanding intensive cooperation among the countries. Governments have realised that only a joint attack against drug trafficking, illegal arms trafficking and terrorism can defeat these new enemies.

Why the UN Register is important to Latin America

In the context of the Western Hemisphere's evolution towards a more cooperative conception of security, the United Nations Register of Conventional Arms is important because it privileges transparency and cooperation. By strengthening peace, the Register indirectly fosters democracy, facilitates integration, and has the potential to make an important contribution to tackling the new threats.

The Register fosters democracy because accountability and transparency are two fundamental components of a democratic regime. Accountability and transparency in security matters, especially in military issues, are the missing elements in some Latin American democracies. The armed forces of many countries are still not under complete civilian control. A full participation in the UN Register offers the armed forces of Latin America the opportunity to commit themselves to transparency and, through the exercise of transparency, to become more involved with democracy.

The corrosive action of corruption against Latin American democracies has been often pointed out. To confront such pervasive and harmful problems, in March 1996 the OAS member countries, under the leadership of Venezuela, adopted an Inter-American Convention against Corruption. In the past, it is precisely in the realm of conventional arms purchases that many allegations of corruption have been made. In providing information on on-going or recently completed weapons acquisition programmes, the Register makes it easier to detect corruption by facilitating transparency which facilitates scrutiny of expenditures and checking of costs. In helping to detect corruption, the Register provides an important contribution to democracy.

The Register also helps economic development, because may act as a deterrent to excessive expenditures in weapons acquisition programmes. To the extent that arms purchases are made public, Governments become more accountable. In fostering transparency, the Register acts as an inhibitor of arm races that, in Latin America, are nowadays unjustifiable. Resources not expended on weapons procurement become available for development programmes.

The Register can foster better understanding and integration among Latin American countries, by promoting better mutual knowledge in an especially sensitive area. It is obvious that mutual knowledge and predictability can be enhanced by this mechanism. The information provided to the Register helps to dispel myths and ignorance about the military might of any given country. To some extent, the Register helps to better understand the military intentions of governments, which in some cases can be determined through the acquisition of military equipment. By strengthening peace, the Register simultaneously develops trust among countries, a basic condition for regional integration.

Difficulties hindering full participation of Latin American countries in the UN Register

Although several Latin American states have consistently participated in the Register, many have not done so far (see chapter 2). In my view there are two factors, in addition to normal lack of awareness and bureaucratic inertia, that are particularly important in hindering participation in Latin America.

Firstly, full participation in the Register requires a certain amount of conformity and support from the countries' armed forces. The national institution which originates arms acquisitions is typically the military institution. In the armed forces of certain Latin American countries, a historical mistrust towards civilian decisions in strictly technical-military matters continues to exist. In this context it is appropriate to ask, are Latin American armed forces participating in the Register with conviction or with suspicion? Participation in the Register requires a change of attitude in the military sector. Traditionally, the armed forces have associated purchases and sales of arms and other military equipment with secrecy. Time is needed so that all the military strata may develop positive attitudes towards transparency and openness.

Secondly, in some countries, difficulties hindering participation in the Register are of legal character and not of political will. This is the case in my country, Venezuela. The Venezuelan Government wants to participate in the Register, but laws regulating military secrecy prevent this from happening. There are countries whose legal regimen punishes the dissemination of information of a military character, particularly information on arms transfers and military arsenals. Governments of these countries would be breaking their domestic law and committing illegal acts if they were to offer information to the United Nations Conventional Arms Register. Thus, some time is needed to study the issue in those countries and to change the law.

The role of the OAS in the development of a regional security system based on mutual confidence and cooperation

The transition toward a more cooperative system directed toward meeting the new threats is being carried out within the framework of the Organisation of American States. The OAS has provided an important contribution to national security by acting as a forum, in its Commission on Hemispheric Security, for consultations and decisions on the subject. It was through the sponsorship of the OAS that the 1995 Regional Conference on Confidence and Security Building Measures, in Santiago, Chile, took place. From this event emerged the Declaration of Santiago, which recommended a range of measures for developing trust among the countries of the Hemisphere (See Appendix 1 for extracts of the Declaration of Santiago).

One of the measures recommended by the Declaration of Santiago is the participation of countries in the United Nations Register of Conventional Arms. Subsequently, the XXVI General Assembly of the OAS, in its resolution 1409, adopted a range of recommendations including that member countries of the Organisation should participate in the Register (See Appendix 2). Recently, on April 28, 1997, the OAS held a special meeting on 'the United Nations transparency and confidence-building measures,' and particularly on the UN Register. [1] At this meeting, the operation of the Register was examined and measures to achieve universal participation in it were considered. The main conclusion of the OAS meeting on the Register was that a greater awareness of its importance for the region should be propitiated.

It is expected that additional measures related to transparency will be discussed at the OAS in the near future. Amongst the most important of these are pre-notification of arms purchases and demonstrations of conventional weapons to neighbouring countries once they have been acquired.

Moreover, OAS states are well-advanced in the negotiation of a Convention Against the Illicit Trafficking of Firearms, Ammunition, Explosives and Other Related Materials. This Convention will oblige States Parties to adopt harmonised legal and other measures to combat such trafficking, including: establishing national registers of manufacturers, traders, importers and exporters of such materials; establish national monitoring and information systems, and effective border controls; and establish national centres to facilitate cooperation on illicit arms trafficking with other OAS states. [2] In addition, it will establish an Advisory Committee which will meet regularly to manage and promote information exchange, further harmonisation of national controls, and coordination amongst parties.

How could the Register be even more relevant to Latin America?

I will end with a subject also dealt with in the recent OAS meeting on the Register. Perhaps a key element missing in the Register is a category related to light weapons. In Latin America, terrorist attacks, internal conflicts, border skirmishes, and violent acts from criminal organisations are conducted mainly with small arms. In addition, since illegal arms trafficking is one of the main security problems in the region - so much so that the OAS is engaged in the adoption of a convention against illegal arms trafficking - the addition to the Register of a category on light arms transfers would be very relevant to Latin America. Transparency in the field of light weapons would help to determine the origin of fire arms used by criminals. Such an addition would significantly enhance the Register's contribution to transparency, to democracy and to greater understanding and integration among the countries of the region, by supporting the Latin American struggle against new, non-conventional security threats.

But even in its current version, the United Nations Register of Conventional Arms is a valuable contribution to transparency, to democracy and to greater understanding and integration among the countries of Latin America. I anticipate that progressive increases in awareness of the governments of the OAS countries about the multiple benefits of the Register will bring their full participation by the end of 1998.

Appendix 1

The 1995 Declaration of Santiago on Confidence- and Security-Building Measures (Adopted by OAS member states on 10 November 1995)

Below we reproduce extracts from the Declaration.

Changes that have taken place in the international arena. The emergence of democratic governments in the Hemisphere, and the end of the Cold War have created a climate conducive to strengthening peace and security in the Hemisphere. The way has thereby been paved for OAS member states to continue the necessary process of reflection to eliminate those factors that breed mistrust among states in the Hemisphere and identify new modalities of cooperation to consolidate peace, ensure effective achievement of the purposes of the OAS Charter and adherence to its principles, guarantee effective compliance with international law, and promote ties of friendship and cooperation, all of which will enhance security in the region.

The adoption of confidence- and security-building measures is a significant contribution to transparency, mutual understanding, and regional security, and to the attainment of development goals, including efforts to overcome poverty and protect the environment. Economic, social and cultural development is inextricably linked to international peace and security.

Confidence- and security-building measures must be adapted to the geographic, political, social, cultural and economic conditions of each region, and they have their own scope, as experience in the Hemisphere has amply demonstrated.

......

The application of confidence- and security-building measures helps create a climate conducive to effective limitation of conventional weapons, which makes it possible to devote more resources to the economic and social development of member states, which is a basic purpose of the OAS Charter.

The strengthening of bilateral and multilateral dialogue facilitates mutual understanding and increased collaboration in the face of the challenges of the next century. Confidence- and security-building measures in the Americas are especially significant for building ties of friendship and cooperation.

The Meeting of Experts in Buenos Aires in March of 1994, as well as OAS General Assembly resolutions, in particular, AG/RES. 1179 (XXII-0/92), AG/RES. 1284 (XXIV-0/94), and AG/RES. 1288 (XXIV-0/94), and the draft inventory submitted by the Inter-American Defense Board to the Permanent Council in compliance with resolution CP/RES. 650 (1031/95), are noteworthy in the process of identifying confidence- and security-building measures.

In accordance with the foregoing, the governments of the OAS member states, meeting in Santiago, Chile, agree to recommend the application, in the manner that is most suitable, of confidence- and security-building measures, among which the following should be mentioned:

a) Gradual adoption of agreements regarding advance notice of military exercises;

b) Exchange of information and participation of all member states in the United Nations Register of Conventional Arms and the Standardized International Reporting of Military Expenditures;

c) Promotion of the development and exchange of information concerning defense policies and doctrines;

d) Consideration of a consultation process with a view to proceeding towards limitation and control of conventional weapons;

e) Agreements on invitation of observers to military exercises, visits to military installations, arrangements for observing routine operations and exchange of civilian and military personnel for regular and advanced training;

f) Meetings and activities to prevent incidents and increase security for transport by land, sea, and air;

g) Cooperation programs in the event of natural disasters or to prevent such disasters, based on the request and authorization of the affected states;

h) Development and establishment of communications among civilian or military authorities of neighboring countries in accordance with their border situation;

i) Holding of seminars and courses, and studies on mutual confidence- and security-building measures and policies to promote confidence involving the participation of civilians and military personnel, and on the special security concerns of small island states;

j) High-level meetings on the special security concerns of small island states; and

k) Education Programs of education for peace.

The measures that have been announced require that a series of actions be set in motion for the monitoring and periodic evaluation of their implementation. To that end, the representatives of the OAS member state governments request the Committee on Hemispheric Security to undertake those tasks and to prepare a report on this subject for consideration by the General Assembly at its twenty-sixth regular session, which will decide, inter alia, whether a regional conference should be held to follow up the Regional Conference on Confidence- and Security-Building Measures held in Santiago, Chile.

In view of the importance of knowing about other measures being applied or that might be adopted, the representatives agree to provide periodically to the OAS Committee on Hemispheric Security information on the application of confidence- and security-building measures so as to facilitate preparation of the complete and systematic inventory of these measures, as instructed by the General Assembly.

...

Appendix 2

CONFIDENCE- AND SECURITY-BUILDING MEASURES IN THE AMERICAS

Extracts from Resolution 1409, adopted by the XXVI General Assembly of the OAS, on 7 June, 1996

THE GENERAL ASSEMBLY,

EMPHASISING the importance of the Declaration of Santiago on Confidence- and Security-Building Measures, adopted on November 10, 1995, which recommended, in the best possible manner, the application of confidence- and security-building measures;

RESOLVES:

1.   To urge all member states to implement, in the manner deemed most appropriate, the recommendations of the Declaration of Santiago on Confidence- and Security-Building Measures and of resolution AG/RES. 1179 (XXII-0/92).

2.   To invite all member states to provide to the Permanent Council's Committee on Hemispheric Security, prior to April 15 of each year, information on the application of confidence- and security-building measures, so as to facilitate preparation of the complete and systematic inventory of these measures, in light of the provisions of the Declaration of Santiago and resolutions AG/RES. 1284 (XXIV-0/94) and AG/RES. 1288 (XXIV-0/94).

3.   To request all member states to provide the Secretary General of the Organization of American States (OAS) by May 15 of each year with the information submitted to the United Nations Register of Conventional Arms in accordance with United Nations General Assembly resolutions 46/32L and 47/52L, and to the United Nations Standardized International Reporting of Military Expenditures, as provided for in United Nations General Assembly resolution 46/25.

4.   To request the Permanent Council, through the Committee on Hemispheric Security, to hold a one-day meeting on the two United Nations confidence and transparency measures cited in the preceding paragraph in order to increase understanding of and participation in the measures and to allow for an exchange of views among the OAS member states.

5.   To urge all member states to increase their mutual exchange of information on defense policies and doctrines so as to contribute to regional openness and transparency on matters of security.

6.   To urge all member states to develop, adopt, and execute, as appropriate, confidence-building measures such as those outlined in the Declaration of Santiago, including prior notification of military exercises, invitations to observe military exercises, the development of means of communication, and special consideration of a process of consultation with a view to proceeding with conventional arms limitation and control.

7.   To request that the Permanent Council, through the Committee on Hemispheric Security and with support from the General Secretariat, draw up general guidelines for an education for peace program within the OAS, for presentation to the General Assembly at its twenty-seventh regular session.

8.   To urge the member states to support and hold seminars, courses, and studies on confidence- and security-building measures and policies.

9.   To encourage an exchange of experience in confidence- and security-building measures with other regions, including, when deemed appropriate, participation by the OAS Committee on Hemispheric Security as an observer in meetings held by other international organizations working on the subject, such as the Organization for Security and Cooperation in Europe.

10.   To request the Permanent Council to establish, through the Committee on Hemispheric Security and with support from the General Secretariat, a roster of experts in confidence- and security-building measures, based on information provided by the member states so that they may conduct outreach courses, seminars, and studies of any measures determined by the Permanent Council.

11.   To instruct the General Secretariat to provide necessary resources, subject to the availability of funds, to support the activities and work of the Committee on Hemispheric Security.

12.   To invite the Inter-American Defense Board to provide advisory and consultative services to the Committee on Hemispheric Security for studies on confidence- and security-building measures, pursuant to resolution AG/RES. 1240 (XXIII-0/93) and when the Committee so requests.

13.   To request the Permanent Council, through the Committee on Hemispheric Security, to continue consideration of this matter, and to report to the General Assembly at its twenty-seventh regular session.

14.   To transmit this resolution to the Secretary-General of the United Nations and to other regional organizations as appropriate.

1   OAS Special Meeting on the United Nations Transparency and
        Confidence-Building Measures, Washington DC, 28 April 1997,
        organised by the OAS Committee on Hemispheric Security.

2   Permanent Council, Organisation of American States, *Draft
        Convention Against the Illicit Trafficking of Firearms,
        Ammunition, Explosives and Other Related Materials,*
        CP/doc.2875/97, 20 March 1997.

CHAPTER 15

The Arms Trade and Security Building in Russia and the CIS

Alexander Nikitin

Five Years of the CIS: Dividing Military Heritage

Five years have passed since the collapse of the Soviet Union, the creation of the Russian Federation as a separate state and the formation of the Commonwealth of Independent States (CIS).This half a decade was marked by intensive restructuring of the security institutions, as well as a change of patterns in arms production and trade in the new independent states.

Restructuring of the security and military configuration on the territory of the former Soviet Union took place in three stages overlapping in time and space. The first stage was essentially an attempt to save and protect a unified military infrastructure in the republics which were on their way towards independence. This period between 1990 and 1992 was characterized by the spread of the notions of *common geostrategic space* uniting republics and *common external borders* of the just created CIS (both notions were used in the early CIS documents), and an attempt to avoid a division of the former Soviet military infrastructure by placing it under *Joint CIS Command* (taking a lead from the former Soviet Ministry of Defence and General Staff).

The second stage had already started in late 1991 and lasted until 1993/1994. It saw the creation of separate and independently controlled armed forces in each new independent state. The Baltic states, Ukraine and Azerbaidjan (each of them for different reasons) were leading the rush to form independent military structures and to supplement the 'divorce' from the old Soviet Union with actual division of the military-industrial complex. This trend towards separation and division prevailed in late 1992-early 1993 when, inside Russia, the newly-formed Russian Ministry of Defense took, one by one, all functions away from the semi-created Joint CIS Command. At that time division within the military-industrial complex had also become inevitable for economic reasons since most of the CIS states were requiring their proportional 'share of military-industrial property'.

The third stage, a process of security and military integration of separated and independent CIS states, had been started by signing the Tashkent Treaty on Collective Security[1] in May, 1992, and continues up to now.

The process of military integration in the CIS grows quite intensively. Its legal basis already includes about three hundred interstate agreements and collective documents on military matters. Almost one third of these are devoted to matters relating to military-technical cooperation, including standardization, arms transfers, cooperation in arms and ammunition, and elaboration and production of armaments.

Specific Features of the CIS Region: Uneasy Challenges to Transparency and Arms Control

The Commonwealth of Independent States is a region which deserves special and high attention from the point of view of arms control, arms limitation and security building, as well as promoting transparency in a sphere of conventional armaments. There are several reasons for this:

- The process of dividing the former Soviet military infrastructure was not in all cases and subregions well planned and fully controlled. There were and still are uncertainties concerning specific quantities of military equipment or ammunition which were 'lost', inappropriately reported or listed in a process of 'sharing a heritage'.

- Large quantities of small arms, artillery and even armoured combat vehicles got into the hands of, or were temporarily used by, unauthorised military groupings, and non-state military forces, especially in Georgia, Armenia, Azerbaidjan, Tadjikistan and North-Caucasian parts of the Russian Federation.

- Many 'barter' transfers of arms and military equipment took place between the new independent states in the period following the creation of independent armed forces. Some of these mutual transfers are not reported internationally and may thus influence the validity of formerly existing open information.

- Large and medium scale armed conflicts in areas like Tadjikistan, Abkhazia, South Ossetia, Transdnestria, North Ossetia/Ingushetia, and Chechnya were accompanied by massive relocation of the armed forces, armaments and ammunition, as well as destruction or damage (in many cases difficult to confirm or deny) of arms. This has led to rapid and continuing constant changes in quantities, location, status of arms arsenals in many CIS states. Internationally reported data soon become obsolete and require correction or regular updating.

- Debates surrounding the revision of the CFE Treaty involved issues of correlation of arms arsenals, distribution of internal quotas on permitted types and quantities of armaments between different CIS states. With the exception of the Central Asian CIS states (which are outside of the geographical area of the CFE Treaty), all CIS countries have provided information within CFE and Vienna document exchanges. The so-called issue of 'flank limitations' is managed partly through the internal redistribution of quotas between Russia and other CIS states and this requires additional attention towards location, methods of counting and transparency of information about arms in the CIS.

Participating in the UN Register

States of the CIS (though not all of them) are participating through the provision of data for the UN Register of arms transfers. Whereas in 1995 only four CIS states (Russia, Ukraine, Byelarus and Moldova) provided reports, by early 1997 ten countries of the CIS reported on arms transfers (namely: Armenia, Azerbaidjan, Byelarus, Kazakhstan, Kyrgyzstan, Moldova, Russia, Turkmenistan, Tadjikistan and Ukraine). Uzbekistan and Georgia did not report, though Georgia was reporting the previous year. Armenia, Azerbaijan and Byelarus were the only CIS countries to provide reports on military holdings.

The three Baltic states (Estonia, Latvia and Lithuania - formerly Soviet Republics, but not members of the CIS) also participated in the Register. All three have been importing arms and military equipment quite intensively, as part of the process of redirecting the residual of the former Soviet military infrastructure towards NATO/Western military standards and suppliers. Thus, after four years of the Register's existence, thirteen out of fifteen newly independent states, created after the collapse of the Soviet Union, were represented at the Register.[2]

It is tremendously important that Russia as the largest CIS arms producer and trader participates in the UN Register. Russia's participation is motivated not only by the fact that Russia is a member of the UN Security Council and typically is quite disciplined regarding UN-sponsored activities, but also by the reasonably developed 'disarmament culture' (including expertise, system of counting and control, and background files of information presented through CSCE and UN channels in Soviet years), as well as by Russia's involvement in the CFE process as one of the chief negotiating parties.

The arsenal of confidence building and transparency measures is developed by Russia not necessarily in direct connection with the UN Register but as part of bilateral US-Soviet, later US-Russian, negotiations, established practice of inspections. An important proportion of Russian participation in the Register is backed by the generally positive practice of participation in nuclear disarmament over almost three decades since the early 1970s.

Return of the Bear: Russian Arms Producers Conquering the World Markets

Currently in 1997, nine Russian companies, including the state-owned 'Rosvooruzhenie' Company, possess legal rights to trade armaments. 15 more companies applied for receiving such rights in the future. In 1996 Russia earned $ US 3.5 billion through selling armaments. $ US 3.4 billion dollars out of this amount were gained by 'Rosvooruzhenie'.

Quite intensive debates are going on whether all trade of armaments should be centralized in the hands of the state-owned structures, or whether other forms of company could be allowed to participate in export/import operations. This issue is to be regulated by the State Law 'On military-industrial cooperation of the Russian Federation with foreign states'. The draft of such a law is currently under consideration in the State Duma (the lower chamber of Russian Parliament).

There is a visible disagreement between different branches of power on the issue of centralization or decentralization of the weapons trade. Vice-Premier of the Russian Government, Minister of Foreign Economic Relations O. Davydov recently expressed his firm support for the rigid state monopoly over any export operations with armaments.[3] He explained that the Ministry does not plan to issue licenses for the arms trade to any companies other than the state-owned 'Rosvooruzhenie'. If such a system would be implemented it could lead to a centralized and reliable system of reporting all export contracts and their implementation. Assuming that the political decision of the Russian government to participate in updating the UN Arms Register would stay firm, such centralization would make all systems of reporting and updating more simple, reliable and operable.

At the same time, other approaches exist among Russian decision-making circles. The Ministry of Defense Industries (before its reorganization in 1997) is interested in supporting more than one company of the large and underused military-industrial complex. Deputy Minister of Defense Industries V. Pakhomov suggested in February 1997, that a system of state licensing should be introduced, and enterprises which passed state licensing successfully should be granted relatively wide opportunities to trade independently on external markets.[4] While broadening the scope of exporters through state licensing, the policy on importing military-related items and armaments could be even more liberal.

The Committee on Industry of the State Duma went even further and, in the hearings with participation from the leadership of the military and arms-producing enterprises, expressed an opinion that the above-mentioned law on foreign military-technical cooperation should be postponed and changed to accommodate more flexible regulations. More than 70 % of the enterprises of the Russian military-industrial complex are converted into share companies or fully or partially privately owned companies. In a situation where state orders for armaments production are dramatically lower than in Soviet years, most military-industrial enterprises are seeking direct access either to foreign investments or foreign markets.

The state-owned giant 'Rosvooruzhenie' is not ready to disperse its attention and resources among hundreds of small contracts and concentrates on dozens of high value deals. The 'Promexport' agency estimates that every year Russia is losing about 1 billion US dollars by not taking up offers on small arms export contracts. In 1996, only 'Promexport' itself left unrealised contracts on 500 million US dollars because of the difficulties with licensing export deals.[5] Of course especially small contracts arranged through side companies are extremely difficult to trace. Implementation of tactics of breakthrough into this market (including supply of spare parts to already purchased armaments as well as modernization of formerly sold equipment) could create real problems with full transparency.

Whether through centralized or decentralized export systems, the Russian government plans to increase quite considerably its presence on the world armaments market. As officials of 'Rosvooruzhenie' quote governmental plans and policy, the target is to double the existing level of $ US 3.5 per year within the next two years and to reach, by the year 1998, a level of armaments exports of $ US 7 billion.[6]

Independent Russian experts, however, express serious doubts as to the feasibility of such plans, although some growth in arms production and trade is expected.

As a matter of fact, the Russian system of state regulation of military-technical cooperation after several years of decay and liberalization has reached a point after which it may stop to be a state system. This is why some state structures are insisting on a new phase of increasing, not diminishing, state regulation of military production and trade.

Geopolitical Aspects of Arms Trade in the CIS and Regional Security

The five years between 1990 and 1994 have by some observers been called 'chaotic years' for arms production and trade in the USSR and the later CIS. Only in 1994-1995 did the situation start to be reasonably controlled by the state again. Transparency and controllability were restored for arms production and trade in Russia, Ukraine and Byelarus, the main CIS arms producers, but not in some other areas of the CIS, like Caucasus or Tadjikistan. What was achieved in Russia is the following (though it is inappropriate to call these changes an 'achievement' because they should be normal practice in a modern stable state):

- elimination of organizational and legal 'loop-holes' for arms sales unsanctioned by the state;

- localization of the internal 'grey' arms trade to mostly North Caucasus and limiting it to the area of small arms;

- virtual elimination of instances where military-industrial enterprizes have reduced the prices of arms sales below market averages in order to increase their profits from stocks which had been produced cheaply during the Soviet years[7];

- pushing of unknown or illegal trade companies out of the arms trade area;

- visible growth of input from state arms sales into the state budget.

In addition, the geopolitical consequences of arms trade policy are raised more and more often in the course of domestic debates in Russia and other CIS states. There are several aspects to this problem:

- Russia and some other CIS states (for example, Byelarus) have among their partners in arms trade a number of states attracting 'special attention' from the point of view of international security, for example, Iran, Angola, Bangladesh, and North Korea.

- Some arms sales are destined for the areas where armed conflicts are going on or tensions exist (for example, Azerbaidjan, Moldova, Middle East states, Iran, Turkey, and Cyprus).

- Central and Eastern European countries aiming to join NATO, as well as the Baltic states, and - on a lesser scale - also Ukraine and Moldova are seeking reorientation in their arms trade away from Russia towards Western countries. CIS states in Transcaucasia and Central Asia are approached by Turkey, China and some other Asian states as markets to be shared with Russia. In both directions, Europe on the one hand and Asia on the other, Russia is losing its former monopoly on arms exports, and consequently looks for creative political and economic strategies to keep the markets, or at least shares of the markets. This fight for markets often takes shape of politicised tensions as can be seen in the economic dimension of NATO enlargement.

- On more than one occasion, the West (and foremost the USA) has exerted political and ideological pressure on the Russian government in relation to arms deals with India, Angola, North Korea, and Cyprus. There are domestic debates whether Russia should withdraw from deals which are suspect to the world community (or at least provide more transparency), or whether national economic interests are currently of higher priority than the image of a 'disciplined trader'.

- Some of the CIS states appear as arms suppliers to different sides of regional conflicts. Relations between Russia and Ukraine were negatively influenced when Ukraine started large military sales to Pakistan while Russia continued to be an active military supplier to India. Kazakhstan does not welcome Russian and Byelorussian military supplies to China. Armenia is trying to influence Moscow and Kiev to stop arms sales to Azerbaidjan. The direction of arms transfers and sales from the CIS states becomes one of the points of disagreement inside the Commonwealth itself.

Creation of the Collective Security System for the CIS, Military-Technical Cooperation and Transparency

Military integration and the development of military-technical cooperation within the CIS creates some important positive opportunities for promoting transparency in the sphere of conventional armaments production and trade, as well as for updating the UN Register.

First of all, the activity of the Staff for Coordination of Military Cooperation in Moscow, where all CIS states are represented by permanent military representatives and which is the highest military executive structure of the CIS, brings a lot of organization, coordination and order into the transfers, sales and relocation of arms on the territory of all CIS states. Internal transparency inside the CIS collective security system on the matters of armaments acquisition, production, exchange and sales by the CIS states is much higher today than it was in the initial stages of concluding the Tashkent Treaty. Transparency inside the system of CIS collective security is provided as a result of intergovernmental coordination through permanent military representatives of each CIS state assigned to the Staff for Coordination of Military Cooperation in Moscow. There is no formal mechanism of exchange of information on arms production among CIS countries, but in a process of coordination of positions of the CIS states on the CFE talks and in the process of elaboration of technical cooperation agreements and treaties there is an intensive exchange of requests, replies and statements of different CIS states.

This internal transparency and exchange of data could be interfaced with UN requirements and contribute to the UN Register. What is needed is a direct dialogue on these matters between UN and CIS structures. Of course, the final decision on submitting or not submitting information stays with participating CIS states but the advice of the influential International Military Staff could be decisive.

The Council of CIS Defense Ministers as well as the Staff for Coordination of Military Cooperation are implementing a list of confidence building measures among CIS states. Among such measures in the CIS are: early notification of military exercises and large movements of troops and armaments, agreed exchange of information necessary to assure the smooth functioning of the collective system of air- and missile-defense of the CIS, as well as systems of early warning on nuclear strikes against CIS states' territories. The CIS countries of Central Asia are exchanging information between themselves and with Russia which is vital for the protection of common external borders of the Commonwealth. Among the examples of mutual confidence building coordination, was an early elaboration of a common CIS approach at the CFE revision talks.

Even Ukraine, which is formally not a signatory of the Tashkent Treaty, is constantly participating in all sessions of the Council of CIS Defense Ministers and takes part in many agreements on military-technical cooperation with other CIS states. All in all, the stabilizing nature of CIS collective security arrangements is without a doubt. CIS integration plays a role in promoting transparency, coordination and attention to international standards in armaments-related activities of CIS states.

The policy on military-technical cooperation elaborated by the CIS structures contains several important limitations on arms trade of the CIS states. These limitations which contribute to international security are, as a rule, the following:

- CIS states are required not to sell any armaments to any countries which are a subject to international embargos;

- supplies of armaments to states which are in a state of external or internal conflict are discouraged (still there are some debates whether supply of armaments to the official central government of a state with an armed opposition should be an exception);

- arms sales to non-state buyers are not encouraged;

- supply of offensive weapons which can seriously influence any regional balance of power is under special consideration and criticism (and cases of supplies to Armenia and Azerbaidjan, India and Pakistan are examples);

- CIS structures advocate official reporting of all arms transfers and sales to the UN Register (and the three biggest arms suppliers - Russia, Ukraine and Byelarus - are setting a positive example on that) and to the CIS military coordination structures;

- CIS states are undertaking collective measures and efforts to limit and diminish any 'grey' flows of armaments inside the CIS and especially any cases of transfer or sale of armaments to unauthorised non-state military groupings.[8]

Over the last decade, between 1987 and 1997, there were 28 conflicts with the use of armed force on the territory of the former Soviet Union. This area continues to contain large quantities of armaments of all types. Yet whereas in the 'chaotic years' immediately after the collapse of the Soviet Union, arms production, transfers, redistribution and sales were very unstable and uncontrollable, these troubles had been clearly localized by the end of the 1990s. CIS military coordinative structures are developing a policy which is generally favorable to international transparency and controllability towards the situation regarding conventional weapons. Major CIS arms producers - like Russia, Ukraine and Byelarus - are participating in the UN Register procedures. All this has set a positive trend. But there is a need for active promotion of further transparency and international control in the sphere of conventional arms in the CIS region to assure security and stability to a region which is undergoing profound social and political change.

1   The Treaty on Collective Security of the CIS states was signed by Armenia, Russia, Tadjikistan, Kyrghyzia, Kazakhstan and Uzbekistan on May 15, 1992 in Tashkent. Three more states - Georgia, Azerbaidjan and Byelarus - joined the process of military integration later. Ukraine participates in some integrative activities and documents without formally having joined the Treaty.

2   Malcolm Chalmers and Owen Greene, *Taking Stock: The UN Register After Two Years*. Westview Press, 1995, pp. 181-205.

3   See O. Davydov's interview in 'Segodnya', 20.02.97, p.1

4   'Pravda', 18.02.97, p.2.

5   'Segodnya', 14.02.97, p.6

6   'Commersant-Daily', Moscow, 01.02.97, p.2.

7   Sales of arms and military equipment using inadequately low prices by certain state structures or private companies are still quite serious for many CIS states, including for example Byelarus, Ukraine, Georgia, and Azerbaidjan. Byelarus reports up to 50 such cases within last 5 years which brought an estimated damage of 15 million US dollars to the Byelorussian state budget. See S. Anisko, 'Byelarus: Problems of Reformation of the Army and Arms Exports', In: *Export of Conventional Armaments*, Moscow, PIR Center, N 1-2 (9-10), 1997, p.16.

8   See more details in D. Evstafiev, 'Arms Trade and Geopolitics of Russia', in *Export of Conventional Armaments*, Moscow, PIR Center, N 1-2 (9-10), pp. 9-10.

Part E: Associated Transparency Measures

CHAPTER 16

Addressing Light Weapons and Small Arms Proliferation

Mitsuro Donowaki

In the immediate aftermath of the Cold War, world leaders were first preoccupied with the threat of possible proliferation of weapons of mass destruction as a result of the disintegration of the former Soviet Union. Then, with the experience of the Gulf war, international transfer of major conventional arms had to be brought under control. As a modest but significant step forward, the UN Register of Conventional Arms was established starting from 1992. It was from about this time that the problems of light weapons and small arms started to draw the attention of world leaders.

In Somalia, where the government collapsed after the fleeing of dictator Mohammed Siad Barre in 1991, chaos, famine, widespread banditry and internecine warfare among various clan-based factions became prevalent. Humanitarian and refugee support activities of the United Nations came to be threatened. The Security Council Resolution 794 of December 1992 determined the situation as a 'threat to peace'. However, the coalition peace keeping forces led by the United States forces had to abandon their job after a bloody gun battle in downtown Mogadishu later in 1993.

In Angola, after the elections held in September 1992, UNITA forces led by Savimbi resumed their struggle against MPLA, and by 1994 when a cease-fire was agreed, another 500,000 Angolans are thought to have died through combat or war-induced starvation. In Rwanda, violent clashes between Hutu and Tutsi tribes in May 1994 resulted in the massacre of an estimated 500,000 Rwandans. In Liberia, where the guerrilla forces of NPFL led by Charles Taylor started to take control of the country at the end of 1989, the subsequent internal factional strife over five years completely devastated the nation. One half of its 2.3 million population are said to have fled their homes and now live as refugees.[1]

A common feature of all these situations was that they were not inter-state conventional wars. Weapons used in these intra-state conflicts were mostly small arms and light weapons that are not covered by the UN Register of Conventional Arms. In fact, few people could foresee the magnitude of the disaster and human suffering that could be caused by such smaller types of weapons. Until recently, it was generally believed that such a scale of human casualties, reaching hundreds of thousands at times, could only be caused, if not by natural disasters, only by weapons of mass destruction or by larger conventional weapons.

The seriousness of the problems caused by the proliferation of light weapons and small arms is not limited to Africa. In Central America where three civil wars recently came to an end, the wide-spread circulation of such arms (at least one million of them according to some estimates) is causing an alarmingly high rate of criminal activities combined with illegal drug trafficking activities. In South West Asia, light weapons and small arms supplied to the Afghanistan government and the Mujahideen guerrillas from outside sources over the years are now said to be spilling over to neighboring countries, causing serious internal security problems. According to reports, over 100,000 Kalashnikov assault rifles are available in Karachi alone.[2]

The UN response

The United Nations Secretary-General Boutros Boutros Ghali was quick to respond to the problems of the proliferation of such arms. In his address to the Advisory Board on Disarmament Matters in January 1994, he stated that 'Regional registers of conventional arms should now be the next step. They have the advantage of allowing the categories of weapons to be registered to reflect the security concerns felt in the region.'[3] Then, in response to the request made by the President of Mali in October 1993 to assist in the collection of light weapons proliferating in his country, the Secretary-General sent an Advisory Mission to Mali in August 1994. This was followed by another Mission sent to six neighboring countries in West Africa in early 1996.

Also, at the beginning of 1995, the Secretary-General published a *Supplement to an Agenda for Peace*, in which he specifically called attention to two categories of light weapons, namely small arms and anti-personnel mines. He concluded that 'Progress since 1992 in the area of weapons of mass destruction and major weapons systems must be followed by parallel progress in conventional arms, particularly with respect to light weapons". He went on to say, 'It will take a long time to find effective solutions. I believe strongly that the search should begin now."

It was in response to this call by the UN Secretary-General that, at the co-sponsorship of Japan and other UN Member States, resolution 50/70 B was adopted by the General Assembly in December 1995. The resolution requested the Secretary-General to prepare a report on the question of small arms and light weapons 'with the assistance of a panel group of qualified governmental experts to be nominated by him on the basis of equitable geographical representation' and to submit the report to the General Assembly to be held in 1997.

Specific issues to be dealt with in the report, according to the resolution, are: (a) 'the types of small arms and light weapons actually being used in conflicts dealt with by the United Nations', (b) 'the nature and causes of the excessive and destabilizing accumulation and transfer of small arms and light weapons, including their illicit production and trade', and (c) 'the ways and means to prevent and reduce the excessive and destabilizing accumulation and transfer of small arms and light weapons, in particular as they cause or exacerbate conflict'.

It is important to note here that the 'panel group of governmental experts' was asked to address the question of small arms and light weapons 'used in conflicts dealt with by the United Nations'. Therefore, its report is not required to deal, for example, with the question of those weapons used for criminal activities in general, or even those used in civil or international conflicts which are not dealt with by the United Nations.

Pursuant to this resolution, the Secretary-General appointed the Panel of Governmental Experts on Small Arms. The Panel members consist of 16 governmental experts - four from Asia (Iran, Japan, Malaysia and Sri Lanka), five from Europe (Belarus, Belgium, Finland, Germany and Russia), three from Africa (Egypt, Mali and South Africa), and four from the Americas (Canada, Colombia, El Salvador and the United States).

The Panel held its first session in June 1996 in New York, during which it had an opportunity to receive briefings from six prominent scholars and experts in the field. [4] The Panel held its second session in January 1997 in New York, and its third and final session will be held July 1997. In addition, the Panel decided to hold three regional workshops in Pretoria, San Salvador and Kathmandu in order to receive inputs from experts of the regions of Africa, Central America and Southwest Asia with the participation of not necessarily all the Panel members. The first two of these workshops were held during autumn 1996, with the third being held in Kathmandu in May 1997. In addition, the Panel held an extra session of three working days in Tokyo also in May 1997.

Measures to address small arms and light weapons proliferation

As the chairman of the Small Arms Panel, I am not allowed to prejudge or present the conclusions to be arrived at by the Panel. Therefore, below I simply aim to give my personal views, based on what I have learned in connection with the Panel's activities.

The first point I wish to stress is that the problems related to small arms and light weapons appear to call for immediate concrete actions to solve them. This is because, unlike major conventional weapons, they are causing day-to-day human casualties in places where there are ongoing conflicts. Moreover, in places where conflicts have come to an end these weapons are causing alarming increases in criminal activities, making the authorities unable to guarantee security to their citizens, and creating severe disruptions in political, economic and social development and stability.

Naturally, 'ways and means to prevent and reduce excessive and destabilizing accumulation and transfer' of such weapons have urgently to be found, rather than the round-about approach of promoting transparency measures,. This is exactly why the Panel on Small Arms was established. In this context, it should also be added that, although transparency measures may be a useful device with respect to larger conventional weapons because they can be used for large-scale cross-border attacks, this may not be the case with respect to small arms and light weapons because they do not cause such concerns.

Secondly, having said the above, the question of transparency with respect to small arms and light weapons will still have to be tackled from various directions. This is for various reasons. For example, as I quoted above, the Secretary-General stated at the beginning of 1994 that 'the regional register of conventional arms should be the next step'. In those days it was often pointed out that the low rate of participation to the UN Register by African States might be due to the lack of the relevance of the Register to the security interests of African States, because many of them do not possess or import the seven categories of conventional weapons that are covered by the UN Register. Small arms and light weapons are the ones they are more concerned about. It was therefore argued that regional registers covering such weapons might have to be developed.

This question was discussed both by the Advisory Board on Disarmament Matters and by the 1994 Group of Governmental Experts. During these discussions, it was recalled that the guiding principles in elaborating the UN Register were 'simplicity and easy to comply with'. Larger conventional weapons are easily identifiable, and their numbers can be counted and registered easily. Compared to them, small arms and light weapons are vastly more numerous, and extremely difficult to be traced and registered even in some of the developed countries. In any event, these are not the type of weapons to be used primarily for large-scale cross-border aggressions.

For these reasons, it was concluded impractical and unnecessary to try to include small arms and light weapons in the global UN Register. The 1994 Group of Governmental Experts on the UN Register also concluded in its report that security concerns specific to some regions or sub-regions 'should be addressed primarily among States in the regions or sub-regions'.[5]

In March 1997, I had an opportunity to attend a Ministerial Consultation in Bamako, Mali, held on the occasion of the first anniversary of the 'Bonfire of Peace', and to speak on the question of a 'Regional Arms Register in West Africa'. On that occasion, I stated that if the establishment of such a regional register was for the specific purpose of bringing under control the proliferation of small arms and light weapons, one would have to start with having close consultations among the military and police officials of the sub-region, including border guards and customs officials. The harmonization of national control laws and regulations of such weapons would also have to be carried out. Exchange of intelligence information as well as cooperation among the authorities of the nations in the sub-region would have to be promoted in order to curb the illicit trade in such arms, and also to combat criminal activities in which such weapons are used. In the process, the introduction of a computerized database would inevitably become a necessity. This kind of regional arrangement may be called a 'regional network of information sharing' rather than a 'regional register'. It should serve the purpose of helping to reduce and prevent the excessive accumulation of such weapons, and to promote transparency in such armaments.

Thirdly, it should also be noted that with respect to some of the larger types of light weapons, transparency can be promoted by lowering the threshold of some of the seven categories of conventional weapons covered by the UN Register. For example, in the deliberations of the 1997 Group of Governmental Experts on the UN Register, a suggestion was made to lower the calibre of 'Large Calibre Artillery Systems', which is currently set at '100 millimetres and above' down to '75 millimetres and above'. If this suggestion were to be approved by a consensus, quite a number of mortars actually being used in conflicts in Africa would become relevant to the Register. Although it would not be possible to lower the thresholds so far as to include typical small arms such as assault rifles, it might therefore be possible to carefully identify and include some of the larger types of light weapons into the categories of weapons to be covered by the UN Register.

Fourthly, I should like to stress that illicit trafficking of small arms and light weapons badly needs to be countered by some transparency measures. The scale of the illicit arms trade is estimated to be between US $ 3 to 10 billion annually. Most of this involves small arms and light weapons, because larger conventional weapons are less likely to be traded without governmental involvement. This may be a trivial figure compared to the estimated US $ 300 billion of annual drug trafficking. However, it is an alarmingly high figure when compared to the estimated figure of roughly US $ 20 billion of the annual arms trade, although there is no way of confirming the amount of illicit arms trade since by definition it defies reliable monitoring.

Illicit arms trade may be defined as a trade conducted without the approval of the authorities of either the supplier state or the recipient state. This is because a covert trade approved by one side but not the other can hardly be called illegal or illicit. This being the case, even in the areas of legitimate trade there appear to be various factors that limit transparency. Therefore, a much higher degree of transparency in the authorized trade in small arms and light weapons would also be required if we are to have better ideas about how to control the flow of small arms and light weapons.

Turning to the illicit trade itself, it is well known that illicit arms trade takes place due to the lack or paucity of national and international regulations as well as vigilance. Some countries have laws and regulations placing fairly strict controls on the trade and production of arms, but this may not be the case with respect to many other nations. Furthermore, even the existence of such laws and regulations does not appear to effectively prevent them being circumvented. Therefore, if the international community is serious about the suppression of the illicit arms trade, concerted efforts to put in place adequate national laws and regulations, to harmonize them and to ensure their effective implementation will be indispensable. It will only be through such concerted efforts that the flow of small arms and light weapons can be placed under better control, narrowing down the room for illicit arms trade.

In this respect, the government of Colombia has over the years been one of the most vocal in advocating the need for the United Nations to take some actions in order to stem the tide of the illicit arms trade. As a result of one of such initiatives taken by Colombia, a Group of Governmental Experts on to study the 'ways and means of promoting transparency in internationals transfers of conventional arms' was established during the period 1991 - 92. The Group produced a report containing well-considered views and recommendations on the question of illicit arms trade.[6] Later on, this report was to serve as a useful basis for the discussions of the issue of the illicit arms trade by the Untied Nations Disarmament Commission (UNDC). Eventually, in 1996 the UNDC was to adopt by consensus a document entitled 'Guidelines for international arms transfers in the context of General Assembly Resolution 46/36 H.' It can be said that these 'Guidelines' represent the common sense views of the international community today on what should be done to combat and reduce illicit arms trade. However, since General Assembly resolutions are no more than recommendations to Member States, what is required of us now as our next step is to work out some concrete actions to be taken by the international community based on these 'Guidelines'.

As my fifth point, I wish to draw attention to an encouraging initiative being undertaken by the Rio Group nations of Latin America (see also chapter 14). A group of experts of the Rio Group has been working on a 'draft convention against the illicit manufacturing, and trafficking of firearms, ammunition, explosives and other related materials', and the draft convention is now said to be ready for signature at its Twenty-seventh General Assembly of the Organization of American States to be convened in Lima, Peru in June 1997. In fact, according to the provisions of the draft convention, most of the measures to combat illicit trade activities are left to national measures to be taken by the prospective States Parties to the convention, in line with its stipulation that 'the illicit manufacturing and trafficking of firearms, ammunition, explosives and other related materials shall mean those activities which are carried out in violation of the legislation of Party States or international law'. However, if the Convention is agreed, an Advisory Committee consisting of one representative each from States Parties will be established and will meet at least once a year in order to promote the exchange of information, to further the standardization of laws and regulations, and such like.

Therefore, the thrust of the draft convention appears to amount to the development of the kind of 'regional network of information sharing' discussed above in connection with the question of a 'regional register'. If this convention comes into force, it will be the first ever international agreement for the control of small arms and light weapons. Unlike General Assembly resolutions, the convention will be a legally binding undertaking even if its application is to be geographically limited. This will certainly take us a step further from the UNDC Guidelines mentioned above.

Lastly, I would like to draw attention to the activities of the Commission on Crime Prevention and Criminal Justice based in Vienna. At its Fifth Session held in May 1996, the Commission received a report entitled 'Measures to Regulate Firearms' prepared at its request by the Secretary-General of the United Nations.[7] This report, based on the information received from 25 Member States, contained statistics on criminal cases, accidents and suicides involving firearms and on transnational illicit trafficking in firearms. It also contained information on relevant national legislation and regulations, and on various national and other initiatives for firearms regulation. In addition, the report referred to some of the activities of the Commission itself. For example, the Commission is considering the possible preparation of a draft declaration concerning firearms regulation, and for this purpose was consulting with the Secretary-General. Also, a database of firearms regulations may be established. Furthermore, an Advisory Group on the Gathering and Analysis of Information on Firearms Regulation was established by the Commission. The Advisory Group started its work in December, 1995, and 50 national consultants would be contracted by the Advisory Group to gather data and other information. The Commission held its Sixth Session in May 1997.

As can be seen, the approach adopted by the Vienna Commission is to deal with the problems of firearms so far as they are related to criminal activities anywhere in the world. Any firearms including those for hunting purposes and even home-made guns will have to be dealt with. On the other hand, the UN's Small Arms Panel has to deal with small arms and light weapons used as primary means of fighting in the conflicts dealt with by the United Nations. Such conflicts are limited to certain geographical areas only, and the weapons that matter are in most cases those made to military specifications. Furthermore, it may be said that while the Small Arms Panel is expected to come up with recommendations for more or less immediate and concrete actions in order to relieve the suffering of nations in troubled regions or sub-regions, the Vienna Commission appears to be dealing with its problems at a slower but steadier pace, first by collecting information on national laws and regulations.

However, it is clear that both groups are dealing with similar problems from different directions, and that some coordination will be needed to avoid unnecessary overlaps. In any event, I should like to stress that the activities of the two groups of the United Nations are basically complementary to each other, and that the Vienna Commission's work will also contribute immensely to the cause of bringing small arms and light weapons under control.

---

1   For case studies of Angola, Liberia, Rwanda and Somalia, see Michael Klare, 'Light Weapons Diffusion and Global Violence in the Post-Cold War Era', Jasjit Singh (ed.), *Light Weapons and International Security*, Indian Pugwash Society/BASIC, Delhi, December 1995, pp 17-21.

2   Jasjit Singh, *Light Weapons and International Security*, ibid., p. X.

3   Address of the Secretary-General to the Advisory Board on Disarmament Matters, *The Disarmament Agenda of the International Community in 1994 and Beyond,* United Nations, New York, 1994. This booklet also contains the Secretary-General's message to the opening meeting of the Conference on Disarmament in 1994.

4   The experts presenting evidence to the first session of the Panel were: Ian Anthony of SIPRI; Natalie Goldring of BASIC; Michael Klare of the Five College Program in Peace and World Security Studies, Amherst; Andrew Latham of York University, Ontario; Andrew Pierre of the Carnegie Endowment for International Peace; and Chris Smith of King's College, Strand, London.

5   UN General Assembly document A/49/316, dated 22 September 1994, paragraphs 36 to 39

6   UN General Assembly document A/46/301, 9 September 1991.

7   UN Economic and Social Council document E/CN.15/1996/14, dated 16 April 1996.

CHAPTER 17

Developing Transparency and Associated Control Measures for Light Weapons

Natalie J. Goldring

Introduction

This chapter identifies opportunities for developing international cooperative mechanisms to improve the transparency of light weapons transfers, as well as obstacles to such efforts. It also suggests some potential associated measures that move beyond transparency to aid efforts to limit light weapons proliferation.[1] Taken together, these measures could help establish an international norm favoring control of light weapons flows.

Current transparency mechanisms provide minimal information about light weapons transfers. In fact, although they are probably responsible for the vast majority of the deaths in conflicts since World War II, until recently light weapons were largely ignored by the international analytic and diplomatic community. For example, the United Nations Register of Conventional Arms is a global register of transfers of major conventional weapons; it does not include light weapons. In 1994, a UN group of experts evaluated the register and considered ways of strengthening it. As part of this assessment, they considered adding anti-personnel mines and other light weapons to the register. Unfortunately, the panel was unable to reach consensus on ways to enhance or expand the register. The 1997 group of experts has a similar charge: to evaluate the register and to decide whether its enhancement and expansion are appropriate. The group's focus has been on the level of information countries should provide with respect to their military holdings and procurement through national production; it has not focused on light weapons.[2]

Definitions

Analysts have not yet reached consensus on clear definitions of light and major conventional weapons. The working definition used by BASIC's Project on Light Weapons defines light weapons as including pistols and revolvers, rifles, machine guns, portable anti-tank and anti-aircraft weapons, mortars up to 100 mm, associated ammunition, and anti-personnel mines. Major conventional weapons are understood to include: tanks, airplanes, ships, helicopters, mortars 100 mm or over, artillery, anti-armor mines, armored personnel carriers, and non-portable missiles and missile launchers.

Light weapons versus major conventional weapons

Recently, analysts have begun to debate the relationship between light and major conventional weapons. One perspective is that light weapons transfers and transfers of major conventional weapons are two quite separate phenomena. The current version of the register is consistent with this perspective: it draws a sharp distinction between major conventional weapons, which are included, and light weapons, which are not. However, there is no such dividing line on the battlefield. In addition, important aspects of the light weapons trade, such as covert transfers to governments or insurgents, illicit transfers, transfers to non-state actors, transfers in return for goods, direct government-to-government transfers, and legal sales by companies, are also key factors in the trade in major conventional weapons.

In recent conflicts, light weapons may well have been responsible for most of the killing, but government forces in particular have regularly been backed up by major conventional weapons, as have some insurgent forces. Excessive and destabilizing accumulations of light weapons and major conventional weapons often occur at the same time and often must be dealt with simultaneously. Unless confidence- and security-building efforts and conflict prevention, conflict resolution, arms control, and disarmament measures take into account the entire range of weapons in use, they will probably fail.[3]

Overview of recent UN activities on light weapons

The United Nations has been increasingly involved in light weapons issues in recent years. In addition to discussions about light weapons in the 1994 and 1997 UN Register review panels, important work on light weapons has been taking place within the UN Disarmament Commission, the Economic and Social Council's Commission on Crime Prevention and Criminal Justice, and the Panel of Governmental Experts on Small Arms.

The UN Disarmament Commission adopted guidelines for international arms transfers in spring 1996 which focused mainly on the illicit trade. These guidelines recommend that states institute a variety of national measures to combat illicit trafficking, including: strengthening national laws and regulations, establishing effective import and export licensing procedures, providing adequate numbers of customs officials, and defining which weapons are legal for civilians and which can be held by military personnel. International initiatives outlined by the Disarmament Commission include: establishing verifiable end-user certificates, sharing customs information, cooperating on border control and law enforcement, complying with UN arms embargoes, developing common legislative and administrative import and export controls, and participating in the UN Register of Conventional Arms.[4]

The second effort is a United Nations firearms survey carried out through the Economic and Social Council's (ECOSOC) Commission on Crime Prevention and Criminal Justice. This inquiry's scope is to exchange data on civilian-owned firearms regulations at national, regional, and international levels, and to establish a database on firearms regulation. An international group of experts, including customs, police and military officials as well as representatives of regional criminal justice institutes, has developed a set of recommendations based on information supplied by approximately 50 member states. On 5 May 1997, the Commission released a draft report of nearly 150 pages that provides a summary of the survey results as well as recommendations for international action.[5]

According to the survey results, major legislative reforms have recently been undertaken in Australia, Canada, the Czech Republic, Estonia, the Russian Federation, and the United Kingdom, while such reforms are pending or under discussion in Brazil, Denmark, Finland, India, Jamaica, Poland, and South Africa. Other initiatives underway include licensing requirements, penalties for firearms offenses and firearms smuggling, and gun amnesties to promote public awareness.[6]

The draft report recommends domestic regulatory policy options, as well as promotion of regional and international cooperation on firearms. It also encourages other international bodies such as the World Health Organization (WHO), the International Criminal Police Organization (Interpol), and the World Customs Organization to provide additional information to supplement the survey.[7]

The Commission reviewed progress on the survey during its sixth session in Vienna, 28 April - 9 May. The edited version of the report is expected to be submitted to the UN's Economic and Social Council in July 1997. Possible future activities proposed by the Secretary-General for consideration by the Commission include expanding the survey to additional countries, initiating a second-round of the survey, publishing a global report on firearms legislation, organizing interregional and national workshops on firearms regulation, improving information exchange through continued development of databases, and developing model agreements on illicit weapons trafficking.[8] A final report incorporating the Commission's comments as well as possible additional survey results is expected by the end of 1997.

At its Vienna meeting, the Commission on Crime Prevention and Criminal Justice adopted a resolution on "Firearm regulation for the purpose of crime prevention and public safety". An early draft of this resolution was submitted by the governments of Japan, Canada, and Mexico; the resolution was eventually sponsored by more than 30 countries. The resolution recommends continued data collection and dissemination on firearms regulation on the part of the United Nations. It also urges member states to institute a variety of measures, including: regulations on firearm safety, licensing of firearm businesses, and the marking of firearms at manufacture and import. Finally, it urges various bodies such as the UN Panel of Governmental Experts on Small Arms, the International Criminal Police Organization (Interpol), the Customs Co-operation Council and other non-governmental organizations to provide the Commission with information and advise it on ways to enhance activities such as sharing information on illegal firearms, and reviewing the effectiveness of controls on international firearms transfers.[9]

Apparently in response to this resolution, the US-based National Rifle Association (NRA) submitted a statement declaring that the conclusions of the firearms survey were "incomplete and inconclusive" and that "Its conclusions are not supported and its recommendations are not warranted at this time."[10]

The third effort is that of the Panel of Governmental Experts on Small Arms. [See chapter 16, written by Ambassador Mitsuro Donowaki for further details.] In brief, the panel's mandate is to address the types of small arms and light weapons being used in conflicts being dealt with by the UN, the nature and causes of excessive and destabilizing transfers of small arms and light weapons and ways and means to prevent and reduce excessive and destabilizing accumulations. As of spring 1997, the panel had agreed on a draft typology of weapons to be covered, and there appeared to be potential for agreement on establishing regional registers on light weapons transfers. However, there was significant disagreement over the nature and causes of conflict and over the panel's recommendations, including whether UN Disarmament Commission recommendations were an appropriate starting point for this panel.[11]

Ways to Increase the Transparency of Light Weapons Transfers

There are many options for increasing the transparency of light weapons transfers, both inside and outside the UN framework. The following section analyzes four options for increasing transparency, focusing primarily on options that can be undertaken under UN auspices. Discussion of each option includes an assessment of its advantages and disadvantages. Following this analysis, there is a brief discussion of other ways to increase transparency.

As often emphasized in UN documents, the objectives of increasing transparency include developing means of detecting excessive and destabilizing accumulations of light weapons in order to prevent such accumulations of weaponry in the future.[12] The UN's stated objectives are to increase stability and security, presumably in the hope of finding ways to reduce the number of people being killed in conflicts around the world. Transparency mechanisms alone are highly unlikely to accomplish this objective, but they are a good first step.

All of the options detailed below deal with the licit, or legal, light weapons trade, and focus on various types of transfers among governments and corporations. Most transfers to or from insurgent groups are not likely to be included in registers. At the same time, however, some transparency measures could make illicit transfers more difficult and more visible, for example, by highlighting discrepancies between declared production and domestic use, stocks, and exports.

Option 1: Include detailed information on light weapons transfers in the global register

This option would involve expanding the UN Register of Conventional Arms to include light weapons transfers. These transfers could be included as a single new category in the register, or as separate categories for each major type of small arms and light weapons.

Advantages of option 1

One important advantage of this approach is that light weapons would be included in the key international transparency measure on global weapons transfers. The existing register deals with only seven categories of weapons systems: battle tanks, armored combat vehicles, large caliber artillery systems, combat aircraft, attack helicopters, warships, and missiles and missile launchers.

By adding one or more categories to the current register, it would be possible to take advantage of the existing mechanism, rather than having to construct new forms, a new forum for their evaluation, and a new process for their submission. In turn, this change would make the register much more relevant to regions such as South America and Africa, where major conventional weapons are less prominent than are light weapons.[13] As UN member states in these regions became aware of this change, they could be encouraged to give higher priority to the register, thus aiding the effort toward universal participation.

Perhaps the most useful and least burdensome means of adding light weapons to the existing register would be to add a single new category, but to mandate that countries provide information on the specific types of weapons transferred. This would present a much smaller administrative burden than establishing six or more new categories for the different types of small arms and light weapons.

Disadvantages of option 1
Perhaps the most significant disadvantage of this first option is that it would require a much greater level of detail than the current register in order to be useful. It would not be very helpful if countries simply reported the aggregate number of light weapons they transferred, for example. Because there are many different types of small arms and light weapons, a register would have to disaggregate them within a single new category or into several additional categories if it were to be effective. Similarly, as long as detailed information about the specific types of weapons being transferred is "optional", there is a risk that some countries would simply lump together all of their light weapons imports or exports, making the data meaningless.

It would probably be more productive substantively to add several categories dealing with light weapons, but this could lead to other problems. This approach could lead to proposals for separate categories for pistols, revolvers, machine guns, portable anti-tank missiles, portable anti-aircraft missiles, launchers for each, anti-personnel mines and mortars smaller than the level covered by the existing register.[14] This could result in more than doubling the number of categories in the register. One of the most frequent complaints about another UN transparency exercise, the register of military expenditures, is that its complexity has hindered participation. Register supporters do not want the register to be viewed in the same light.

Adding several categories to the register to deal with light weapons could also lead to demands for significantly more detail with respect to the remaining register categories, perhaps requiring wholesale revision of the existing register. In addition to being a very time consuming task, this seems unlikely given the current political environment, and the early opinions of the 1997 experts' group. Several experts interviewed after the first panel meeting in March 1997 were quite skeptical about adding light weapons to the UN Register. However, an expert from Africa questioned their assessment, saying, "There seems to be an implication that this [light weapons] should be left to some regional register....Why should my safety be downgraded to regional?"[15]

This option also has the disadvantage of requiring significant change in the global register and financial resources for implementation. Currently, many governments apparently wish to make at most modest changes and do not wish to incur additional financial commitments to the United Nations.

Option 2: Develop sub-regional or regional registers with common forms that are then compiled into and published as a global register, under UN auspices

This option would involve the development of standard forms that could be used by interested regions to register their light weapons imports and exports. If resources permitted, these forms could then be compiled into a global register of light weapons transfers. The decision about participation would rest with the regional or sub-regional organizations.

There are several possible ways to develop the necessary common forms. A UN group of governmental experts could take the lead in developing a draft form, which could then be circulated to interested regional and sub-regional organizations for comment. Another option would be for an experts group to develop a basic form, which regional or sub-regional organizations could supplement with additional information if they wished. Alternatively, one region with particular interest in light weapons control could spur the process by developing a draft form to present to UN member states for review.

Advantages of option 2
This approach would have the advantage of retaining a global perspective and UN sponsorship. It could also be relatively easy to implement, because it would not be necessary to accept the forms and inherent weaknesses of the current register, especially in terms of the very limited level of detail called for in the current forms. Instead, the regional registers could be designed to provide much more detail. The development of common forms would increase significantly comparability across regions. This option would also help increase regional awareness of the importance of openness and transparency as confidence-building measures. These registers could focus either on the weapons that are not covered by the UN Register, or on all weapons transfers.

The implementation of regional registers would provide more flexibility than the global register. Communications and coordination could be easier with fewer countries involved, and there could be more room for individual country initiatives. For example, countries could report more than once per year. Countries could also couple the regional register with other regional confidence- and security-building measures (CSBMs). Discussions in the Association of South East Asian Nations (ASEAN) and in West Africa appear to be following this track by pursuing registers and CSBMs simultaneously.[16]

Disadvantages of option 2
The main political problem with this approach is convincing developing country representatives that regional registers would be taken seriously at the United Nations. In interviews, some developing country representatives have expressed concern that developing regional registers would imply that their weapons were less important than those in the "real" register.

In addition, this option could be fairly expensive. To increase comparability across regions, the forms would probably need to be developed by the United Nations. The United Nations would also need to appropriate funds for oversight and reconciliation of returns. It is not clear whether it would be possible to maintain the same administrative structure for compiling the regional returns as exists for the current register. Because there are many types of light weapons, and there is a high volume of transactions, the task of verifying regional light weapons registers is likely to be more complex than for the global register of major conventional weapons. This means that more staff could be required for verifying returns. At a time of budgetary cutbacks, it could be difficult to fund this type of venture.

Option 3: Create separate regional or sub-regional registers, not under UN auspices

This option is similar to option 2 in its focus on regional and sub-regional registers. However, with this option, the registers would be developed independently in each separate regional or sub-regional setting. In addition, the registers would not be developed or paid for by the United Nations.

Advantages of option 3

This option would allow each regional or sub-regional grouping to decide what information would be most useful in its political and military context. Officials and analysts would be able to tailor each register to the specific needs of the area.

This option would require less centralized bureaucracy than either option 1 or 2. It gives each regional or sub-regional association the opportunity to determine whether there is sufficient interest to proceed with a regional weapons register. This may help develop regional arms control expertise and interest.

Regional registers could also avoid the potential burden of UN-style consensus, which often has paralyzed arms control efforts. The governments in each region would presumably pay for their own efforts, and would only need to contribute modest amounts of money to facilitate regional compilations. Interested governments or NGOs could work with existing regional organizations to increase the validity and comparability of the resulting data and to increase support for the exercise.

Disadvantages of option 3

The primary disadvantages of this option are related to questions of legitimacy and comparability. This option loses the legitimacy of being a UN exercise, and probably loses the global reach of UN-associated efforts as well. This is a serious disadvantage; global actions are often better publicized than regional actions, and frequently have more political force.

While allowing each region to tailor a register to its needs provides flexibility, publishing separate registers also increases the likelihood of comparability problems. This problem could be resolved at least in part by establishing a separate system for cross-checking returns. However, such a system would require countries to agree on what types of cross-checking to allow. It would also require significantly more financial assistance from the participating countries than for simply compiling the returns as received.

Option 4: Suggest the voluntary provision of information within the global register

This option would consist of inviting countries to include information on light weapons transfers in their optional submissions of background information to the UN Register. This information would be requested, not mandated.

There could be, but need not be, a standard form for such submissions; an alternative would be a simple request for information. In either case, the experts' group would need to reach consensus on recommending this addition to the register, while also suggesting how it might be implemented.

Advantages of option 4

The main advantage of this option is its simplicity. It would begin the process of increasing light weapons transparency with a minimum of bureaucracy, but would still keep it within the UN context. It would allow expansion and enhancement in later years.

This option would set the important precedent that accumulations of light weapons should be monitored, because they can be destabilizing. It could bring global attention to the light weapons issue, and could increase pressure on governments to find ways to restrain light weapons transfers.

There is already precedent for this type of endeavor in the register itself. Roughly one third of the countries providing returns to the register also submit background information on their weapons trade practices, weapons holdings, and/or procurement through national production.

Disadvantages of option 4

This is likely to be the least useful option in terms of being able to compare information across countries or regions. In addition, the arguments in favor of this option parallel those for beginning the UN Register with minimal information -- that later enhancement and expansion will occur. The fact that such expansion has not yet occurred with the UN Register undermines arguments for using that arrangement as a model for future transparency efforts.

Analysis and recommendations

It is important that the Group of Governmental Experts on the UN Arms Register deal directly with the issue of light weapons transfers. Even if the experts' group recommends the least ambitious proposal described in this chapter, it will send an important message about the significance of light weapons. Any of the four options described above would be an improvement over the current situation, in which there is no official international source of information on light weapons transfers. Conversely, if the experts' group ignores the issue, and assumes that it will be dealt with on the regional level, it will undermine efforts to control light weapons.

Option 1, full expansion, is the most ambitious, but it also deals most directly with the weapons of concern. Negotiating such a change in the register would require a great deal of effort from the members of the panel of experts, but it is feasible given adequate political will. Option 2, developing regional registers that would then be integrated into a global register, is the best fallback. While not as immediately useful as option 1, it would still strengthen the existing register significantly, and could be developed in parallel with it.

Options 3 and 4 are both significantly less attractive options than options 1 and 2. Option 3 would, however, allow regions with more political will to take the lead, with other regions joining in somewhat later. Option 3 is weakened by not being under UN auspices. It would also be quite difficult to ensure comparability among regions, which would probably inhibit efforts to move from option 3 to a global register.

Option 4, requesting voluntary provision of information as part of countries' background materials, could be useful as a stopgap measure, if consensus were not reached on any of the other options. It is the weakest option, but could be a first step toward greater transparency. One advantage of option 4 over option 3 is that it would establish the precedent of including light weapons in the global register, even if only in the background information.

Other methods of increasing transparency

In addition to regional or global registers, there are many other methods of increasing the transparency of light weapons transfers. Many transparency proposals focus on obtaining and publicizing information about countries' policies and laws related to light weapons. These proposals are based on the assumption that openness ("sunshine") favors restraint -- that public scrutiny leads to more care in decision-making.

In some countries, it may be necessary to begin by establishing or strengthening national laws providing for oversight of the light weapons trade. If countries are lacking administrative procedures for documenting imports and exports of light weapons, they may not have the information necessary to participate in transparency regimes.

Other proposals emphasize the importance of developing reliable data on light weapons transfers and better understanding the dynamics of light weapons flows through country case studies. Individual case studies often provide detailed information about one or two countries, including key actors, motivations for weapons transfers, and economic considerations affecting recent weapons imports and exports.[17] By building an inventory of such cases, analysts should be able to prepare regional or global assessments of the light weapons trade. Such analyses should include problems and opportunities associated with past attempts to limit light weapons transfers, while also suggesting better routes for the future. In addition, case studies of key conflicts, such as the former Yugoslavia or Northern Ireland, may also help with formulating policy proposals for specific situations.

It is also important to learn from prior successes and failures. Comparative case studies of successful demobilization and/or disarmament after conflicts have ended can be used as the basis for policy recommendations for future negotiations. Similarly, in-depth critiques of demobilization or disarmament failures may help prevent similar problems in other countries.

Beyond Transparency

Transparency is only a first step toward limiting light weapons transfers. This section highlights some additional policy options, that, coupled with increased transparency, may help limit light weapons proliferation. These measures have been developed in discussions among participants and advisors of BASIC's Project on Light Weapons. Some of these proposals focus on individual types of weapons, others focus on national and international control processes, and still others focus on conflict. As with the proposals for increased transparency, these proposals are neither mutually exclusive nor collectively exhaustive; they simply indicate a range of possible means of decreasing light weapons flows. It will be difficult to implement these proposals without better transparency mechanisms, as the transparency measures would be necessary for monitoring and verification.

Controlling individual types of weapons

One option is to ban entire categories of weapons that are especially indiscriminate in their effects. Efforts to ban landmines and blinding weapons are underway; there has been particular success with the campaign to ban anti-personnel landmines.

Limiting ammunition holds promise in helping to break the cycle of violence. Because light weapons often last for decades, even if all transfers of light weapons were stopped today, the world would still be "awash" in them decades from now. But ammunition is rapidly consumed in conflict. Ammunition is also unattractive for smuggling, since it has relatively high weight and relatively low dollar value. Reliable (safe) ammunition is also difficult to produce. Ammunition also has a significantly shorter shelf-life than the weapons in which it is used. For all of these reasons, limitations on ammunition supplies may be more feasible than limitations on the weapons themselves.

Another option is to limit transfers of light weapons that use advanced technology. "High-tech" light weapons such as portable surface-to-air missiles threaten civilians as well as military forces. The threat to civilians is one of the reasons the US Central Intelligence Agency is reportedly still trying to buy back the highly capable Stinger anti-aircraft missiles that the US government transferred to the Afghan mujahideen in the 1980s. Because high-tech light weapons are made by fewer suppliers than lower-tech weapons, and because they have not yet been widely disseminated, they may be more readily controlled. To prevent further dissemination, it would also be useful to prohibit coproduction and codevelopment of high-tech light weapons, and to establish controls on transfers of new light weapons technologies.

Focus on national and international control processes

A focus on national and international processes to control light weapons transfers could have several dimensions, including: greater oversight of existing national control and enforcement mechanisms, harmonizing national measures in bilateral, regional and global frameworks; and/or enhancing national policies.[18]

The direct relationship between lax US gun laws and illicit trafficking in US weapons suggests that to control light weapons internationally, it will be necessary to control them nationally. It will be difficult, if not impossible, to control the illicit market in light weapons without monitoring and controlling domestic access to weapons. To have effective international controls, it will also be important to enforce existing laws governing sales of weapons and to provide sufficient resources to monitor and police national borders.

One example of attempts to tighten domestic controls is the proposed US "one gun a month" program.[19] Laws limiting purchasers to one gun per month are already being implemented in several states in the United States; the proposed legislation would implement a similar plan on the national level. Such legislation has already decreased gun running in the affected states; national legislation would make it more difficult to obtain the large quantities of weaponry that make illicit trafficking financially attractive. Coupled with enforcement of existing guidelines governing the domestic sale of weapons, this could make it much easier to limit the international trade in these weapons.

For those in countries with strict gun control legislation, of course, "one gun a month" seems like a weak control measure. However, it is also important to understand the extent of change from existing practices that this proposal represents. At present, in almost every state in the United States, an authorized purchaser can make bulk purchases of literally dozens of weapons at one time. This makes diversion to unauthorized purchasers a relatively simple task.

Another effort to tighten domestic controls is the proposed UK handgun ban. In February 1997, a new UK law banned private possession of handguns of greater than .22 caliber. Just after his election in May 1997, Prime Minister Tony Blair reiterated the Labour Party's support for a total ban on handguns. Ironically, while this may aid domestic weapons controls, it may undermine efforts to limit light weapons transfers. At present, there is no provision for destruction of the banned weapons, and their export will be allowed under the normal export procedures. This risks creating a situation in which weapons not considered safe for UK citizens will be exported: a questionable moral standard.

A promising way to decrease access to light weapons is by controlling and destroying the large stocks of surplus weapons that have resulted from force reductions. At present, these weapons are often kept in poorly guarded warehouses. At the first sign of tension, the warehouses can be broken into and the weapons stolen, as has occurred recently in Albania.[20] Destroying surplus stocks, or at a minimum establishing better controls, can also decrease the damage caused by these weapons.

To ensure that weapons are taken permanently out of circulation, destruction of weaponry can also be incorporated into other efforts to control light weapons flows. In Australia, a gun buyback program has been initiated to collect weapons prohibited as the result of new gun control legislation. Both public opinion and foreign policy considerations were factors in the decision to require that all weapons collected from the buyback be destroyed. The only exceptions are weapons of particular historical interest which may be purchased by museums, and non-military-style weapons that can be consigned to dealers for overseas sale. In the latter case, however, if the weapons are not sold within one year, they must be returned to the buyback program and destroyed. So far an estimated 383,000 guns have been destroyed in Australia as part of the buy-back program.[21] Proposals for similar destruction of banned weapons are under consideration in the United Kingdom, in an effort to increase the effectiveness of the new gun control law described above.

Other useful national controls could include verifying end-user documentation on transfers and developing strategies for controlling diversion and theft, increasing efforts to uncover and destroy illegal weapons, and imposing stronger penalties for illegal possession of weapons and smuggling. All of these proposals could present more effective barriers to theft and diversion of light weapons, while also making such attempts more costly. The credibility of such efforts would be enhanced if governments simultaneously eliminated covert aid and transfers.

One approach that combines national and regional elements is the "Draft Convention Against the Illicit Manufacturing and Trafficking of Firearms, Ammunition, Explosives and Other Related Materials," prepared by a group of experts of the Permanent Mechanism of Political Consultation and Consensus (the Rio Group) in March 1997.[22] The text was submitted by the Rio Group to the Organization of American States (OAS) for their consideration that month, was debated at a permanent council meeting and was referred to a working group chaired by Mexico. [See Ricardo Rodriguez' chapter for additional information about Latin American efforts to deal with light weapons.]

Taking its lead from UN General Assembly resolutions on illicit weapons trafficking, the draft convention outlines ways to combat the illicit trade on a regional basis. It outlines both national and regional steps, including: standardization and revision of national laws; standardization of import and export permit systems; improved border control; and the establishment of a national register of manufacturers, importers and exporters. It also recommends establishing an advisory committee to coordinate information exchange and investigations, promote cooperative training, and ensure enforcement of the convention. Countries have been invited to provide their comments on the draft convention. The proposal may be considered for adoption at the OAS Summit in Lima in June 1997.[23]

Since 1993, an experts group within the OAS has also held a series of meetings to discuss the development of model regulations on firearms issues. In Caracas in mid-1996, they agreed to develop model regulations on a "harmonized import/export certificate system," including provisions on trans-shipment. A drafting group is currently preparing a final report to be presented to OAS countries for their consideration.

Focus on conflict

With respect to conflict, the most important actions are those that focus on preventing it from occurring. In this regard, regional confidence- and security-building measures can be quite useful, as can efforts to prevent destabilizing accumulations of weaponry. Once conflicts begin, it may be necessary to declare and enforce bans on weapons transfers to all parties to the conflict. At all stages -- before, during, and after conflicts -- more effective border controls will help prevent illicit imports and exports of light weapons. Such controls are especially important in unstable regions such as the Great Lakes region in Africa, where weapons circulate from one conflict to another.

A particularly important post-conflict measure is increasing the effectiveness of disarmament after conflict settlement by ordering the return and destruction of weapons as part of disarmament processes. Put simply, destruction prevents reuse. Many of the weapons at use in conflicts today are actually "recycled" from other conflicts. We can avoid this by ensuring that when conflicts end and combatants are demobilized, their weapons are destroyed, not stored or sold. In Mali in March 1996, more than 2500 weapons were destroyed as part of a disarmament process -- an excellent precedent.

Conclusion

In its current form, the UN Register misses key dimensions of weapons procurement and transfers. It is time to make the register more relevant to today's conflicts by including light weapons, which are probably responsible for the vast majority of the killing in conflicts today. Since the stated intent of the register is to discern excessive and destabilizing accumulations of weapons, light weapons must be included, either in the register itself or in an associated measure.

The 1994 experts' panel did not succeed in enhancing or expanding the register. If the 1997 panel also becomes deadlocked, the register may atrophy. It is not and cannot be a static instrument -- either it expands to deal with member countries' concerns, or participation will likely decrease over time.

---

1   The author gratefully acknowledges Susannah Dyer's research assistance in preparing this chapter.

2   For further information about the 1997 review panel, see Dr. Natalie J. Goldring, 'UN Register Experts Argue over Expansion', *BASIC Reports,* no. 57, 1 April 1997

3   For more information about the interaction between light and major conventional weapons, see Dr. Natalie J. Goldring, 'Bridging the Gap: Light and major conventional weapons in recent conflicts', Paper prepared for the annual meeting of the International Studies Association, Toronto, Canada, 18-21 March 1997.

4   'Guidelines for international arms transfers in the context of General Assembly resolution 46/36H of 6 December 1991', reprinted in 'Review of the Implementation of the Recommendations and Decisions Adopted by the General Assembly at its Tenth Special Session: Report of the Disarmament Commission', A/51/182, 1 July 1996, pp. 64-69.

5   'Draft United Nations International Study on Firearm Regulation', prepared by the Crime Prevention and Criminal Justice Division, United Nations Office at Vienna, E/CN.15/1977/CRP.6, Commission on Crime Prevention and Criminal Justice, 25 April 1997.

6   'UN International Study on Firearms Regulation', UN Backgrounder: Firearms (Vienna: UN Information Service, no date).

7   'World Crime and Justice Issues to be Discussed at Two-Week UN Session in Vienna', UN Press Release SOC/CP/197, 28 April 1997

8   'Criminal Justice Reform and Strengthening of Legal Institutions: Measures to Regulate Firearms', Report of the Secretary-General, E/CN.15/1997/4, UN Economic and Social Council, 7 March 1997.

9   'Firearm regulation for the purpose of crime prevention and public safety', E/CN.15/1997/L.19, 30 April 1997.

10   'Statement submitted by the National Rifle Association of America - Institute for Legislative Action (roster), a non-governmental organization in consultative status with the Economic and Social Council', 28 April - 9 May 1997.

11   For further information about the small arms panel, see Dr. Natalie J. Goldring, 'UN Small Arms Panel Makes Progress', *BASIC Reports*, no. 56, 11 February 1997.

12   See, for example, General Assembly resolution 46/36L, 9 December 1991, which established the UN Register, declaring the United Nations' 'determination to prevent the excessive and destabilizing accumulation of arms, including conventional arms, in order to promote stability and strengthen regional or international peace and security...'.

13   In interviews after the first meeting of the 1997 panel of experts, one African participant said flatly, "The register does nothing for Africa." Interview with the author, 25 March 1997.

14   At present, artillery of 100 mm and larger size is covered, but the 1997 review panel may well decide to include all artillery 75 mm and larger in the Register.

15   Interview with author, 25 March 1997.

16   See, for example, 'India, Myanmar for ASEAN Regional Forum', *Jane's Defence Weekly*, 22 May 1996.

17   In the United States, for example, the Arms Project of Human Rights Watch has published an extremely valuable series of country case studies covering light weapons transfers and violations of the laws of war in countries such as Angola, Turkey, and Rwanda. Their work also addresses particular light weapons such as landmines, blinding lasers, and cluster bombs.

18   For an excellent analysis of the potential for such measures in South Africa, see Jacklyn Cock, 'A Sociological Account of Light Weapons Proliferation in Southern Africa', in Jasjit Singh, ed., *Light Weapons and International Security*, New Delhi: Indian

Pugwash Society and British American Security Information Council, 1995.

19   H.R. 12, 'Twelve is Enough Anti-Gunning Act', January 7, 1997.

20   See, for example, Christine Spolar, 'Many Guns, Few Solutions in Albania: Looting of Armories Litters Chaotic Country With Weapons', *Washington Post*, March 12, 1997, and Mike O'Conner, 'Albanians, Struggling to Survive, Sell Stolen Rifles', *New York Times*, April 24, 1997.

21   Geralidine O'Callaghan correspondence with Rebecca Peters, Chair, Coalition for Gun Control, Australia, 1 May 1997.

22   'Draft Convention Against the Illicit Manufacturing and Trafficking of Firearms, Ammunition, Explosives and Other Related Materials', OEA/Ser.G CP/doc.2875/97, 20 March 1997, Organization of American States Permanent Council.

23   Interview with Organization of American States official, Susannah Dyer, 30 April, 1997.

CHAPTER 18

A Nuclear Weapons Register: Concepts, Issues, and Opportunities

Harald Müller and Katja Frank

Introduction

A nuclear weapons register has been proposed in different contexts and with different purposes in mind. In the view of the authors, the register is a multiobjective transparency measure of great utility that would considerably contribute to international security, to more equitable relations among states with different nuclear status, and, as a highly useful, if not even probably indispensable, precondition to future progress in nuclear disarmament.

The paper builds upon a previous version written by one of the co-authors.[1] It discusses the origins of the idea and the interests of the parties that put it forward on various occasions. We then elaborate the four purposes a nuclear arms register would serve: a reduction of discrimination; accountability; security; and disarmament. The third part discusses the possible scope(s) of the register, and how scope could be expanded in different stages of its development; also, the tricky issue how to include the de-facto nuclear weapon states is tackled. Next, the utility and modalities of verification of a register are scrutinised; in this connection, light is shed on the relation of the register to other disarmament measures such as a cut-off, nuclear arms reduction treaties between two or more of the nuclear weapon states, and an international plutonium regime. We also try to explore how a register could work in the last stages of the disarmament process. Before the final conclusions, we investigate in which institutional context the nuclear arms register idea might be best pursued.

As we describe a system that does not yet exist, and talk about its development in a way that presumes political contexts that lie far in the future, our discussion has some visionary, if not utopian, touch to it. This is inevitable if one desires to discuss a future that is not yet here (as is usually the case for the future, anyway). Yet, throughout the discussion, we have tried to exert as much intellectual discipline as possible, and to keep our discussion as much down to earth as the lofty area of the non-existing does permit. In doing this, we feel as much, if not considerably less, vulnerable as those hard-nosed, extremely realistic classical defense analysts who talk about the close-to-bloodless, quickly victorious wars that will be fought in far-away quarters from the continental US in the not-too-distant future, using technology that is 'at hands'. Our discussion at least is not less realistic than that, only because we employ the instruments of peaceful change rather than those of military hardware.

From this it emerges clearly that the authors are not neutral as to the register idea. They are convinced that this concept holds considerable promise and is a useful addition to world security, even if it starts as a rather modest and limited system.

Where did the 'register idea' come from?

On December 16, 1993, German Foreign Minster Klaus Kinkel pronounced a major 'nonproliferation initiative'.[2] This was a significant move, since his predecessor, the formidable Hans-Dietrich Genscher, whom Kinkel had succeeded not too long ago, had seized this field with his usually energetic style in the late eighties, and had steered its course with great determination. Minister Kinkel's taking action in this realm was therefore a serious attempt to prove his worthiness as Genscher's successor.

The initiative contained ten points, among them the German support for the indefinite extension of the NPT and for a Comprehensive Test Ban Treaty. Point eight reads as follows:

> 'Establishment of a nuclear weapons register. Thereby we implement/translate into action the demand for transparency in the stockpiles of nuclear weapons. This transparency is important with regard to international confidence-building in nuclear disarmament of the nuclear weapon states: Only when the stocks are known the success of nuclear disarmament can be measured. The idea of a nuclear weapons register is the logical continuation of our initiative to implement a register for conventional weapons in the UN context.'

This proposal fits well the context of a long-standing and consistent German policy in the nuclear sector.[3] While Germany has always supported nuclear arms control and given - at least rhetorically - its approval of complete nuclear disarmament, activities and genuine initiatives are mainly found in two subsectors: tactical nuclear weapons in

Europe and transparency and verification in the nuclear weapon states. Germany has been a vocal promoter during past NPT Review Conferences of the expansion of IAEA safeguards in the civilian nuclear sectors of Nuclear Weapon States; it has stubbornly requested a verification regime for the fissile material coming out of nuclear disarmament (International Plutonium Regime, another of Kinkel's 10 points) and has pursued the transparency issue energetically in the Vienna nine-parties-talks that might result in guidelines for civilian plutonium users; it has fought, to the dismay of even some non-nuclear weapon states for the 'universality principle' in the 93 plus 2 negotiations on improving IAEA safeguards NPT parties, and for it has succeeded in putting the recognition in the preamble of the resulting protocol that 93 plus 2 measures shall be applied, to the extent possible, universally, that is, in the nuclear weapon states as well. In its negotiations with Russia about the supply of MOX technology for the disposal of weapons plutonium, Germany has insisted that such material must come under IAEA safeguards. In this policy, the German government was guided by two interests: the conviction that enhanced transparency in nuclear weapon states was an important contribution to international security; and the desire of a large non-nuclear weapon state with a strong civilian nuclear industry to suffer as little discrimination as against the nuclear weapon states and to afford them as little privileges as possible. (For the same two reasons, Germany also supported strongly the inclusion of an 'erga omnes' clause in the Nuclear Suppliers' Group guidelines that forces suppliers not to turn a blind eye to transfers to NWS, but to scrutinise whether such transfers might engender a proliferation risk).

Immediately after Kinkel's speech, German diplomats in the capitals of allied nuclear weapon states suffered badly. Part of the reason was a lack of consultation beforehand. No one likes surprises in an issue that is seen as closely related to the national interest. But the opposition was partly grounded in the deep-rooted NWS reluctance to enter any multilateral undertakings that give away their complete freedom of action, and their deep instinctive fear to compromise both their privileged position and their national security by granting anything resembling transparency. This attitude is no absolute, and it varies considerably among them - with the US under the courageous leadership of former Secretary of Energy Hazel O'Leary making the greatest efforts to be accountable both to the international community and to the American people.

Anyway, highly unfriendly reactions were reported to Bonn from Washington, D.C., London and Paris. The French reaction was so strong that the then German ambassador in Paris threatened not to follow instructions in the future that would force him to take the issue up again. As a consequence, the German government decided to bury the issue for the time being.[4] While the idea still enjoys support within the Ministry and other parts of the German government, the risks of sticking out the German neck against the united front of the three most important Western allies is seen as too high as compared against the weight of the issue.

About the same time, Argentina issued a proposal to discuss establishing a nuclear arms register in the CD. As far as we understood the Argentinean approach, it would have been more appropriately depicted as a nuclear disarmament register. The nuclear weapon states should register the nuclear weapons deactivated and dismantled as a consequences of nuclear disarmament agreements. Over time, the expectation went, such annual registrations would create enhanced transparency and thereby contribute to the international climate for disarmament. It can also be assumed that Argentina wanted to have the CD more involved in the nuclear disarmament process, thereby improving the climate among nuclear and non-nuclear weapon states during the debate about the extension of the NPT, a treaty that the country had acceded to only recently, and that Buenos Aires turned out to be a staunch supporter of. The Argentinean initiative, however, drew no consequences in the ensuing years.[5]

A third approach was taken by Egypt. During the deliberations of the group of experts tasked with reviewing the experiences of the UN Arms Register and developing suggestions for improvements, Egypt proposed to add weapons of mass destruction to the register. The Egyptian motivation was and is most likely an attempt to exert additional pressure on Israel. Israel, generally credited with a nuclear weapons arsenal of at least 50-100 warheads, is the only country with this capability in the Middle East. While Egypt is at peace with Israel, it is not willing to condone this difference of capabilities and has taken several initiatives to force Israel to make concessions. Israel, however, while principally admitting to its intention to eventually become non-nuclear, has declared the consolidation of peace, including the countries still hostile to its mere existence, a precondition for nuclear disarmament. On this basis, both the global (NPT) and regional (Nuclear Weapon Free Zone) strategies had met Israeli refusal, and the negotiation track of the Arms Control and Regional Security Working Group has run into stalemate over the Arab reluctance to agree to confidence-building measures and conventional arms reductions as long as Israel objects to even discussing the framework of a nuclear-weapon free zone, and Israel's staunch refusal to discuss any nuclear matters as long as the peace process has not reached a much more advanced stage. The nuclear weapons register, it thus appears, offers Egypt still another approach.[6]

Thus, the idea of a nuclear arms register has come from different quarters, fed by various motivations and taken several distinct shapes. No progress has been made in terms of preparing a legal instrument that would establish accountability of the nuclear weapon states to the world community. However, in the meantime, some additional transparency has been achieved by other means. Four nuclear weapon states, as other countries possessing Plutonium in civilian uses, have entered the habit of declaring annually their holdings. The United States has publicised a considerable amount of data on its past production and present holdings of Plutonium and Highly Enriched Uranium, both in civilian and military uses. The planning data given by the three Western nuclear weapon states about the future size of their nuclear arsenals makes it possible to narrow down the range of estimates as to their weapon holdings. This progress should be noted, but it falls short of what we could expect from a nuclear arms register.

However, it is true that the range of interests that was behind the objections of the nuclear weapon states is still around. The 'haves' are concerned that revealing information might compromise their national security. Some elements of the secrecy syndrome are obviously exaggerated and treated as a symbol of the privileges that nuclear weapons are supposed to convey to their possessors. But other aspects deserve more serious consideration. Particularly the smaller nuclear weapon states may fear that giving away data about their nuclear weapon holdings may make them more vulnerable. It might even be that some of them wish to avoid embarrassment if their arsenals are smaller than the world presently believes, and they might fear that the value of their deterrent might be devalued by exposing its small size.

This might also be true for the de-facto-nuclear weapon states. In addition, as will be elaborated further below, the world community, including even their neighbours, might share an interest with these countries in keeping their nuclear weapon complexes in some stage of opacity. In any negotiation on a register, these interests must be recognized and thoroughly cared for.

Rationales for a Nuclear Arms Register

In the discussion of the origins of the German initiative, some of the rationales for establishing such a register were touched upon. They will now be discussed in a more systematic way.

Reducing Discrimination

An obvious - though not the strongest - objective of a register is to reduce the discrimination embedded in the distinction between nuclear and non-nuclear weapon states as defined by the NPT. Misgivings about this discrimination are shared by nonaligned and industrialized non-nuclear weapon states, though not necessarily with the same degree of intensity. One aspect of the inequality is that NNWS are totally transparent as to their holdings of military fissile material - namely zero - and civilian fissile material, that is scrupulously accounted for by the countries and their operators and registered and verified by the IAEA and respective regional organizations. Concerning the nuclear weapon states, no such transparency is available, with the exception of Britain and France, where civilian fissile material is under EURATOM (but not IAEA) safeguards, and the few examples mentioned at the end of the introduction. The voluntary safeguards agreements concluded by the NWS and the IAEA do not really yield much, as they have led only to sporadic inspections at single sites. No systematic register of fissile material can be constructed this way. And, of course, the military sector was completely opaque.

Much of this is unnecessary and not at all justified by any security and nonproliferation gains. There is no good reason why the world should not know how much fissile material - civilian and non-civilian - is in the hands of the NWS, nor do these appear there to be security threats emerging from openness about the total number of nuclear warheads owned by the Five. The surprising gain in transparency made by the voluntary accounts given by the US Department on Energy under Hazel O'Leary's leadership is telling in this respect. In other words, the present level of opaqueness appears to be kept as an unjustified privilege rather then emerging, by necessity, from the distinction of nuclear and non-nuclear weapon state, like those formerly derived from noble birth. Since they detract from the cohesion within the NPT community, they should be abolished. A nuclear arms register would make a reasonable contribution to that abolition.

Accountability

Secondly, the register would establish an important principle: that of accountability of the nuclear weapon states to the international community. The present situation is highly contradictory. On the one hand, the Five have requested - and obtained - a transitory recognition of their status by way of the NPT. By the accident of their being also the five permanent members of the UN Security Council, (never forget that it is an accident, as the Five do own their status to the fact that they are the victorious powers of the Second World War, not to their nuclear weapons that did not exist when the UN Charter was written), they bear a particularly grave responsibility for world peace and security. And they (or some of them) have themselves repeatedly stated that, in contrast to the purported 'rogue states', they are handling these awful weapons with the appropriate responsibility.[7] Yet when the world community puts forward requests for a higher degree of transparency as a proof of this responsibility, the nuclear weapon states tend to respond with: 'this is our national business'. This contradiction is a shortcoming of the international security order; not the least because what has become known about the treatment of ecological safety, human health, accountancy and physical security of the nuclear weapons complexes in several of the nuclear weapon states does not at all engender confidence that the standard of 'responsibility' is as high as we might wish. It is thus time - and appears to be in the nuclear weapon states' own enlightened interest - to accept the principle of accountability. A nuclear arms register is an instrument for the NWS to prove their accountability in a very important way. Other instruments are binding negative security assurances, more explicit positive security assurances, and regular explanation of nuclear doctrine and strategy; but those steps are not the subject of this paper.

Security

Third, as has already been mentioned, accountancy and physical security is not assured by a law of nature in the NWS. It is an old experience of both democracies and non-democracies that bureaucracies and organizations working outside of the realm of public scrutiny - be they military or civilian, public sector or private - tend to loose quality, establish sloppy and at times dangerous practices, and perform suboptimally. There is thus no a priori reason to believe that granting complete secrecy to the nuclear weapon complexes will result in optimum physical security of nuclear weapons and related materials. The present state of affairs in the former Soviet Union, notably Russia,[8] illustrates this problem. A register is not only a transparency measure to the outer world, though it is important in this capacity; it is also an instrument forcing the nuclear weapon states and their diverse, at times rivalling, bureaucracies to get their act together and to establish and/or maintain a working and regular system of accounting and controlling warheads and materials. This may even help central authorities to control reticent bureaucracies at the functional, regional or local level.

Paving the way for nuclear disarmament

Lastly, a register is related to disarmament. Unfortunately, the connection between transparency and disarmament is not all too well understood by the most ardent supporters of a nuclear weapon free world, as is demonstrated, inter alia, by the curious indifference of some nonaligned countries towards a cut-off. In their zeal to achieve complete nuclear disarmament in a single, or at most a few, steps, disarmers tend to overlook that nuclear weapons, being so much engrained in the security policies of the nuclear weapon states and their allies, will only be abolished if the conditions are built under which those countries feel secure even in the absence of such weapons. Among the concerns is the fear that a present nuclear weapon state (de jure or de facto) could cheat on its undertakings and hide, or quickly reconstitute, a part of its arsenal, thereby creating a nuclear monopoly with grave consequences for the balance of world power and world security. This fear derives, to a very large degree, from the present lack of transparency that surrounds the nuclear weapon complexes. Only if opaqueness is overcome and full transparency established and proven through a series of nuclear arms control/arms reduction/confidence building steps will a sufficient majority in those countries support going to zero. In this context, a register is a very useful step as it begins to establish baselines against which disarmament progress can be measured. A register provides signposts of transparency that can be expanded, through amendments of the register as well as through complementary measures until all countries are sufficiently confident that they understand the (hopefully shrinking) size and composition of the other nuclear weapon states' posture and the related fabrication and storage complexes. (A cut-off would considerably add to that transparency, which - in our view - would be its main accomplishment[9]). Seen from this perspective, a nuclear arms register is certainly a necessary, though by no means a sufficient, condition of nuclear disarmament.

Scope

The concept of a nuclear arms register sounds straightforward, but it is a very complex issue. From the above it has become clear that a register should cover both actual warheads and weapons-usable fissile materials not presently under international safeguards. There is also the issue of launchers. Starting from this comprehensive approach, a register could be constructed with increasing degrees of comprehensiveness in detail. It is possible to conceive of a register that starts at a fairly general level, but becomes more detailed through amendment over time, thus enhancing the degree of transparency as the disarmament train moves forward.

The 'de-facto-nuclear weapon state problem'

Another very tricky issue is the way in which the de-facto nuclear weapon states are to be included. This might prove, conceptually, the most difficult issue connected with the register. The country pushing presently hardest for the whole concept, Egypt, is clearly interested in getting a handle on its nuclear armed neighbour. But it is not only unlikely that Israel, India and Pakistan can be forced into the open on the numbers of nuclear weapons they own, it may be counterproductive to do so. For they are still legally counted as non-nuclear weapon states. There may be some merit in preserving this status. First, as the South African and the Ukrainian examples have proven, it is easier to turn to non-nuclear status if no different legal status is implied. Also, domestic opposition might be less emphatic in cases where the nuclear weapon status had never become official. Secondly, offering data about the size of nuclear weapons in these three countries might create public pressures for proliferation in the respective regions. This would run contrary to the process of nuclear disarmament and could finish this process for good.

On the other hand, it would be inconsequential to ignore these countries altogether. The arguments made for transparency in the nuclear weapon states, at least those on security and disarmament, if not even all four, apply here as well. In addition, as the number of nuclear weapons comes down, the nuclear weapon states will increasingly be reluctant to both further disarm and continue to provide data about their residual forces if other countries stay in a state of complete opaqueness. Not including the de-facto nuclear weapon states would prove, again, a stumbling block for nuclear disarmament. We should not forget that the nuclear weapon states - supported by many non-nuclear weapon states - stated during the run-up to the NPT Review and Extension Conference that there could be no disarmament without nonproliferation. This relationship applies in our context as well.

What is the way out of this dilemma? First, one should not be shy of establishing negotiation fora which can fully address the problems that the Three have in common with the five nuclear weapon states: Such negotiations might be kept informal, in order to prevent any symbolic political damage. During the CTBT negotiations, many deals were done among the P-5, even though, officially and legally, the Ad-hoc Committee and its working groups under the friends of the chair were the only fora for negotiation. Second, one should be careful so that the results that become part of international law do not accord a special status to the three. Between these two imperatives, it is a tightrope walk, but this is inevitable.

We propose to have the Three participating only in the part dealing with fissile materials, not in the warhead registry. The register should thus be called 'Register of nuclear arms and fissile materials not covered by international safeguards'. This is neutral enough to avoid the pitfalls envisaged above, but, if accepted, would still yield highly useful information.

Staging the register

Stage I
On the basis of these considerations, one could imagine the register starting with the most general information in the two main categories: number of warheads and total amount of Plutonium and highly enriched uranium (including, where applicable, U 233) not under international safeguards. That would include all such materials, whether in warheads, in fabrication, refabrication or dismantlement processes, in reserve or disposal storage, in scrap, in submarine fuel or even in the civilian fuel cycle but not safeguarded by the IAEA. No further information would be given at the beginning. In fact, this information is less than that now available about US warheads and fissile materials stockpiles those days, and it is even less than the US had envisioned when it proposed 'stockpile transparency' measures to Russia some years ago.[10] It should also be noted that the draft convention on the safety of spent fuel and radioactive waste, presently under negotiation in Vienna, is likely to cover spent all civilian fuel in all states parties, NWS and NNWS, with an explicit preambular option to also submit, on a voluntary basis, data on inventories of spent fuel from military production in parties' annual reports. This means that

another part of the 'register material' might be submitted to transparency by another instrument.[11]

However, it might be useful even at this stage to give an assessment of the confidence the reporting states have themselves in their own figures. They could state the range of uncertainty for both figures. One would hope that for the first item, warheads, this figure would be zero. For the fissile material reporting, this is unlikely to be the case, as all production facilities are bound to show some material unaccounted for due to measurement uncertainty, production losses, and material retained in the plant (e.g. in curved pipes). De-facto nuclear weapon states would just fill the 'fissile material' form and leave the warhead account vacant. Since the fissile material total would include material in warheads or other military state of use, it would reasonably enhance transparency without the political risks that admitting the actual possession of nuclear weapons might entail.

Stage II

At a second stage, warheads might be broken down by type. Type would include the military name of the warhead and the launcher to which this warhead is assigned. At this stage, it would be useful to distinguish between deployed and reserve warheads. It would also be useful to account for the platforms and launchers not contained in the UN Arms Register (if a country includes holdings in its UN reply, nuclear bomber aircraft, nuclear-capable artillery, missiles and their launchers and nuclear weapons carrying ships, surface and submerged, will be included in its annual declarations). However, as long as the UN register does not necessarily contain information on weapon types, this might be seen as too unspecific. In this case, it would be useful to enumerate types and numbers of platforms and launchers as well. Again, a distinction between deployed and nondeployed weapon systems would be recommendable.

For fissile material, the following breakdown of the total might be possible: material in civilian uses; material in military non-weapons uses, such as navy fuel; material in reserve; material destined for disposal (that is scrap, material from dismantled weapons, other excess material) and material in 'other uses' which would most likely cover fissile material in warheads, in fabrication and refabrication. The label would avoid the touchy certainty of de-facto-nuclear weapon states' real status, while enhancing transparency considerably. At the same time it would prevent the precise assignment of a given amount of material to a given number of warheads, which could enable people to calculate the precise composition of Highly

Enriched Uranium (HEU) and Plutonium per type of warhead, information that is generally regarded as a military secret. It might be debatable whether such information would have any military significance, as countries would hardly be in a position to refabricate a similar warhead on the basis of such information, particularly in the absence of nuclear tests. However, as long as not all these countries are parties to the CTBT, it might be argued that this information could give away militarily significant data. On top of this, some might object that giving out this information would not be compatible with article I of the NPT.

Threshold countries could still participate in the registration of their fissile material. The way the categories have been framed would permit this. On or more governments might object that, in revealing the total amount of their 'material in other uses' rather than hiding it in the larger total, might show how little they have really got, drastically reducing the deterrent value of their opacity. One should wait and see which positions these countries take once that moment approaches.

It might be useful, at this stage, to include some information about the methodology used to calculate the amounts of material, to assess prospects to arrive at greater accuracies, and to spell out steps taken in this direction. In addition, as reporting would be periodical - that is, annual - there would be the need to explain changes in the numbers of platforms and launchers, for example due to export or scrapping.

Stage III

Stage three contains some very daring suggestions that may never work. Nuclear weapon states may just consider the information involved, or part of it, too sensitive to reveal short of total disarmament. Yet it is not inconceivable, the international context permitting, that classification rules will be much more relaxed, and readiness to admit much larger transparency will be considerably enhanced, due to the experiences in stages I and II, and to the repercussions of other disarmament steps taken in parallel.

Stage three information would contain all details from stage II, plus rough parameters for the warheads (yield, size) that would make it possible to distinguish them visually. It might even be possible to announce the precise amount of fissile material per warhead, though this information might be given only in a separate part of the register privy only to the five nuclear weapon states. In addition, the location where the warheads are stored and deployed would be revealed.

Location would also be identified for all fissile material. This would require the dissolution of the 'other uses' category as for material in fabrication, refabrication and actual warheads. The last veil of opacity concealing the de-facto nuclear weapon states' status would thus disappear. This is only advisable and possible if a stage is reached when nuclear disarmament is far progressed, and if the three de-facto nuclear weapon states are fully integrated into the disarmament process. In other words, stage three is conceivable only as the jumping board into the very last phase before a zero-nuclear weapon world will be achieved. Only at this point will the revelation about the de-facto nuclear weapon states come at very low political cost, as the end of their nuclear weapon status will be already in sight. Only then, too, will the nuclear weapon states consider giving away information that would, under other circumstances, be certainly seen as strictly classified for national security reasons.

Verification

Whether this register needs verification, and at what stage, is certainly a matter for discussion. If we conceive of it as a voluntary transparency measure meant to contribute to confidence building among the eight countries that have, or might have, nuclear weapons, that is, modelled on the UN Weapons Register, then verification is not warranted, at least not in the beginning. Politically, there is much to be said for not insisting on a verification system initially. The matter concerns an area of the highest sensitivity for all countries concerned. A verification system meant to make sure that all warheads have been effectively declared, and all weapons-usable fissile materials honestly accounted for, would almost certainly meet considerable resistance in all countries concerned. The character of the register would change, because the most difficult and secretive type of information would be required from the beginning: the precise location of all items to be verified. It is inconceivable that Russia, the smaller nuclear weapon states - China in particular - or the three de-facto nuclear weapon states would be willing to join a register under these circumstances. To request a verification system would thus prevent the register a priori from ever coming into being.

In addition, negotiating a verification system would lead to enormous delays in an otherwise quite straightforward process of establishing the register. Stage 1 follows a very simple concept that presents little obstacles and stumbling blocks to agreeing quickly, and implementing expeditiously, the scheme of declarations implied by it. Success hinges completely on the political will (or lack thereof) of the parties involved. It has little to nothing to do with the intrinsic complexity of the subject, which is largely absent. This picture would change completely if verification requirements were added. Such requirements would lead to long and drawn-out bargaining, with uncertain to unlikely chances of success and an even more uncertain start to implementation.

For these reasons, it is strongly recommended not to ask for register verification at the beginning of the process. If - as is hoped - confidence is built through the process itself, and supplemented through other nuclear arms control and disarmament measures (see below), then a register even without verification is quite worthwhile considering. Again, it will be difficult to muster the political will required even for this, very modest, purpose. We should avoid all steps that would make it more difficult for the sympathetic decision makers in the eight countries to persuade their peers to go along with the register idea.

At stage III, however, we can expect that verification will have become intensive, largely because of developments in other arms control and disarmament negotiations and because that stage, as analysed above, is hardly conceivable short of the firm determination of all participants to lay down their nuclear arms. For this reason, it can be expected that, if that stage is reachable and realizable at all, it will be as well verified as a precondition to go from there to zero.

Relation to other nuclear disarmament measures

Postponing the introduction of verification measures may be made easier by the precedence of the UN Conventional Arms Register, introduced without verifying the data submitted by the participating countries, and continuing without such a system after five years of its existence. There is a second aspect that might facilitate acceptance of the world community of establishing a verification-free nuclear weapons and related materials register without too much misgivings. This is the prospect that, as arms control and disarmament measures multiply, much of what is included in the register may come under verification anyway, if incrementally.

The START process
Let us assume that the START process continues. The most recent proposal submitted by the United States foresees, for the first time, a binding commitment to dismantle the nuclear warheads deployed on those

launchers that are to be destroyed under START II. It is the focus on first dismantling the warheads that permits the postponement of the initial target date for launcher destruction (covering, in the first place, all heavy, MIRVed intercontinental ballistic missiles) without suffering increased insecurity. Dismantling those warheads removes the option of breaking out of START II limits by reloading the missiles with those warheads. In order to implement this commitment in an orderly fashion, one would assume that the parties to START II will need verification to ensure that the warheads to be dismantled are indeed warheads from and for the heavy missiles. That goes a considerable way into establishing the verification measures needed for a register.

If reductions cross the crucial 1000-warheads boundary, the 'breakout problem' created by the potential for reloading missiles that could carry more warheads than they actually do becomes more and more strategically significant. Likewise, the possibility to fly strategic bombers back from their first strike missions, reload them, and use them anew in a follow-on strike will concern strategic planners. While this sounds like 'Dr.-Strangelove' considerations, we must realize that this is, and will remain until complete nuclear disarmament is achieved, a core problem of nuclear strategy. In order to limit the uncertainties and insecurities emerging from these possibilities, nuclear weapon states participating in global nuclear disarmament agreements will desire to limit not only deployed warheads, but reserve warhead holdings as well. By the same token, the fissile material in reserve that could be used to produce warheads for reserve and active forces would be included. Again, verification measures would become necessary that would cover most of what a register - even a stage II or III register - would require.

Separation of launchers and warheads

Among the proposals coming from recent studies on nuclear disarmament that have attracted considerable public attention, none is closer related to strategic stability than the one recommending a separation of launchers and warheads in order to eliminate all fears of an impending nuclear attack.[12] While it might be possible to verify a related commitment just ex negativo, that is by focusing on the launchers and ensuring that no warheads are mounted on them, verification might well go beyond these limitations. Particularly if certain distances were prescribed for the separation system, the location of warheads would have to be known, and some regular activity would be needed to ascertain that the warheads were actually in these storage places and not closer to the launching sites than permitted. This, in turn, would create information that is only foreseen for the third stage of the nuclear arms register, as described above.

Limiting tactical nuclear weapons

Additional impulses could emerge from ancillary arms limitations and disarmament measures. For example, it has been repeatedly proposed that holdings of tactical nuclear warheads should be limited. This is a wise suggestion, as those weapons lend themselves to easier use and often contain less advanced electronic locks to prevent unauthorized use and less sophisticated safety technology to exclude explosion by accident. Again, any limitation agreement would require measures to make sure that actual holdings are not larger than permitted, and that dismantlement would proceed as foreseen - a task very closely related to the reporting going on under a register in all three phases.

A fissile material cut-off and other measures to control fissile materials

A fissile material cut-off treaty would definitely bring some material presently out of safeguards under the purview of the International Atomic Energy Agency. This relates to all fissile material in peaceful purposes and declared excess by the nuclear weapon states. The same applies to the guidelines for the handling of Plutonium that have been negotiated between the users of Plutonium, including the five nuclear weapon states, over the last few years in Vienna.

In the last stage of nuclear disarmament, the register, as conceived in stage III, and the disarmament process are likely to converge. The risk of cheating and breakout would loom large at this stage, and participants as well as the world community would wish this risk to be excluded with as much certainty as possible. This would presume reliable inventories of both nuclear warheads and fissile material and an intrusive and dense verification system to make sure that these inventories were complete and correct. The difficulties in achieving this should not be underestimated, particularly in the light of the present range of estimates for the holdings of the nuclear weapon states.

The Forum for Negotiating a Nuclear Arms Register

Where could or should a register be negotiated? Several possibilities offer themselves: the expert group tasked with improving the UN Conventional Arms Register could suggest amendment of the initial resolution to include nuclear weapons and fissile materials; the UNGA could agree on a new resolution, creating a separate register; the CD could install a nuclear disarmament ad-hoc committee with explicit mandate to discuss such a register; the enhanced NPT review process could be used for this purpose; it could be left to the P-5 plus the three de-facto-nuclear weapon states; or the P-5 could start among themselves and invite others to join, as appropriate.

Using the Conventional Arms Register process

The suggestion has been made to amend the Conventional Arms Register so as to contain a section on weapons of mass destruction. The advantage is to use an instrument easily available, the administration of which is established. In the long run, such a register would develop into a world inventory of arms. In addition, concessions by the nuclear weapon states might induce other countries to be more forthcoming with respect to the inclusion of data they regard as intimately related to their own national security (e.g. weapons production and holdings).

However, the UN Conventional Arms Register is possibly not the best place to start this approach. First, the qualitative distinction between conventional and weapons of mass destruction, particularly nuclear weapons, should not be blurred. This speaks for a separate rather than an integrated solution. Secondly, it might be preferable to keep register undertakings equal for all participants. Since only a few countries are supposed to report under the nuclear weapons register, such equality could not be maintained. Thirdly, and more importantly, the Conventional Arms Register is primarily concerned with exports and imports and may remain so for an extended period. Yet, the export of nuclear weapons is categorically prohibited under the NPT, to which all nuclear weapon states belong. The export of fissile materials that could be used for weapons purposes to non-nuclear weapon states (as defined by the NPT, that is, including the three de-facto nuclear weapon states) is already registered through the IAEA, as this falls under the safeguards obligation of Art. III of the NPT and the related Safeguards Agreement INFCIRC/153. Fourth, while the UN Conventional Arms Register is based on voluntary participation, it is likely that participants in the nuclear weapons register would wish some guarantee for the participation of at least the other nuclear weapon states, if not even the de-facto nuclear weapon states, in the form of a legally binding undertaking. Finally, it is not clear whether the Group of Experts - experts mainly on conventional weapons - is an ideal body to prepare the details of a nuclear arms register.

The UN General Assembly and the First Committee

For similar reasons, while the UNGA should certainly endorse a register agreement, if proposed as a draft resolution, it appears not to be the ideal body to negotiate the details. Nor is its First Committee in a good position to do so. Either should consider and discuss whatever concept emerges from other negotiation bodies. But if such bodies do not come up with a useful and well-worked out proposal, the UNGA does not have the capacity for detailed negotiation.

The Conference on Disarmament

Using the CD looks like a better option. CD parties are quarrelling about the installation of an ad-hoc committee on nuclear disarmament. While the nonaligned countries, supported by some northern non-nuclear weapon states, wish to see tangible action on nuclear disarmament, nuclear weapon states are concerned about a 'slippery slope' and do not want to subject themselves, on an issue which they regard as closely related to their own national security, to a multilateral body that might be insensitive to their interests.

The solution might be to install a nuclear disarmament committee with a specific mandate to develop the proposal for a nuclear arms register, rather than negotiating nuclear disarmament per se. The rationale is the intimate relationship and instrumentality of such a register to the disarmament process, as elaborated at length above. The CD certainly contains the expertise in matters nuclear to discuss the matter in a meaningful way. Given continued stalemate on both the fissile material cut-off and the ban on anti-personnel landmines, such an approach would also prevent the danger that the CD, the only multilateral disarmament body, would be devalued by lack of purpose.

If it proves unworkable to put the item under the headline of nuclear disarmament because of certain objections, then it could be usefully examined under the heading of 'transparency in armaments' also on the CD agenda. This item has been largely idle during its creation, not least because of the reticence of the nonaligned countries to grant more insight into what they view as pertaining closely to their own security unless there is movement on the nuclear disarmament side. Taking up the nuclear arms register in this context might thus be viewed as an adequate quid pro quo.

Negotiations among the P-5 or the P-5 plus 3

It could be argued that the expertise necessary to work out the details of a register lies exclusively with those countries that possess nuclear weapons, because only they know about both the possibilities and risks of revealing specific information about the arsenals and the materials of which they are made. Likewise, the argument could be made that among them, they would feel less inhibitions to discuss this matter frankly, not the least because Art. I of the NPT would not apply (this, however, would not be valid for a forum in which the three de-facto nuclear weapon states would participate, as they are non-nuclear weapon states under the definition of the NPT). Because of these advantages, a small forum, consisting only of the 'haves' might be better capable to solve the issues connected to establishing a register quicker than a multilateral forum with wider membership.

While it should not be denied that this is a possibility, there are nevertheless reasons why a multilateral forum with strong non-nuclear weapon states' participation is preferable. First, a register is meant, inter alia, to work as an instrument of accountability of the nuclear weapon states toward the world community. Consequently, it would be appropriate to have this community present when the parameters of the register are defined. Secondly, a certain pressure on the nuclear weapon states might help to create the register in a more open and informative shape than if the nuclear weapon states, that share an interest to keep accountability limited, decide everything among themselves. Third, the value of the register as an instrument of both security and its role in the disarmament process might be better understood by a broader range of actors if these actors had a say in bringing it about. Fourth, a multilateral forum - notably the CD - would automatically grant the presence of the three de-facto nuclear weapon states. And, finally, for all these reasons the cohesion of the nonproliferation regime might also be improved.

Within a multilateral negotiating body, the P-5 or the P-5 plus three have ample opportunity to discuss issues, as appropriate, among themselves in a limited caucus. This was done extensively - some would say too extensively - during the test ban negotiations. However, in contrast to this precedence, great care should be taken to include, rather than exclude, the three de-facto nuclear weapon states in this caucus, less they would feel alienated from the substance of the talks and refuse acceptance of the final product. The experiences with the test ban contain a serious warning in this regard.

However, the CD operates under unanimity rule. For this reason, the attempt to extract a negotiation mandate from this body might fail. Certain non-nuclear weapon states might be dissatisfied with a more limited definition of the subject of negotiations and could thus object. One or a few of the nuclear weapon states or the de-facto nuclear weapon states may not be willing to let negotiations start. In these cases, it might be the better alternative to restrict the talks to a smaller circle. If the political will existed, this could be done through a parallel to the Ottawa process, that is, within a group of like-minded countries. It goes without saying that this would have little meaning unless a considerable part of the eight countries of concern take part. If, outside of a formal multilateral body, they would prefer to discuss matters among themselves, such a process, if it yielded meaningful results, would be preferable to no register at all. And likewise, a system that would start among the P-5 in which the three de-facto nuclear weapon states would not participate initially, would be preferable to the lack of transparency presently obtaining, particularly if it were established in such a way as to admit and facilitate later accession by the three. Again, something would be better than nothing, but we recognize that countries in regions adjacent to the de-facto nuclear weapon states may set priorities differently.

Using the enhanced NPT Review process
It has been suggested that the enhanced Review Process, that was agreed to in the context of the indefinite extension of the NPT and that has started in April 1997 with the first session of its preparatory commission, should be more extensively used as a negotiating body for nuclear disarmament issues. This suggestion has gained some strength through the present stalemate in Geneva. However, there are principled reasons why this suggestion should be treated with great reluctance and why, in our particular context, its implementation might quickly prove counterproductive.

First, the review process is no process of negotiation. It would be artificial to transform it from its primary task of scrutinizing the implementation of a specific treaty and proposing steps to enhance this implementation to a forum where other international instruments would be worked out. Secondly, such a practice would devalue the CD as the authoritative multilateral negotiation body - without a tangible advantage, as the rules of the Review Conferences would presumably also contain the consensus clause. While past rules of procedure permitted voting in extreme circumstances and as the consequence of an elaborate sequence of procedural steps, this rule was never used. Since negotiating would be an innovative mission for the Review, it is likely that new, specific rules would be set up for this purpose, and it can be excluded that the nuclear weapon states would accept any negotiation on a nuclear weapons issue that would not afford them a veto. Finally, and perhaps most importantly, the three de-facto nuclear weapon states are not parties to the NPT and its review process. They would be excluded from the beginning, and the prospects of their ever acceding to an instrument in the negotiations of which they would not have had a say are extremely dim indeed.

As a result of these considerations, using the CD would certainly be the preferable option. An Ottawa process, or the Conventional Arms Register review process could be used as substitutes, though it is hard to see how the latter could succeed where the CD had failed. An arrangement between the P-5 plus three or at least the P-5 that would, its successful conclusion provided, be submitted to the UNGA would be better than nothing.

Conclusion

A nuclear weapons register is an idea whose time has come. It enhances international security, corroborates the principle of accountability of the nuclear weapon states vis-à-vis the world community and is a stepping stone, and eventually a precondition, for nuclear disarmament. By the same token, if conceptualized appropriately and with due respect for the present concerns and sensitivities of those countries possessing nuclear weapons or unsafeguarded fissile material, such a register could be introduced without any loss of security for these countries, and it could evolve as confidence is built, relaxing these concerns and sensitivities beyond the limits presently obtaining.

For reasons of acceptability for the countries concerned and the integrity of the legal construction of the nuclear nonproliferation regime, it would be wise to limit the undertakings of the three de-facto nuclear weapon states to reporting their fissile material holdings out of safeguards. Some differentiation in these reports is still possible by shaping the reporting form appropriately - i.e. the 'other uses' category - without having them state precisely their (supposed) nuclear weapon holdings.

The register should start without a verification obligation, again accounting for the sensitivities of the eight countries concerned. Verification measures could be added, by agreement, as the register evolves. It can also be expected that aspects covered by the register come under bilateral, multilateral or international verification as a consequence of other nuclear arms control and disarmament measures. Verification will become indispensable in the last stages of nuclear disarmament.

For reasons of practicability, the register should be established as a separate body. The CD route appears most appropriate. Other forums hold disadvantages. To limit the forum to the eight or five countries immediately concerned may facilitate its creation in some aspects, but would come at the cost of confidence and accountability and would thus remove some of the improvements that could otherwise be expected in the relation between nuclear and non-nuclear weapon states.

As in all nuclear disarmament, here again the best is certainly the enemy of the good. An ideal register would be a stage III one, bolstered by verification and complete information about all participating countries. This is much too much to ask for in the present situation. It is thus strongly suggested to consider the much more moderate, but still very useful, system developed under the stage I label.

1   'Transparency in Nuclear Arms: Toward a Nuclear Weapons Register', in *Arms Control Today*, Vol. 24, No. 8, October 1994, pp. 3-7.

2   *Deutsche 10-Punkte-Erklärung zur Nichtverbreitungspolitik*, Bonn, Auswärtiges Amt, 15. December 1993, Point 8

3   Harald Müller and Wolfgang Kötter, *Germany and the Bomb: Nuclear Policies in the Two German States, and the United Germany's Nonproliferation Commitments*, PRIF Reports No. 14, Frankfurt/M. (PRIF) 1990; Alexander Kelle and Harald Müller, 'Germany', in: Harald Müller (ed.), *European Non-Proliferation Policy 1993-1995*, Brüssel, European University Press, 1996, 103-127.

4   'Befehl verweigert', in *Der Spiegel*, No. 15, 1994, p. 16.

5   Argentina Working Paper, *Conference on Disarmament*, Ad hoc Committee on Transparency in Armaments (CD/TIA/WP.14), 3 August 1993.

6   Malcolm Chalmers and Owen Greene, *The UN Register in its Fourth Year*, Bradford Arms Register Studies, Working Paper 2, November 1996, pp. 31-32.

7   For this argument, see. Joseph S. Nye, Jr, 'Nuclear Proliferation: A Long Term Strategy', in *Foreign Affairs*, Vol. 56, Spring 1978

8   *Deutsche 10-Punkte-Erklärung zur Nichtverbreitungspolitik*, op. cit.

9   Harald Müller, 'Doomed Prospects? On a Ban for the Production of Fissile Materials for Weapons Purposes', *PPNN Issue Brief*, Southampton 1997, forthcoming.

10   Interview, US Department of Energy, 1996.

11   Ann MacLachlan and Gamini Seneviratne, 'Draft of Radwaste Management Treaty Ready for IAEA Board', *Nucleonics Week*, Vol. 22, No. 9, May 5, 1997, pp. 10-12.

12   See the related proposal in the Canberra Commission on the Elimination of Nuclear Weapons, *Report of the Canberra Commission on the Elimination of Nuclear Weapons*, August 1996.

Appendices

Appendix A: List of Participants of the Workshop on Transparency in Armaments

Government Officials

Argentina:

Mr. Rafael M. Grossi Counsellor, Argentine Embassy in Belgium

Australia:

Dr. Ronald Huisken, Assistant Secretary, Alliance Policy & Management, Department of Defense

Brazil:

Mr Jose E. M. Felicio Minister Plenipotentiary, Permanent Mission of Brazil to the United Nations

China:

Mr. Hu Xiaodi Deputy Director-General, Department of International Organizations and Conferences, Ministry of Foreign Affairs of the People's Republic of China

Cuba:

Lt. Col. Jose Rufino Menendez Hernandez, Deputy Executive Director, Centre for the Study of Disarmament and International Security

Egypt:

Mr. Maged A. Abdelaziz, Counsellor, Permanent Mission of the Arab Republic of Egypt to the Untied Nations

France:

Mr. Jean-Paul Credeville, Assistant Director, International Relations Division Ministry of Defense

Gabon:

Lt. Col. Sava Matthias Mounange-Badimi, Director for International Relations, Ministry of National Defense and Security

Germany:

Col. Wolfgang Richter, Military Adviser, Permanent Mission of the Federal Republic of Germany to the United Nations Office in Geneva

India:

Mr. A. Manickam, Counsellor, Permanent Mission of India to the United Nations

Iran:

Mr. Gholamhossein Dehghani, First Secretary, Permanent Mission of the Islamic Republic of Iran to the Untied Nations

Israel:

Mr. David Danieli, Minster Counsellor, Delegate to the Conference on Disarmament, Division of Arms Control and Disarmament, Ministry of Foreign Affairs

Italy:

General Giuseppe Grandi, Armament Material and Export Control Unit, Ministry of Foreign Affairs

Japan:

Amb. Mitsuro Donowaki, Ambassador and Special Assistant to the Ministry of Foreign Affairs of Japan

Pakistan:

Mr. Shafqat Ali Khan, Assistant Director, Disarmament Division, Ministry of Foreign Affairs

Poland:

Mr. Kazimierz Tomaszewski, Advisor to the Minister, Ministry of Foreign Affairs of the Republic of Poland, Department of the United Nations System

Romania:

Dr. Gheorghe Chirila, Minister Counsellor, International Organization Division, Ministry of Foreign Affairs

Russian Federation:

Mr. Nikolai Revenko, Head of Division, Department of Security and Disarmament, Ministry of Foreign Affairs

United States of America:

> Mr. Giovanni Snidle, Senior Foreign Affairs Officer, Weapons and Technology Control Division, Nonproliferation and Regional Arms Control Bureau, United States Arms Control and Disarmament Agency

United Nations Secretariat:

> Ms. Hannelore Hoppe, Secretary of the Group of Governmental Experts of the UN Register of Conventional Arms

Consultant:

> Mr. Terence Taylor, Assistant Director, International Institute for Strategic Studies

Academics and NGO Representatives

> Prof. Amitav Acharya, York University, Canada

> Dr. Malcolm Chalmers, University of Bradford, UK

> Dr. Katja Frank, Research Fellow, Peace Research Institute of Frankfurt, Germany

> Dr. Natalie Goldring, Deputy Director, BASIC, Washington DC, USA

> Dr. Owen Greene, University of Bradford, UK

> Amb. Tomoya Kawamura, Director, Centre for the Promotion of Disarmament and Non-Proliferation

> Prof. Harald Müller, Director, Peace Research Institute of Frankfurt, Germany

> Dr. Alexander Nikitin, Director, Centre for Political and International Studies, Russia

> Dr. Ravinder Pal Singh, Director, Arms Procurement Project, SIPRI, Sweden

Dr. Ricardo M. Rodriguez, (Venezuela), Minister-Counsellor, Mission to the Organization of American States, (ex-Chair of Working Group)

Air Commodore Jasjit Singh, Director, Institute for Defense Studies and Analysis (IDSA), New Delhi, India

Prof. Herbert Wulf, Director, Bonn International Conversion Centre, Germany

Appendix B: Participation in the Register 1993-1996

	Reply for 1992	Reply for 1993	Reply for 1994	Reply for 1995
EUROPE (38)	31	31	32	32
Albania	*			*
Andorra			*	*
Austria	*	*	*	*
Belgium	*	*	*	*
Bosnia				
Bulgaria	*	*	*	*
Croatia	*	*	*	
Cyprus		*	*	*
Czech Republic	*	*	*	*
Denmark	*	*	*	*
Finland	*	*	*	*
France	*	*	*	*
Germany	*	*	*	*
Greece	*	*	*	*
Holy See				
Hungary	*	*	*	*
Iceland	*	*	*	*
Ireland	*	*	*	*
Italy	*	*	*	*

	Reply for 1992	Reply for 1993	Reply for 1994	Reply for 1995
Liechtenstein	*	*	*	*
Luxembourg	*	*	*	*
Malta	*	*	*	*
Macedonia				
Monaco				*
Netherlands	*	*	*	*
Norway	*	*	*	*
Poland	*	*	*	*
Portugal	*	*	*	*
Romania	*	*	*	*
San Marino				
Slovakia	*	*	*	*
Slovenia	*	*	*	*
Spain	*	*	*	*
Sweden	*	*	*	*
Switzerland	*	*	*	*
Turkey	*	*	*	*
UK	*	*	*	*
Yugoslavia	*	*	*	
ASIA AND OCEANIA (34)	21	22	21	23
Afghanistan		*		
Australia	*	*	*	*
Bangladesh				

	Reply for 1992	Reply for 1993	Reply for 1994	Reply for 1995
Bhutan	*	*	*	*
Brunei				
Cambodia				
China	*	*	*	*
Cook Islands				*
DPRK				
Fiji	*	*	*	*
India	*	*	*	*
Indonesia	*	*	*	*
Japan	*	*	*	*
Laos				
Malaysia	*	*	*	*
Maldives	*	*	*	*
Marshall Islands	*	*	*	
Micronesia				
Mongolia	*	*	*	*
Myanmar				
Nepal	*	*	*	*
New Zealand	*	*	*	*
Pakistan	*	*	*	*
Palau				
Papua New Guinea	*	*	*	*
Philippines	*	*	*	*

	Reply for 1992	Reply for 1993	Reply for 1994	Reply for 1995
Republic of Korea	*	*	*	*
Samoa		*	*	*
Singapore	*	*	*	*
Solomon Islands	*		*	
Sri Lanka	*			*
Thailand		*	*	*
Vanuatu	*	*		*
Vietnam			*	*
AMERICA (35)	17	17	19	15
Antigua & Barbuda		*		
Argentina	*	*	*	*
Bahamas			*	*
Barbados			*	*
Belize			*	
Bolivia	*			
Brazil	*	*	*	*
Canada	*	*	*	*
Chile	*	*	*	*
Colombia	*			
Costa Rica				
Cuba	*	*	*	*
Dominica	*	*	*	*
Dominican Republic		*		

	Reply for 1992	Reply for 1993	Reply for 1994	Reply for 1995
Ecuador			*	
El Salvador			*	
Grenada	*	*	*	
Guatemala				
Guyana			*	
Haiti				
Honduras				
Jamaica	*	*	*	*
Mexico	*	*	*	*
Nicaragua	*			
Panama	*		*	
Paraguay	*	*	*	
Peru	*	*	*	*
Saint Kitts and Nevis				*
Saint Lucia	*	*	*	
Saint Vincent & the Grenadines		*		*
Suriname				
Trinidad & Tobago		*		*
USA	*	*	*	*
Uruguay				
Venezuela				

	Reply for 1992	Reply for 1993	Reply for 1994	Reply for 1995
FORMER SOVIET UNION (15)	6	5	9	13
Armenia		*	*	*
Azerbaijan				*
Belarus	*	*	*	*
Estonia			*	*
Georgia	*	*	*	
Kazakhstan	*		*	*
Kyrgystan				*
Latvia				*
Lithuania	*			*
Republic of Moldova			*	*
Russian Federation	*	*	*	*
Tajikistan			*	*
Turkmenistan				*
Ukraine	*	*	*	*
Uzbekistan				
SUB-SAHARAN AFRICA (48)	9	12	5	9
Angola				
Benin				
Botswana				
Burkina Faso		*	*	*

	Reply for 1992	Reply for 1993	Reply for 1994	Reply for 1995
Burundi				
Cameroon			*	
Cape Verde				
Central African Rep				*
Chad		*	*	
Comoros		*		
Congo				
Cote D'Ivoire		*		
Djibouti				
Equatorial Guinea				
Eritrea				
Ethiopia				*
Gabon				*
Gambia				
Ghana				
Guinea				
Guinea Bissau				
Kenya		*		
Lesotho	*			
Liberia				
Madagascar		*		*
Malawi		*		
Mali				

	Reply for 1992	Reply for 1993	Reply for 1994	Reply for 1995
Mauritania		*	*	
Mauritius	*	*		*
Mozambique				
Namibia	*			*
Niger	*	*	*	
Nigeria	*			
Rwanda				
Sao Tome & Principe				
Senegal	*			
Seychelles	*			
Sierra Leone		*		
Somalia				
South Africa	*		*	*
Sudan				
Swaziland				
Tanzania	*	*	*	*
Togo				
Uganda				
Zaire				
Zambia				
Zimbabwe				
MIDDLE EAST (18)	8	3	3	2
Algeria				

	Reply for 1992	Reply for 1993	Reply for 1994	Reply for 1995
Bahrain				
Egypt	*			
Iran	*	*	*	
Iraq				
Israel	*	*	*	*
Jordan		*		*
Kuwait				
Lebanon	*			
Libya	*		*	
Morocco				
Oman	*			
Qatar	*			
Saudi Arabia				
Syria				
Tunisia	*			
United Arab Emirates				
Yemen				
TOTAL	92	90	95	94